feisworx.

oregon champ. feis

x 600

$$600 \overline{)\begin{array}{r} 16 \\ 10000 \\ 600 \\ \hline 4000 \end{array}}$$

Jewish Agricultural Utopias in America, 1880~1910

Jewish Agricultural Utopias in America, 1880~1910

by Uri D. Herscher

HEBREW UNION COLLEGE — JEWISH INSTITUTE OF RELIGION

WAYNE STATE UNIVERSITY PRESS   DETROIT 1981

Library of Congress Cataloging in Publication Data
Herscher, Uri D
  Jewish agricultural utopias in America, 1880–1910.

  Bibliography: p.
  Includes index.
  1. Agricultural colonies—United States—History. 2. Farmers, Jewish—United States—
History. 3. Jews in the United States—History. I. Title.
HD1516.U6H4   338.1'0973   81–462
ISBN 0–8143–1678–6   AACR1

Grateful acknowledgment is made to the Morris and Emma Schaver Publication Fund for
Jewish Studies for financial assistance in the publication of this volume.

Contents

Acknowledgments   7

Introduction   9

*Abbreviations Used in Text,
Picture Credits, and Notes   12*

1 A Condition of Imbalance   15

The Jew in Russia, Early 1800s   16
Refugee Assistance in America, 1880s   21
Agriculture: A Means of Resettlement   22

2 "Our Russian Colonies"   28

Jewish Settlements in America: Early Plans   29
    Ararat, New York   29
    Zeire Hazon and Sholem, New York   29
    American Hebrew Agricultural and
        Horticultural Association, New York   30
Jewish Farming Settlements in America,
1880–1910   31
    Alliance Israélite Universelle: Its Role   32
    Sicily Island, Louisiana   32
    New Odessa, Oregon   37
    Crémieux, South Dakota   48
    Bethlehem-Jehudah, South Dakota   52
    Am Olam Group Settlement, Arkansas   52
    Cotopaxi, Colorado   55

Palestine, Michigan   *61*
Painted Woods and Iola, North Dakota   *70*
Chananel, North Dakota   *71*

3 New Jersey: "Every Beginning Is Difficult"   *73*

Alliance   *73*
Woodbine   *84*

4 The American Experience   *108*

Settling Jewish Colonists as Farmers: Problems   *109*
Failures of Jewish Communal Farms: Causes   *111*
Jewish Agricultural Utopias: An Assessment   *114*
Colonization in Palestine/Israel and America:
   A Comparison   *115*

Appendix 1: Jewish Farming Colonies in New Jersey   *123*

Appendix 2: Sidney Bailey's Memoir   *133*

Notes   159

Selected Bibliography   183

Index   191

Acknowledgments

I cannot begin to name everyone who was helpful in the preparation of this work, but some deserve special mention. At the Hebrew Union College-Jewish Institute of Religion, I am grateful for the good counsel of Samson H. Levey, of the Los Angeles faculty; Jacob R. Marcus and Herbert Paper, both of the Cincinnati faculty; Abraham Aaroni and Fritz Bamberger, both of the New York faculty; and Harold Epstein, of the national administration. In addition, Ezekiel Lifschutz, former archivist of the YIVO Institute for Jewish Research, New York City, provided valuable assistance.

Very special thanks go to Stanley F. Chyet, of the College-Institute's Los Angeles faculty. As a close friend and editor par excellence, he gave generously of his time and vast fund of knowledge. I was deeply encouraged by his guidance and inspiration.

Appreciation is extended to the YIVO Institute for Jewish Research for its permission to publish my translation of the Sidney Bailey memoir, and to Tel Aviv University for its permission to include my translated excerpts of Herman Rosenthal's *The Jewish Farmer*, which were first published in *Michael: On the History of the Jews in the Diaspora*, vol. III, edited by Lloyd P. Gartner (Tel Aviv: Diaspora Research Institute, Tel Aviv University, 1975). Special credit is due, respectively,

ACKNOWLEDGMENTS

to Hebrew Union College-Jewish Institute of Religion, the American Jewish Historical Society, YIVO, the American Jewish Archives, the New York Public Library, Temple Beth El (Birmingham, Michigan), the State of Michigan Archives, Yuri Suhl, and Adam Yarmolinsky, for permission to publish rare photographs.

I am also grateful to Janice Vrancic, of Cincinnati, for the devoted care she gave the typing of my manuscript.

Finally, my thanks to my wife Ellie for her unfailing encouragement and support.

Introduction

Jewish history is in its way the antithesis of the hermetic. As the Franco-Jewish orientalist James Darmesteter wrote nearly a century ago, "the historian's special interest in the Jewish nation is due to its being the only one that is met with at every turn of history. In following the course of this nation's destinies, [the historian] is successively brought into contact with nearly all the great civilizations. . . . The Jewish people, enduring through all times, has helped to shape all great events that have had their day: it is a perpetual and universal witness of all these dramas, and by no means an inactive or mute witness, but closely identified with them in action or in suffering."[1]

Darmesteter had in mind "dramas" of a religious and intellectual character. But there is no reason why his assertion would not apply to the socio-economic and political dimensions of the history of Western civilization. That, at any rate, is the assumption which underlies this essay in late nineteenth- and early twentieth-century Jewish history: in the Jewish experience is reflected in some substantial manner the experience of the larger gentile society.

The focus on the link between Jewish and general experience is not merely theoretical. It springs from a sense of the often enough furious upheaval, psychic as well as socio-

9

economic and political, which technological change has introduced into human patterns of living.

No society has adapted comfortably to the industrial revolution. Indeed, the East European experience was in this respect quite unexceptional. Post-Napoleonic Russia's troubled entry into the arena of Western civilization, the arena of industrialism and capitalism, made for convulsions in the Romanov empire. Political agitation bestirred itself; anxious dreams of a utopian future were pitted against the reality of czar and boyar and archimandrite and serf. A limited abolition of serfdom was declared, railroads were built, and factories were put into operation. But the old elemental Russia struck back with a swelling Pan-Slavic mystique and a mounting fury against religio-ethnic as well as political dissidence. The crisis received particular expression in its effect on Jewish life in the empire. For the Jews, the empire's classical pariahs, the earth began shaking underfoot. In unprecedented numbers they began making their way across the frontiers, most of them westward bound.

If the crisis which convulsed late nineteenth-century Russia, the struggle between the socio-economic patterns of the *ancien régime* and the aspirations of the modernists, found a parallel in the imbalance and insecurity imposed on Jewish life in the czarist territories, America, too, had its Jewish resonance or summation. In the late nineteenth century America's Western frontier vanished and was replaced by a new industrial frontier concentrated in the Northeast, a development reflected in the rush of Jewish immigrants into the needle trades centered in the metropolises of the East Coast. The uncertainty, indeed the fear, which the new industrial capitalism evoked in the more traditional agrarian, commercial American society has indicia in the sinister image widely imputed to Jews at this stage of American history.

But there is also a Jewish "index" to the farm crisis which America's conquest by industrialism involved during the postbellum decades. Some of the Jewish immigrants, never very many, were determined to avoid the pavements of the urban West and instead to make a life for themselves in one or another western wilderness overseas: in Louisiana, in Oregon, in Colorado, in Michigan, in Kansas, in South Carolina, in the Dakotas, in New Jersey. For they had been touched, these few, by a special revolutionary passion and a special dream of utopia. They wished, as Mark Wischnitzer has said, "to initiate a renaissance of Jewish life through productive labor" in collective agricultural settlements,[2] though what productive farming meant was something they had insufficient experience to anticipate. Indeed, in the trans-Atlantic West they would find encouragement from their settled, prosperous, bourgeois co-religionists, mostly of Central rather than East European origin, who might not see fit to pursue utopian schemes for themselves but would find it possible to believe such ordeals suitable for refugees from Stepmother Russia. The efforts by this immigrant minority and its Americanized sponsors to establish Jewish agricultural colonies on American soil proved abortive more often than not, but such failures are not understood without reference to the depressed condition of American agriculture in the late nineteenth century.

In the story of these agricultural undertakings, many strands converge. First is the precarious situation of Jews in Eastern Europe, as the Sidney Bailey memoir (Appendix 2) recapitulates it. Second is the yearning of some Jews for what they thought of as normalization and for utopian solutions, as Herman Rosenthal's *The Jewish Farmer* (Appendix 1) documents them. Third are the anxieties as well as the idealism of Jews well settled in America. And, finally, is the understanding—among Jews in America, too little and too late for permanent effect—that in an industrial age even a farm commune in a remote district offers no escape from industrialism. Such divergencies spell out the experience of East European immigrants among the nineteenth-century American utopians who, in the words of a contemporary writer, "finding themselves utterly out of place and at a discount in the world as it is, rashly concluded that they [were] exactly fitted for the world as it ought to be."[3]

In all quotations throughout the text, appendixes, and notes, my interpolations appear in brackets, while those by the respective authors appear in parentheses.

11

Abbreviations
Used in Text, Picture Credits, and Notes

AIU	Alliance Israélite Universelle
AJA	American Jewish Archives
AJHQ	American Jewish Historical Quarterly
AJHS	American Jewish Historical Society
ALT	Alliance Land Trust
CCAR-YB	Central Conference of American Rabbis Year Book
DAB	Dictionary of American Biography
DAH	Dictionary of American History
DNB	Dictionary of National Biography
EAH	Encyclopedia of American History
EB	Encyclopaedia Britannica
EJ	Encyclopaedia Judaica
HEAS	Hebrew Emigrant Aid Society
HIAS	Hebrew Immigrant Aid Society
IESS	International Encyclopedia of the Social Sciences

JE	Jewish Encyclopedia
MAAS	Montefiore Agricultural Aid Society
MDS	Michigan Department of State, State Archives
NYPL	New York Public Library, Manuscript Division
ORT	Organization for Rehabilitation and Training
PAJHS	Publications of the American Jewish Historical Society
TB	Temple Beth El, Birmingham, Michigan
UJE	Universal Jewish Encyclopedia
WBD	Webster's Biographical Dictionary
YIVO	YIVO Institute for Jewish Research

1 A Condition of Imbalance

The 1880s have a large significance in modern Jewish history, marking the beginning of the mass East European Jewish emigration to the United States. It was also at this time that the Jewish farm movement became a substantial force but in no sense an historical accident. To understand what lay behind not only the unprecedentedly sizable migration from Eastern Europe but also the smaller-scale effort to establish Jews on the land and thereby effect what Victorians saw as the "normalization of Jewish life,"[1] the position of the Jews in the Eastern Europe from which they fled in such numbers must be examined.

The bulk of European Jewry in the nineteenth century was concentrated in a zone which, before the late eighteenth-century partitions by Austria, Prussia, and Russia, had been part of the old Polish kingdom. This zone constituted the "center of gravity" of the Jewish population in Eastern Europe. Together with Galicia (Austrian Poland, with a quarter of a million Jews), the "Pale of Settlement" (the Russian territories of Congress Poland, Lithuania, Byelorussia, and the Ukraine) formed the vast reservoir from which the great majority of Jewish immigrants to the United States was drawn.[2]

15

The Jew in Russia, Early 1800s

The economic, political, and social conditions prevailing in the Russian empire in the first half of the nineteenth century realized the ideal of one of the czars, Nicholas I: "Russia is to be kept frozen." Economically, what the freeze meant was the absence of industrialization and the continuance of serfdom and of pronounced economic conservatism. Political autocracy was in full sway; the czar remained absolute in power, for there was no constitution or legislative body to check his authority. His chief supporters, the nobles and the higher clergy, enjoyed extensive privileges. Even though they occupied the highest level in the social order, they were nevertheless state officials as much subject to the will of the czar as any merchant, townsman, or peasant. Civil liberties were nonexistent, and while in Western Europe the trend was toward separation of church and state, in Russia the state employed the church as a prime agent in enforcing its will. With great fervor the church preached implicit obedience to the czar, the "Little Father," as a religious duty. Acting on the theory that the only true Russian was a communicant of the Orthodox Church and that everyone else was, if not quite a heretic, at the least a foreigner or outsider, the church assigned all non-believers an inferior status and not seldom subjected them to persecution. Moreover, by the ruthless suppression of the national feeling of the many diverse non-Russian ethnic groups within her borders, Russia not only cut herself off from the Western current of European life, but ran counter to it. The French Revolution which had swept over Europe had stopped at the doors of Russia. Democracy and secular nationalism had never entered. What prevailed instead was "the old Trinity of true-Russian Principles: Orthodoxy, Nationality, Autocracy."[3]

Beginning with the 1860's, however, the picture had changed. One sign was Czar Alexander II's Emancipation Edict, aimed at solving the perennially thorny land-tenure problem Russia confronted. The czar sought a compromise between the interests of the landowners and those of the serfs, but the defects of the edict far outweighed its accomplishments. Legally serfdom was abolished and the erstwhile serf gained a previously unknown degree of personal freedom. But even so, the peasant often remained bound to the soil by the requirements of a government passport; he could not in any case hope to become a proprietor because ownership of the land was vested in the *mir*, a village commune of peasant farmers. "The serf of the manorial village," as one authority has said, "did not become under the terms of the Emancipation a free-moving, landless man."[4] The peasant, moreover, remained a serf mentally and in the modesty of his demands.[5] The most significant result of the edict was that it created a potential source of labor. The emancipation left the industrial peasants, the so-called free hired laborers, with allotments generally even smaller than those of their agricultural neighbors, and sometimes with none at all. The "courtyard people," landless serfs totally dependent upon the landlord, drifted away to the slums and factories of the towns, to what has been called "the recruiting ground of the new industrial army."[6] This potential source of labor made possible the establishment of factories, the growth of towns and a money economy, and some increase in the size and influence of the middle classes. It is at this time, in the 1860s, that one meets in Russia early signs of capitalism.[7] Industrial growth did not, however, reach its stride until the last decade of the nineteenth century, when vast quantities of French capital were poured into Russia.

In the period immediately preceding Jewish mass emigration, Russia, then, was in the throes of a nervous transition from feudal agrarianism to a more modern industrial character. She was still, of course, predominantly agricultural, with three-fifths of her population engaged in agriculture and 85 percent of her exports agricultural products.[8] Her methods of cultivation were primitive and crude. Systematic fertilization, deep plowing, and a complex diversification and rotation of crops were on the whole beyond the power of the Russian peasant and even beyond his knowledge and desire.[9] The conditions of modern life had yet to be created. In this world, which the French historian Leroy-Beaulieu described as being "on the opposite pole of modern civilization with the United

States,"[10] the Jews played a part, small in total numbers but rather large in impact.

Russia was a vast land of many millions, and the Jews formed only 4 percent of the total population. The distribution of the Jews was such that some 95 percent of them lived in the Pale.[11] Both within the Pale and without, however, the Jews pursued primarily industrial and commercial occupations. Within the Pale, they predominated as petty artisans, traders, and merchants. In the empire as a whole, they played a significant part as manufacturers and wholesale merchants, but a negligible number earned their living as farmers. The Jews, to be sure, occupied an important role in the empire's agricultural life, but it was in the capacity of middlemen. Thus, there were twenty-six times as many Jews as non-Jews supporting themselves as grain dealers in the Pale, while three-fourths of all dealers in cattle were Jews. As such statistics emphasize, Jews formed a nonagricultural minority in an agricultural society.

Few were the Jews who achieved any notable economic success, but Jews often possessed liquid wealth, however modest, to a greater extent than did nobles or peasants. Being a "commercial" people and given to non-agrarian pursuits, the Jews congregated largely in towns and cities. They formed 12 percent of the total population within the Pale, but 38 percent of the town population. Jews formed 4 percent of the population of the whole empire, but 51 percent of the Jews lived in incorporated towns, while only 12 percent of the non-Jews lived in towns. Their concentration in towns gave Jews a cultural position and influence far out of proportion to their numbers.[12] The Jew was often enough the antithesis of the non-Jewish peasant. He tended to be relatively bourgeois in aspiration, proportionately more "urban," more familiar with town life; and he included in his ranks a larger percentage of intellectuals, or at least of people who were literate. In short, the Jews exhibited what by non-Jewish standards was a condition of socio-economic imbalance, a condition which resulted from the repressive policies Russian governments had adopted toward the Jews for some centuries. By governmental decree, the Jew had been denied the right to engage in agriculture and, up to the era of emerging capitalism, had been virtually condemned to a life of tavern-keeping.[13] Yet there did exist within the Russian empire a group of Jewish farmers, admittedly small in number, but nonetheless significant.

The story of Jewish agricultural efforts in Russia would deserve a full exposition here if it could be shown that the Jewish farmers of the Southern Ukraine were the very ones who, upon coming to America, engaged in agriculture. Incontrovertible evidence exists, however, to indicate that, in general, there was no link between the Jewish farmer in the Russian empire and the Jewish farmer in the United States. Those East European Jews who participated in the various colonizing experiments of the 1880s and 1890s in the United States were virtually without exception inexperienced as farmers and were drawn from the artisan and intellectual classes.

The history of Jewish agriculture in Russia is a checkered one, filled with hopes and disappointments. From Czar Paul's appointment in 1799 of a commission to study what the government regarded as the problematic nature of Jewish life and that commission's recommendation in 1802 that Jews be encouraged to take up agriculture, right up to the infamous May Laws of 1882 which put an end to all such efforts, there runs a single thread.[14] That was the belief that, by permitting the Jew to go into agriculture and to work on the land, his position in Russia would be "normalized." On returning to that basic occupation upon which all else depends, he would become, or be made, productively useful in terms more readily understandable to a pre-capitalist, pre-industrial structure like Russia's in the early 1800s. Czars Paul and Alexander I hoped agriculture would contribute to a healthy Jewish communal life while Nicholas I hoped it would break down Jewish isolation and Jewish separateness and thus act as a stepping stone in the Russification of the Jew. Whatever the ultimate objectives of these czars, each recognized that barring the Jews from farming imposed on them an inevitable and uncomfortable economic and social difference. By 1856, according to one source, the number of Jewish farmers in Russia was 65,000.[15] Another places the number in 1865 at only 33,000.[16] In all likelihood, it was due mainly to the harshness of the government's policy that the number was not larger. Unfortunately, the tensions and instabilities plaguing the empire made it impossible for the czarist government to adopt a consistently intelligent and humane policy on this question.

By 1881, it was apparent that the Jewish problem, of which agriculture was only one facet, was still stubbornly unsolved. A number of indications were present in the 1870s, however, to suggest the turn the solution might take. In 1871, for example, a serious outbreak against the Jews had taken place in Odessa, but it was minimized by the leaders of Russian Jewry and passed off as little more than an anachronism. Influenced by Czar Alexander II's reformist tendencies, Jewish leaders were encouraged to believe the day of medieval pogroms had passed. Certainly it is noteworthy that, while anti-Jewish factors had always been present, it was more than a century since popular animosity toward the Jews in Russia had resulted in any widespread violence.

During the 1870s, too, the pseudo-science of *Rassenkunde* ("racialism") was being exploited in Germany by Adolf Stoecker, Heinrich von Treitschke, *et al.*, all of whom were influenced by the French racialist Count Arthur de Gobineau and his belief in an "Aryan" superiority. These potentially vicious new racist doctrines of Nordic supremacy had found their way into Russian circles as well and thus paved the way, psychologically, for the atrocities which became all too common under Alexander II's successors.

Above all, there was the personal anti-Jewish background of Alexander III, who came to the throne in 1881 after the assassination of his father. This prince had for his tutor none other than Constantin Pobyedonestsev, the head of the reactionary party and an arch-Judeophobe. Pobyedonestsev's influence, which included unrelenting efforts to link the czar's assassination to Jewish sources, virtually insured a violent "solution" to the Jewish problem. Even as crown prince, however, Alexander III had been a comfort to the anti-Semites. In 1876 he had subvented the work of Hippolyte Lutostanski, who published a scurrilous pamphlet entitled *Concerning the Use of Christian Blood by the Jews*. In 1879 he had looked with favor on the scandalous spectacle of a blood libel charge—the trial of ten Jews for the "ritual murder" of a

Christian child—at Kutais in the Caucasus. He had also approved the Judeophobic propaganda of the informer Jacob Brafman.

The oppressed and ignorant Russian peasant was invited to vent his resentment against a minority that enjoyed a slightly better economic status than his own. Anti-Semitism was finally the inchoate expression of resentment by the masses against their own misery. The true source of their wretchedness lay elsewhere, but, as had been done in Russia and elsewhere in the past, the Jew was made a scapegoat.[17]

The pogroms of 1881 were the most virulent form Judeophobia had taken in the nineteenth century. The ranking American diplomat in Russia spoke of them as "more worthy of the dark ages than of the present century." But apparently what troubled the czar most was not the human crisis which the pogroms bespoke; it was that because of the attacks on Jewish lives and property his government had "to defend the Jews." Based on a variety of factors, psychological, religious, economic, social, and political, the riots burst upon the Jews of Russia, and their effect was cataclysmic.

Refugee Assistance in America, 1880s

The mass response was emigration, flight from the scourge. At first, as all records testify, this emigration was wild, chaotic, and disorganized.[18] Thousands, for example, descended upon the Galician town of Brody, whereupon the Austrian government threatened to send them back to Russia unless the congestion were immediately relieved. The necessity for organized action was apparent. The Franco-Jewish Alliance Israélite Universelle (AIU), therefore, came to the rescue by sending its representative, Charles Netter, to remedy the situation at Brody. His efforts enabled 1,500 refugees to come to the United States. What Netter attempted was yeoman work, but the number helped was insignificant in contrast to the thousands who needed aid. Moreover, he could not help the thousands who fled from Russia and who managed to find their way to western Europe or to the United States, but who lacked support once they had arrived.

To assist the victims of czarist oppression, committees

throughout Europe and the United States were hastily formed. Primarily, their object was to render immediate aid to the newcomers. Thus in New York City the Russo-Jewish Committee was set up. (Similarly, in London the Mansion House Committee was established to take care of the unexpected influx.) An eyewitness reports:

> The condition in which they arrived [at New York] baffles description. Terror was written all over their faces, as they knew not whither they were going or what was to become of them. Many of them had been arbitrarily separated from their wives and children and were fearful of what had become of them. Castle Garden—now the Aquarium—was then the place of entry. . . . They were permitted to remain in Castle Garden for days, sleeping on the floor or on boards as best they might, with such covering as was at hand or as kindly people in the city provided.[19]

Because of their plight, their numbers, and the lack of a quota system, the Commissioner of Immigration permitted them to remain in Castle Garden. In the meantime various B'nai B'rith branches offered to take in families. In the fall of 1881, the Russian Emigrant Relief Fund Committee on Behalf of the Russian Exiles was organized in New York City at the Young Men's Hebrew Association. Some two months later, on November 27, 1881, however, because of the continuing influx from Russia and the apparent need for a more basic solution to the problem than that provided by temporary shelter, the Hebrew Emigrant Aid Society (HEAS) was formed. The charter of the organization stated that its purpose was "to afford aid and advice to emigrants of the Hebrew faith coming to the United States from countries where they have suffered by reason of oppressive laws or hostile populace; [and] to afford aid and advice to emigrants desiring the help of the society in settling in the United States upon lands of the society or otherwise."[20]

Agriculture: A Means of Resettlement

The HEAS was to be larger than the Russian Emigrant Relief Fund Committee on Behalf of Russian Exiles, and was to devote itself primarily to agricultural work for the Jews.[21] The stress upon agriculture is understandable when one considers that the social critic Henry George's impressive *Progress and Poverty* had appeared just a few years before the pogroms of 1881. George was convinced, and convinced others, that the only way to remedy "the unequal distribution of wealth . . . the curse and menace of modern civilization" was to "substitute for the individual ownership of land a common ownership." Earlier, arguing for a reform of American land policy, he had insisted that public lands should be given not to speculators or industrialists but exclusively to "actual settlers," and that "our great object should be to give every one an opportunity of employing his own labour, and to give no opportunity to any one to appropriate the labour of others."

The American Jewish philanthropists who stood behind an agency like the HEAS might have been wary of George's political radicalism, but they would not have failed to see the application of his ideas to the immigrant problems they hoped to solve. Farming seemed the answer, farming which, as late as 1906, was still thought to be the most important industry in the United States. No wonder late nineteenth-century immigrant relief agencies, reflecting the upper-class anxieties as well as idealism of their leaders, saw in agriculture a way to prevent repetition of the unhappy history of the Jew in Eastern Europe, "to afford opportunities in which the highest capacities of mind and heart will be more rapidly developed than our present life admits."

Even before the Russian crisis of the early 1880s, an editorial in *The American Hebrew,* a New York weekly, saw in Jewish agricultural settlements a chance "to furnish a profitable and useful opening for the able-bodied poor who find the avenues of petty traffic already too crowded for them." Such an enterprise, "the healthy, invigorating and independence-fostering avocation of the farmer," would save "the thousands of poor Israelites who live and die as pedlers and small hucksters . . . from the slough of pinching privation and mind-debasing penury." The editorialist despised "the mob of pedlers and petty traders" who, presumably, dominated the Jewish street in urban America: what a blessing to be confronted no longer with "the paper muscle and pack-thread sinews of your average tenement house peddler."

A sophisticated communal worker and agriculturist like Hirsch L. Sabsovich knew, of course, that Jewish farming in America could not be considered "the result of a spontaneous movement . . . but . . . the result of certain philanthropic efforts to . . . prevent . . . an unnecessary waste of means, energy and enthusiasm [among immigrant Jews] in their efforts to better their material conditions." For the most part, Sabsovich was right in considering "Jewish farming as one of the preventive measures which present themselves to Jewish philanthropy in the United States."

Louis Mounier, of Vineland, New Jersey, who, like Sabsovich, was eager to advance the South Jersey agricultural colonization designs, conceded that "the colonization was . . . the result . . . of dire necessity—a means to remove 'a thorn in the side' of people who saw in the [immigrant Jewish] congestion of the large cities a danger to the Jewish cause." Mounier, a non-Jew, was well enough acquainted with the American Jewish scene to recognize how much importance the leaders of American Jewry attached to avoidance of urban "congestion."

In the fall of 1881, one American Jewish spokesman described "the position of the Jews in America" as "not such that they can well afford to run any risk of incurring the ill-feeling of their fellow citizens." Still, even among Jewish newcomers, agriculture might be viewed with a reverence that was nothing less than religious. A member of the pioneering Am Olam utopians summed up the agricultural orientation with eloquence in a diary he kept: "Our motto is labor in the fields, and our goal is the physical and spiritual rejuvenation of our people. In free America . . . we Jews . . . shall find a corner in which to rest our heads. We shall prove to the world that we are qualified for physical labor."[22]

In short, all these energies were harnessed to achieve that "normalization" of Jewish life toward which the earlier agricultural efforts of the nineteenth century had been directed. For two years, from 1881 to 1883, the local branches of the AIU and the HEAS were the chief organizations devoted to the aid of the immigrants. Later, other societies, among them the Montefiore Agricultural Aid Society (MAAS) and the Baron de Hirsch Fund, were set up to participate in the task of helping immigrant Jews establish themselves securely in the New World.[23]

What all these efforts amounted to was an attempt to "repeal" the lengthy socio-economic history that had seen the evolution in Europe of a Christian policy designed to drive the Jews off the land, deny them agricultural experience, and confine them to commercial activities. In Eastern Europe, the Jews were, for the most part, no longer needed to develop the economy of the area for its rulers. Indeed non-Jewish German settlers had come to be looked to for that. The Jews were employed to manage the latifundia of the nobility, to fill the invidious function of tax-gathering, and to provide the peasants with small loans and cheap merchandise. The well-to-do, Westernized leaders of the AIU, the HEAS, the Baron de Hirsch Fund, and similar agencies wanted to do away with this whole unsavory history of socio-economic grotesquerie. Sabsovich put the matter thus: "For the *general Jewish welfare* we must . . . have a farming population, as we will stand better with our [non-Jewish] neighbors when we are able to point out that the agricultural industries are taken up by us as a life vocation." But he went on: "From an *economic standpoint*, farming, as a new Jewish trade, is . . . an absolute necessity."

Not all the immigrants saw farming as Sabsovich did. Not many could share his essentially utopian wish to "de-commercialize" and to "re-agriculturize" Jewish life. The preponderant majority of nineteenth-century non-Jewish immigrants from lands like Ireland, Italy, Germany, Sweden, and Poland were people of peasant stock driven off their ancestral farmsteads by higher birthrates, changes in agricultural technology, and famine. Even they were not notably attracted to farming in America, but at least they would have known how to make use of any good agricultural opportunities America offered. Most of the East European Jewish immigrants, however, were incapable of imagining themselves as farmers. During the first decade of the twentieth century, for example, Jews constituted scarcely more than 1 percent of the nearly 1,400,000 agriculturists who immigrated to the United States during those years. Jews thus, almost as a matter of course, sought to establish themselves in the burgeoning urban centers of the New World.[24] They would

25

have agreed with the poet Eliakum Zunser that the Jews, those "hitherto Russian slaves," had become "giants . . . under the bright sun of free America" and could now "progress and advance along the road of true civilization, culture, art and industry."[25]

Not everyone, however, was willing to seek self-fulfillment in an urban setting like the Lower East Side of New York. A much smaller, yet hardly inconsequential group was determined to look up to the bright sun of free America not from a crowded, malodorous urban pavement but from the land itself, the fields and forestland, that lay waiting beyond the borders of the city. The members of this group would attempt in a more literal way to strike roots in American soil. They would seek to maintain themselves and their families through cultivation of the soil, more often than not communally or collectively. The *goldene medineh*, the Eldorado, of the newly emergent American industrialization which had its reflections in city life meant little to them, or meant something they felt compelled to negate. The merest handful had had any farming experience at all, but many of these would-be cultivators had been influenced by earlier nineteenth-century utopian thinkers like Charles Fourier and Robert Owens. The established Jewish community they found on their arrival on American shores was unlikely to have known very much about Fourierist and Owenite goals, but included people influenced by the related, though quite contemporary, utopianism of the American social thinker Henry George.

Thus, not the direct ferment of the industrial revolution and the new urbanization, but an older, reactive, and more utopian or more messianist tradition lived in the would-be farmers and their sympathizers. Their salvation was to be through giving oneself, one's hopes and energies, to an agrarian way of life in the New World.[26]

Newcomers to the New World, enroute to becoming "giants . . . under the bright sun of free America." (Courtesy AJA, Cincinnati)

2 "Our Russian Colonies"

For utopians among the immigrant Jews from Eastern Europe and for the Western Jews willing to aid them, an agrarian way of life in the New World meant colonization, establishing cooperative farming enterprises, more often than not in the trans-Mississippi West. Of course, the core of such ventures is a communal thread, a common bond. The bond need not be, though generally is, economic; but more important are the social and spiritual ties. Colonization, wrote the German Zionist and sociologist Arthur Ruppin,

> is not only a matter of promoting agricultural development but of *creating genuine communities*. Its primary object must, therefore, be the creation of such conditions as will enable people to live together with a minimum of friction. Wherever the general social requirements are not properly satisfied, colonization must fail, however well it may have been planned.[1]

Although Ruppin had in mind the Jewish agricultural efforts in Palestine, not those which took shape in America, as a social scientist he understood that the creation of a community is the essence of colonization anywhere in the world. The nature of the bonds, economic or spiritual, uniting the colonists might vary: "socialistic" colonies, and "individualistic" colonies, "atheistic" colonies, and "orthodox" colonies. But, whatever the bonds, there had to be the common aim of creating a community.

A *sine qua non* for a successful colony is planning. The frequent failures in Jewish colonization attempts in the United States during the last two decades of the nineteenth century resulted, to no minor degree, from poor business planning. The extent to which these failures stemmed from social inadequacies seems to have been slight.

Jewish Settlements in America: Early Plans

Ararat, New York

The year 1881 has been regarded as the date of the establishment of the first Jewish farm colony in the United States, but an earlier date would be defensible. Probably the first such scheme was the abortive project of the New York Jewish playwright-politico Mordecai Manuel Noah, who in 1825 proclaimed the establishment of Ararat, a Jewish colony on Grand Island in the Niagara River, a largely unpeopled region near Buffalo in northern New York State. Noah wanted Grand Island publicized as a place where refugee Jews could "till the soil, reap the harvest, . . . raise [their] flocks . . . and [enjoy] their religious rights, and . . . every civil immunity." Noah's program aroused some controversy. Most of his contemporaries thought the scheme ridiculous. However, Ararat seemed anything but chimerical to one Eliezer Kirschbaum, a Galician Jewish poet and medical student, in whose memory the vicious anti-Jewish riots of post-Napoleonic Central Europe were no doubt quite fresh. Kirschbaum, even before the Ararat proclamation, had published a Hebrew pamphlet praising Noah for his efforts. Redemption was at hand, Kirschbaum believed: the United States government would allow 35,000 Jewish newcomers "to organize a state." It would be easy to realize the project: what was needed was 6,000 families, half of them "agriculturists"; the others would come on their own, "and thus the Jews will have a state."[2]

Zeire Hazon and Sholem, New York

Twelve years after Ararat, in 1837, a group of German Jewish immigrants in New York City organized the Association Zeire Hazon ("Tender Sheep") whose purpose was "removing West, and settling on some part of the Public Lands, suitable for agricultural purposes." These German Jewish "tender sheep," many of them members of New York's Anshe Chesed Congregation, had as "one of [their] leading objects . . . the formation of a Congregation, wherever they may locate." Nothing came of this design either, but a year later a number of Anshe Chesed members formed the nucleus of a colony called Sholem in Wawarsing, not far from Ellenville in Ulster County, New York.

In the cases of Ararat and the Zeire Hazon, the plans never got beyond the stage of proclamation. In the case of Wawarsing's Sholem colony, the story remains something of a mystery "clouded in rock and humus," but by 1847 the colony had disappeared.[3]

American Hebrew Agricultural and Horticultural Association, New York

In 1855, nearly two decades after Sholem was planted, another group of Jews, all of Central European origin and B'nai B'rith members, issued in New York City "a call to establish a Hebrew Agricultural Society to encourage agriculture amongst the Israelites of America." No doubt frightened by the anti-immigrant agitation of the "Know-Nothings" and their sympathizers during the troubled decade preceding the Civil War, these proponents of farming claimed that the lack of Jewish agriculturists led to Jews being "looked upon as transitory inhabitants, having neither the desire nor the capacity to settle as permanent citizens." Moreover, "the exclusive pursuit of commerce" promoted "a course inimical to the wellfare (*sic*) of our country": accumulating wealth "without the acquirement of permanent interest in the soil of the land which constitutes the real title to citizenship and to the full enjoyment of civic rights." Eager "to change this undesirable state of affairs" and

> to create a taste for and encourage agriculture amongst our people, a calling so honorable and ensuring the greatest degree of independence and happiness and finally in order to employ the newly arrived emigrants, and the working man generally in want of employment and to give them a chance to

gain by honesty and industry a comparatively happy living and to wean them from beggary and from becoming a burden to our charitable institutions,

the New Yorkers proposed the establishment of an American Hebrew Agricultural and Horticultural Association. The new society was to purchase land at the earliest opportunity and employ "a competent and reliable manager to superintend [its] whole property." The people sent there to cultivate the land were to be "of good character" and capable of "diligent and honest labour." Instruction, both theoretical and practical, in horticulture and agriculture would be offered "those desirous to turn agriculturist." The apologetic tone of the proposal stirred up considerable controversy, especially in the city's Jewish periodical *The Asmonean*. An association actually came into being, but nothing more is known about it.[4] Before very long the entire project appears to have been abandoned.

Jewish Farming Settlements in America, 1880–1910

More is known about the Jewish agricultural colonies established a half-century later. One similarity is common to all these East European immigrant colonizing efforts of 1880–1900. All experienced the same vicissitudes: a premature birth, a brief struggle, and an abrupt death. They were conceived in haste and planned in stress. Indeed, their organizers tended to ignore or discount the complexities and dangers, the depressed state, of post-Civil War American farming.[5] Notwithstanding the record of failure, their story is a memorable one, expressive in a poignant way of the yearnings to which East European Jewish idealists gave themselves. Some of these idealists, even before the pogroms of 1881, could think of America as a "great and glorious land of liberty, whose broad and trackless acres offer an asylum and a place for . . . courageous souls, willing to toil." America, "the sacred soil of George Washington," promised a freedom which would enable Jewish settlers on the "western lands" to "become new created for the great struggle of life." Sixty years after Noah and Kirschbaum, the dream of a Jewish territory in America was still alive.[6]

The first of the ventures to settle East European Jews upon American land in the 1880s was undertaken by Herman Rosenthal on behalf of the Franco-Jewish Alliance Israélite Universelle. Rosenthal, who had come to the United States early in 1881, had an unusual personal background. In the Ukrainian city of Kiev, he had been both a successful merchant and a *litterateur*. Like many a contemporary East European Jewish intellectual, he had been an ardent Russophile, but the threat of an anti-Semitic reaction in Russia even prior to the violence of the 1880s had disenchanted him and made him break away. In 1880, he was an organizer of the Am Olam group,[7] whose chief aim was to transplant East European Jews to other lands, either to Ottoman Palestine or to the United States, and to settle them in socialistically planned agricultural colonies, the sort he advocated in his Yiddish journal *The Jewish Farmer*, published in 1891.

Early in 1881 Rosenthal arrived in America as the advance agent of the Am Olam pioneers group and, while here, induced the AIU to assist the 124 colonists who were following him. The AIU, founded in 1860 to promote educational, industrial, and agricultural work among needy Jews, had engaged in emigration work in 1869–71 and was responsible for the establishment of the Mikveh Israel agricultural school near Jaffa in Ottoman Palestine. The interest of the Franco-Jewish philanthropists in aiding refugees had already been demonstrated by Charles Netter's work at Brody in Austrian Poland. The AIU was probably the most responsible Jewish agency in existence at the time and met Rosenthal's appeal without delay, if also without enthusiasm. Some of the philanthropists to whom Rosenthal turned reportedly laughed and said, "Let the Russians become peddlers, they can never be farmers."

Sicily Island, Louisiana

In the summer of 1881, the central office of the AIU authorized its New York branch to grant the prospective colonists a loan of $2,800. The money was used to purchase a tract of land, approximately 5,000 acres, located on Sicily Island in Catahoula Parish, Louisiana, some 400 miles upriver from New Orleans and Baton Rouge. According to a contemporary account, "the land abounded in swamps and marshes and was three days journey from a city with no train service."[8]

There are conflicting accounts as to why this particular tract of land was selected. One source claims it had been the voluntary choice of the geographical committee, a committee of the prospective colonists which had corresponded with leading Jews in various parts of the country. Another source would have it that the selection had been forced upon the committee because the sale was to the advantage of a "politician,"[9] allegedly the governor of Louisiana,[10] though there appears to be little basis to the charge. Governor Samuel D. McEnery is known to have offered the colonists a tract of land, but his offer had been rejected because the land was deemed infertile. The governor, it is true, spoke highly of the land finally selected, and he promised the local New Orleans immigrant aid committee that he would encourage the immigrants and do all in his power to make the colony a success.[11] Subsequent events, however, proved that the selection of the land had been injudicious.

Estimates of the extent of the Sicily Island acquisition vary. Leonard Robinson said it amounted to 5,000 acres. The colonists gave it, variously, as 1,000 or 2,400. The HEAS, in its report of 1882, states that 2,800 acres were involved.[12] No land office records exist. That the colonists themselves were so uncertain of the land they had purchased suggests the nature of the group that set out on its unique experiment. The "American Chalutzim," as Leonard Robinson designates them, comprised twenty families and several single men. In Eastern Europe, they had been students, teachers, artists, merchants, craftsmen, and peddlers.[13] It is significant that none of them had ever farmed previously and few were accustomed to manual labor. This assorted group, enthusiastic and ignorant, was given a cordial reception by the Jewish community of New Orleans, and after leaving most of the women and children behind in the Louisiana port, forty-two of them went on to their new abode. Upon reaching the site, an old plantation abandoned since Civil War days, they set about organizing themselves.

On November 16, 1881, the *chalutzim* ("pioneers") incorporated themselves in Louisiana as the "First Agricultural Colony of Russian Israelites in America." The object of the association was "the improvement of the moral and intellectual condition of its members and families."[14] The newcomers were empowered to found a colony on Sicily Island, "there to purchase lands, apportion the same, erect dwellings, farm houses, [and] a school house for the education of the children"; they were also to "establish a library for the common use of the colony" as well as "supply money, farming utensils, or other articles of husbandry, household furniture and stock," and "generally do and provide for . . . the furtherance of [the colony's] aims and purposes . . . whatever shall be necessary." A governing board of seven members was set up to administer the business and to settle disputes. Article 7 of their constitution reflected an intention of carrying out the socialist ideals of the Am Olam group:

> All money belonging to individuals of the colony which had been deposited with the Immigrant Aid Society of New Orleans [the committee of the New Orleans community set up to deal with the problems of the new arrivals] will remain as a general fund for the benefit of the colony; but each member will be entitled to a special credit on the books of the association for the amount deposited less the costs incident to his voyage and support.

According to Article 8, "all supplies sent to the colony by the Immigrant Aid Association shall be charged to the colony and to the members receiving them," but, Article 9 continued, "any member having to his credit a larger amount than any of his associates shall not for that reason be entitled to draw more supplies than is necessary for his needs, unless by special authorization from the I.A.A. [Immigrant Aid Association] committee of New Orleans." No member would be "allowed to sell, barter, or offer for sale anything within the boundaries of the colony"; any commercial enterprise would require approval by two-thirds of the colonists, and distilling was to be forbidden.

In order to work more effectively the three tracts of land purchased, the colonists divided themselves into three groups. All resources were pooled. The business and any profits were to be divided on an equal basis. At the outset, individuals were to have no shares of their own; ultimately, when the colony had achieved a strong foundation, each person was to be established on an individual basis.[15]

The local committee of the AIU dealt with the basic problem of supplies by furnishing the colonists with lumber for their homes as well as horses, farm implements, cattle, and poultry. A German farmer was hired as an agricultural adviser, but since he would come only once or twice a week, his instruction proved of limited value. The colonists, nonetheless, set about clearing the land, which contained excellent timber. They tilled the soil and planted corn, cotton, and vegetables. Ten houses were also put up, but the original plan of erecting forty small houses, each to serve a family or four single men, would never be realized. A general store was opened and stocked with things "necessary and unnecessary." In all, the picture seemed encouraging. "There is no winter here," one of the colonists assured correspondents in the Russian capital. "Trees blossom all year around."

The social aspect of the colony's life appeared rewarding. Evenings the colonists gathered for discussions and debates in one of the three big houses remaining from the Civil War. One member, Borowick, an opera star in Russia, entertained with song. Another, Herman Rosenthal himself, read his poems to an appreciative audience. The community life was reflected in a weekly news bulletin written in Russian and offering a humorous view of life. For the children, who were gradually brought from New Orleans, a school was organized in Rosenthal's house, and two of the members who knew English served as teachers. The adults, too, applied themselves to learning the language of their new home, and many a night was spent in study and reading.

The spring of 1882 saw the prospects of success diminish. The colonists began to complain of the heat. Coming from Russia's colder climate, they were not accustomed to the high Louisiana temperatures. Moreover, snakes and mosquitoes added to the discomforts of life, and malaria struck down a number of children. "Young men of strong physique and possessed of knowledge," reported one observer, "were shattered like a broken pitcher from the asthmatic sickness" they contracted in the colony. The natural high spirits of the colonists were considerably dampened. The letters they received from their city relatives telling of jobs, homes, and opportunities only added to the discontent. After they had exhausted any comfort they might have derived from one another, they had no one else to turn to. Their neighbors were, in the main, blacks whose pattern of life diverged widely from their own. Rosenthal, too, became disheartened: "A viler spot on God's earth it would be hard to find," he wrote in late May.

These factors might not have spelled doom for the colony. What destroyed it was that as farmers the colonists were to achieve no success. Originally cotton and corn were planned as the main cash crops, with small-scale gardening for home use. According to Robinson, a prominent New Orleans Jew had offered to pay $2,000 for the first bale of cotton grown by the Jewish colonists, though the prevailing market price was $40 a bale. The offer was never realized, however, since in the spring of 1882 before a single bale of cotton had been picked a flood washed everything away: houses, cattle, implements, and small crops. The Louisiana colony was quickly abandoned. Even at the end, others had to come to the aid of the colonists. Rosenthal and a friend went to New York to raise funds for the transportation of the pioneers elsewhere. At a meeting in New York City on May 24, 1882, Rosenthal spoke of the colony as "a piece of Jewish history."[16] Thus passed out of existence the first agricultural colony of Russian Jews in the United States. One of the colonists summed up the experiment as "work, mostly useless, hope, despair, love, songs, poetry, happiness and misery—life as we lived it there in Louisiana."[17]

Why had the Louisiana enterprise failed? The organization backing the colonists in New York and in New Orleans was highly effective. The New Orleans Jewish community was responsive. The internal organization of the colonists was competent. Herman Rosenthal, their leader, was a capable, self-sacrificing individual. They had not planned to become dependent on a single crop, but rather on a variety of agricultural efforts. The land was cheap. They had immediate lodging. Necessary supplies were furnished at the outset. All these advantages, however, could not offset the basic factors of harsh environmental conditions, heat, floods, and disease, combined with the lack of agricultural experience and the social isolation of the community. Even so, it appears, some of the colonists were not discouraged. Believing a new start could be made elsewhere under more favorable conditions, some went on to Arkansas, others to Dakota, and still others to Kansas.

New Odessa, Oregon

The anti-Semitic storm which broke over Russia in 1881 led to the formation of more Am Olam groups. In September of that year one of them, made up of sixty-five young people, left Odessa and crossed the Austrian frontier to Brody. There they were met by a representative of the AIU who directed them to the next stop on their long journey to the United States. On their arrival in Berlin, the travelers found that certain Orthodox Jewish leaders, forewarned of their nonconformist views on religion, balked at helping them; but using the limited means they possessed, they were able to go on and landed at New York in January 1882. In February 1882 a second group reached New York, and two others soon followed. When the colony of New Odessa was founded in remote Oregon, its membership stemmed almost entirely from these four groups.

The reception these Am Olamites had received in New York was none too cordial. This time it was not religious traditionalists but the conservative and insecure German leaders of the HEAS who looked askance at the plans of the Russian Jews. There were, however, in the New York community two individuals whose sympathies were won over. These two, the liberal publicist and philanthropist Michael Heilprin and the lawyer Dr. Julius B. Goldman, deserve to be remembered as responsible for the unique agricultural experiment of New Odessa.[18] Heilprin indeed exerted himself to such an extent that his biographer claims that his work in behalf of the Russian refugees brought on his premature death.[19] Abraham Cahan in his memoirs recalled him as the most beloved figure among the immigrant masses of the 1880s. Heilprin had been a follower of the Hungarian revolutionary Louis Kossuth, and no doubt his experiences in the Hungarian uprising of the late 1840s made him a sympathetic friend to the Jews leaving the czarist empire four decades later. Moreover, Heilprin was a passionate believer in agricultural colonization for Jews. It is understandable that this band of idealists won his devotion.[20]

Like their predecessors who had undertaken the unfortunate Louisiana venture, this Am Olam group had neither funds nor training. Unlike the Louisiana colonists, however, they set about their Oregon enterprise somewhat more systematically. Some of them saw that the immediate task was to gain experience as farmers, and so they set about acquiring it by actual work on farms on Long Island and in Connecticut and Indiana. One is said to have refused a good city job and to have gone to work on a farm in Vincennes, Indiana, for a pittance. Others, however, felt that obtaining funds was at the moment more essential than agricultural experience. They remained in New York City to take positions that paid more than farm work, but the money they earned was deposited into a general fund. The city members, sixty of them, kept together by organizing what they called "The Commune." They rented a house on Pell Street, and the manner in which they ran it was a foretaste of the life they expected to lead in the future. Household tasks were divided, earnings were pooled, and at night educational meetings were held to formulate plans for the colony.

Another question to be solved was the selection of land for their colony. Here, possibly due to the guidance of Heilprin, who had by this time succeeded to the secretaryship of the HEAS, sound judgment was exhibited. Two groups of prospective colonists were sent out: one, to the Midwest and to Texas; the other, to the Northwest, to Washington and Oregon. The members of these groups worked on the farms of their particular regions for three months and then sent reports back to their confrères in New York. The Texas group reported the land there was arid. The Washington-Oregon group held that the land in Douglas County, Oregon, was fertile and desirable. It was thereupon agreed that Douglas County was to be the home of the New Odessa colony.

The colony might have died stillborn at this juncture if not for Heilprin's effort to raise $2,000 of the $4,800 purchase price.[21] The land selected 250 miles south of Portland, Oregon, consisted of 760 acres, 150 of them fit for immediate cultivation. The rest was virgin forest containing excellent timber. As the Oregon and California Railroad was under construction nearby, the colonists reasoned they could obtain much-needed capital by cutting wood from the forests and selling it to the railroad for ties. At the same time, for home consumption they could raise wheat, oats, peas, beans, and a variety of vegetables. As the land was rich and well-watered, the physical conditions appeared to be most promising. There was one physical factor whose importance they underestimated: the colony's distance from markets.[22]

In July, 1882, twenty-five Am Olamites started for Oregon. On their arrival in Portland, some eight of them proceeded immediately to the site of the colony; the others remained behind to earn money and to learn English. Their plan was for small groups to go from New York to Portland and remain there until called. They were not to be idle, and it was agreed that, whatever their earnings, part would go to support the New Odessa colonists.

From this point on it becomes difficult to reconstruct a detailed story of these pioneers, particularly for the period between July 1882 and the spring of 1883. Occasionally New York's *Jewish Messenger* published a fleeting reference to "our Russian colonies."[23] In the spring of 1883, forty to fifty people inhabited the colony.[24] They had erected a large two-story frame building. The upper story was used as a dormitory, and the lower consisted of a communal kitchen, dining room, and assembly hall. They had already begun raising wheat, oats, peas, and other crops, but marketing the yield proved a formidable problem, since the cost of transportation was extremely high. It was, not so incidentally, the opinion of Julius Bien, one of the HEAS leaders, that inaccessibility to markets and to avenues of communication had to be counted among the chief reasons for the failure of all the colonization attempts. It undoubtedly contributed to the difficulties faced by the New Odessa colony.[25]

The colonists, despite all hazards, were able to pay off $1,000 for the land. In two years they grossed an income of between $7,000 and $8,000 for the sale of 4,000 cords of wood to the Oregon and Pacific Railroad. In 1884 it appears the railroad was willing to contract for the delivery of more lumber. The offer was rejected, because to carry it out would have required the erection of an expensive sawmill. Correspondence between the colonists and the MAAS[26] was exchanged in reference to this proposal, but the negotiations failed. The reasons given for the failure vary. Some of the colonists resisted committing themselves to the railroad through a contract extending over a term of years. Others doubted that the funds necessary for the sawmill could be raised. There is evidence to support their doubts, for it was at this time, in November 1883, that Heilprin's *Appeal to the Jews* appeared. In it he stated that the New Odessa colonists

> have done a great deal of hard work, their zeal has not abated, and the future of the colony is promising. It is able to maintain itself in spite of trying privation and scantiness of means. It furnishes the Oregon and Pacific Railroad wood for fuel, and if possessed of the necessary steam-saw machinery, could also supply the railroad with the sleepers required for its extension.[27]

In view of the title Heilprin gave his tract it might be thought that inadequate finances alone were holding up the construction of the mill. It was, however, not the lack of a sawmill which brought about the end of the New Odessa venture in 1885. Neither want, privation, crop shortage, hostile climate, nor physical exhaustion could be held responsible. Nor was there a threat of foreclosure hanging over them. On the contrary, in 1885 the owners of the land offered to extend the mortgage for fifteen years if necessary, and several local merchants as well as two prominent Portland Jewish businessmen offered the colonists credit in an effort to save the colony. If the physical and financial conditions were

Herman Rosenthal, Am Olam founder.
(Courtesy AJA, Cincinnati)

Julius Goldman, champion of colonies in
Oregon and New Jersey. (Courtesy AJA,
Cincinnati)

Abraham Cahan. More than a new kind of life for Jews, he sought "sound socialist ideas." Drawing by Saul Raskin (1923). (Courtesy AJA, Cincinnati)

William Frey, the Saint of New Odessa. (Courtesy William Frey Papers, Manuscripts and Archives Division, New York Public Library, Astor, Lenox and Tilden Foundations)

Michael Heilprin, beloved by immigrants, tireless supporter of New Odessa. (Courtesy AJA, Cincinnati)

William Frey in his last days, ca. 1888. Pencil sketch by Prince Peter Kropotkin. (Courtesy William Frey Papers, Manuscripts and Archives Division, New York Public Library, Astor, Lenox and Tilden Foundations)

William and Mary Frey, founders of New Odessa. (Courtesy William Frey Papers, Manuscripts and Archives Division, New York Public Library, Astor, Lenox and Tilden Foundations)

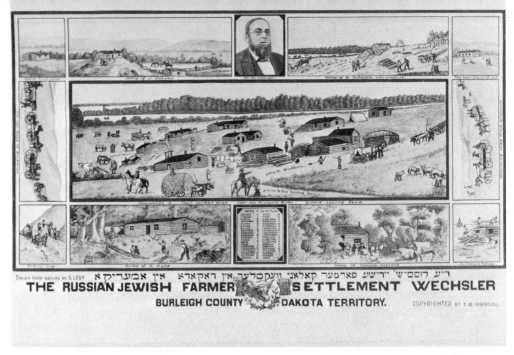

Memento of the Wechsler settlement, Dakota Territory, 1880s, founded by Judah Wechsler, liberal rabbi. (Courtesy YIVO)

Colonist workers at a mine near Cotopaxi Colony, Colorado. (Courtesy AJHS)

reasonably favorable, why then did the colony fail? The answer lies largely in the social and spiritual domain.[28]

The New Odessa colony, like the earlier Louisiana experiment, had been conceived as a communistic effort. But the Sicily Island venture had not aimed to establish a colony in which pure communism, a thoroughgoing collectivism or equalization of wealth and income, would be put into immediate practice. At New Odessa, the Marxist creed of "from everyone according to his ability, and to everyone according to his needs" was applied literally. Pure communism was an immediate objective. There were fixed hours of labor, and specific tasks were assigned on the farm, in the forest, and in the kitchen.

The leading spirit of this undertaking was a non-Jew of upper-class antecedents, William Frey, born Vladimir Konstantinovich Geins, a former officer in the czarist army and professor of mathematics in the military academy at St. Petersburg, the Russian capital. Abraham Cahan wrote of him as a moral giant, the greatest figure among the immigrant masses of the 1880s. Staunch believers in the humanist positivism of the nineteenth-century French philosopher Auguste Comte, Frey and his wife, Maria Slavinskaya, had come to the United States in 1868 and had spent some ten years in rural communes in Missouri and Kansas. It was Frey who set the tone for this band of pioneering Jews whose rather reluctant leader he now became. Frey professed extreme simplicity in thought and deed, but doubted that the Am Olamites would be able to pattern themselves after him. Would he not be "a living reproach to their consciences"? But the Jewish newcomers were adamant, and Frey, together with Maria, and with his mistress Lydia Eichoff, settled at New Odessa.

The Am Olamites strove to vindicate his decision. They agreed to "dispense with bosses or employers, renounce personal property, receive no salary, [and] have one purse for all." Even though the land was fruitful, the idealistic colonists insisted on leading a frugal existence. Their diet was confined to beans, peas, and coarse bread. The cost of feeding one person per day did not exceed five cents. When the food budget rose to eight cents, it was considered gross extravagance. These exponents of the selfless Comtean discipline of the religion of humanity would not live lavishly while millions starved. The New Odessa colonists, said Cahan in later years, had "had the beautiful expectation of providing the egotistic, unhappy world with an inspiring example of how to live in equality and brotherly love."[29]

For two years the group apparently worked in harmony and with sizable success. Diversions within the colony were largely intellectual. Nights were given over to discussions, debates—generally about Auguste Comte's philosophy of positivism and the religion of humanity—and the inevitable self-criticism and mutual criticism often associated with earnest, self-searching intellectuals. These meetings, Cahan reported, were "designed to provide a reciprocal examination of individual morals in order to cleanse the entire colony," but "people are people, so that often the member at whom the speaker aims his criticism listens not in a brotherly spirit but with a rising anger." There were also sexual jealousies arising from the paucity of girls which left the "young men . . . moody, jealous, [and] isolated." Respect for privacy seems to have been conspicuous by its absence.

Since the aristocratic Maria Frey, a musician, entertained with recitals one night a week on a pipe organ which had been presented to the colony, the social life could not have been as forbidding or cheerless as might be thought. Indeed, many an American farmer travelled long distances to spend a social evening at New Odessa, especially for the dances given there at the assembly hall. According to one visitor, an itinerant non-Jewish farm expert, the group never quarreled, was constantly cheerful, and was extremely idealistic. Clearly, the spirit of brotherhood prevailed in the New Odessa colony. "Everyone labored to save the world." A German-born Reform rabbi, Judah Wechsler, visited New Odessa in the fall of 1884, but was not quite sure what to make of the colonists:

> They are good mechanics and do all their own repairing. They even built a small grist mill themselves. They live, eat, and drink together harmoniously like members of a vast family. They have an excellent library. They believe in no religions, keep no Sabbaths, and do nothing that would distinguish them as Jews.[30]

It is a tribute to this band of idealists that they held together in a voluntary association for two years in such a spirit of harmony, but Frey's frail health alarmed the colonists. Moreover, as Cahan puts it, "mounting dissatisfactions began to eat at the heart of the commune, devouring it as rust devours iron." When the break came, as it did in 1884, it came over ideological differences. By this time at least two distinct schools of thought had developed. One banded around the arch-idealist Frey and followed him in his spartan code of simplicity. Few of them, Cahan suggests, may have actually subscribed to Frey's positivism, but not many had the heart to offend this man whom they revered as a saint, and "besides, he was a gentile and an aristocrat."

The group which did muster the fortitude to break with Frey was led by Cahan's friend Paul Kaplan, one of the organizers of the colony, and was composed of those who were "positive but not positivistic." They were idealists, too, but a shade more earthy. Comprised largely of the younger element, they were interested in marriage and increasingly frustrated by the scarcity of eligible young women. Apparently they were ambitious and wanted to return to their careers. Some felt that the goals of the colony were aimed much too high; that farming and communism were not the only instruments through which real happiness could be obtained.

The chasm between Freyites and non-Freyites proved unbridgeable. In an atmosphere lacking in malice, and in one of profound pain at separation—one of the colonists reported that "the tears fell like rain"—Frey and fifteen of his followers departed New Odessa. He and Maria settled in London, where he died, at the age of forty-nine, in November 1888. Kaplan, however, was unable to improve matters in Oregon, and it was probably not long thereafter that a non-Jewish observer offered readers of the *San Francisco Overland Monthly* a rather grim picture of the colony, or what was left of it:

> Nearly all members eat, and sleep, and stagnate—for [one] can hardly speak of it as living—in a large hall of rough boards and unplaned planks and containing only two apartments, the lower story being the dining room and kitchen in one, and the upper story a large sleeping room without partitions.

47

This writer, too, like Rabbi Wechsler, noted the group's atheism, saying that they had no religion, no political organization for management of their affairs, and no defined code of morals other than "to be good."[31]

The loss of over one-fourth of the colony's membership was a serious blow to the enterprise, but it need not have been fatal. It was not their miniscule numbers that hindered the colonists; it was their lack of unity in thought and action. Still, the *coup de grâce* came from another direction. The community building, which housed the most valuable possession of the group, the library which had so impressed Rabbi Wechsler, was destroyed by fire. The loss of companionship with a lively part of the band was thus intensified by the loss of intellectual contacts with the outside world. To geographical isolation was now added spiritual isolation, a situation which proved intolerable; and the colonists began to disperse. One group of irrepressible idealists went to San Francisco and then on to New York where they revived the collectivist "Commune" experiment, this time a steam laundry on Essex Street. Others realized earlier ambitions: three became doctors; two, lawyers; two, pharmacists; one, a dentist; one, a chemist; one, an engineer; and one, an educator. By 1885, the New Odessa enterprise which had started out with such high hopes had, like Sicily Island in Louisiana, become another false start, or, as Israel Mandelkorn, one of the colonists, would put it, "What began as an experiment ended as an experience."[32]

Crémieux, South Dakota

Thus far, in Louisiana and in Oregon, the attempts made to settle the Russian refugees had been on privately owned tracts of land. Shortly after the New Odessa colony was initiated, however, the United States government threw open for settlement a former Indian reservation in the Dakota Territory. Since 1862, indeed, all government land had been placed within the reach of the small cultivator by an extremely liberal land policy. By the terms of the Homestead Act of 1862, a quarter-section, 160 acres of land, was granted free to the head of a family or a person over twenty-one who was a citizen of the United States or who had filed his intention of becoming one, if for five years he resided on the land and cultivated it. If, however, after six months of cultivation, the occupant desired to acquire full title to the land, he might do so by buying it at the low rate of $1.25 an acre. Settling on such government land seemed to Rabbi Isaac M. Wise, editor of Cincinnati's *American Israelite*, "the main enterprise" which would enable East European immigrants "to become independent men." Wise, busily promoting a Cincinnati-sponsored Homestead Act design, the Beersheba colony, in western Kansas, argued that a settler who took advantage of the act could be "sure of success in the end, sure of a living for himself and family, and of perfect independence."[33] It was this prospect of free or cheap land which motivated two pioneer Jewish families to set out from New York City on July 1, 1882, for the town of Mitchell in the Territory of South Dakota. The community which they helped to establish was the transient but memorable colony named in honor of the late president of the AIU, Adolphe Crémieux.[34]

After the breakup of the Louisiana colony in the spring of 1882, Herman Rosenthal had returned to New York City to arrange for the relocation of his unfortunate comrades. But he was far from abandoning colonization altogether. Rosenthal ascribed the failure of the Sicily Island colony to the region's oppressive heat and malaria; the next attempt, he felt, should be in a temperate climate, one more like the climate to which the colonists were accustomed in Eastern Europe. The possibility of newly available Homestead land in the Dakotas was a powerful magnet to attract a man of ambition, energy, and ideals like Rosenthal. It was with hopes of taking advantage of the generous policy of a hospitable government that he determined on land near Mitchell in Davison County, South Dakota, as the desirable site for a new colony.

Rosenthal's scheme of settlement in South Dakota attracted support from the indefatigable Heilprin and the earnest young Benoir Greenberg, the son of a noted architect and bridge-builder in Russia. Greenberg had been brought up in wealth, luxury, and culture, but like other young intellectuals in Russia he had become disillusioned as a result of the pogroms and had turned to the Am Olam organization. The three, Rosenthal, Heilprin, and Greenberg, formed the MAAS, which was later to supersede the HEAS. Both Rosenthal and Greenberg took part in the actual colonization, while Heilprin remained in the East to propagandize for the design. Greenberg's was one of the two families to arrive in Mitchell. Upon arrival, the two were greeted by a local Jewish businessman named Weil, with whom the families had corresponded, as well as the entire population of Mitchell. Weil provided temporary quarters for the two families, and they spent a week in Mitchell obtaining information for their venture and awaiting the arrival of Rosenthal eight days later.[35]

The tract of land selected for Crémieux was fertile and virgin, located in prairie country. Word was sent back to New York City that the site had been chosen and families began to come out. After 200 persons had settled in the colony, the area that finally came under the colonists' control covered fifteen square miles. Each man settling and cultivating the land acquired title in his own name. Thus, in contrast to the Louisiana and Oregon attempts, land was not held in common, though it was still possible for the colonists to work cooperatively, sharing tools, seed, livestock, and, in the end, profits and losses.

Lack of trained leadership and ill-advised expenditures militated against the success of the project, but these factors were not irremediable. Scarcely had the colonists succeeded in making their homes habitable, however, when a prairie fire broke out on Yom Kippur, 1882. Every bit of standing hay was destroyed, and the cattle were left utterly without feed. Rather than bewail their loss, the colonists were grateful for their personal rescue and solved the problem of feed by purchasing it from local farmers.

The first winter of 1882–83 in South Dakota was long remembered for its severe cold. The kerosene froze in the lamps, and the water that was drawn turned to ice unless one drank it immediately. Obtaining water was a difficult task even under normal weather conditions, for there were no surface springs and wells had to be dug fifty or sixty feet deep. Only the wealthiest of the group, Rosenthal and Greenberg, could afford the enormous sums of two to three hundred dollars that well-digging entailed. The other settlers had to rely upon a small spring a little over three miles distant. In sub-zero temperatures the intrepid soul who ventured this distance brought back ice. All the colonists were spiritually and physically hardy, for despite the formidably low temperatures and raging blizzards, they came through the first winter without losing a single member. Encouraged no doubt by their apparent triumph over nature, the colonists set to work planting their crops, mainly corn, flax, wheat, and some vegetables, in the spring of 1883. With the autumn harvest, however, the colonists derived little more than the moral satisfaction of knowing that they were capable of functioning as farmers. Unfortunately, their wheat found a depressed market (the period was one which saw the curve of farm prices in steady decline), and the pioneers received little for their exertions. Since flax had brought a better return, the following spring more flax was planted, and of course, the inevitable wheat.

Amidst their planting and reaping, the band of colonists found time for an active social life. The pattern was much like that of New Odessa; there were lectures, discussions, debates, concerts, and dances. The colonists threw themselves with equal enthusiasm into their work and play, and many of the native farmers were drawn to this odd, exciting group. While there was plenty of communal life, there was no organized religious life. The only religion the Crémieux idealists believed in was that of an empirical humanism. Metaphysics was nonsense; synagogue, a rabbi, a shochet ("ritual slaughterer") would have been superfluous. Apparently, the social life they led was all-sufficient, since there is no indication of ideological strife or dissension among them.

In the autumn of 1884, a hailstorm destroyed the entire flax crop. Hopes for the second year faded, and some of the older men became discouraged. By now all but a few families were heavily in debt. While money was available, the rates of interest were notoriously exorbitant. The mounting burden of indebtedness was disheartening, and, inevitably, in 1884 the exodus began.

Those who hung on saw all their efforts come to naught the following year when the Hessian fly destroyed the wheat, and drought and intense heat killed off most of the livestock.

As the supply of food and water dwindled, many of the farmers sold what remained of their stock. It became impossible to meet the interest on the mortgages, and so by the end of 1885 the Crémieux venture, which started out with such promise, had taken its place beside that of the other abandoned colonies.

Bethlehem-Jehudah, South Dakota

Thus far, the two attempts at colonization under the auspices of the Franco-Jewish Alliance, Sicily Island in Louisiana and Crémieux in South Dakota, had been unsuccessful. The AIU's last venture along these lines was brief and on a less pretentious scale, and it, too, ended in failure.

In 1885, a group of single men had settled near Crémieux on a tract of Davison County land which they called Bethlehem-Jehudah. Here with the support of AIU funds, they attempted to carry on a fully collectivist life. Bethlehem-Jehudah was to demonstrate to anti-Semites the world over that Jews were capable farmers; every colonist was expected to farm, and commercial activity was "absolutely forbidden." Women, moreover, were to "enjoy equal rights with men." To a colonist in nearby Crémieux, "these brave youths" at Bethlehem-Jehudah testified that "the great spirit of Israel is still alive." Unfortunately, however, the colony's brief year and a half of existence was marked by strife, discontent, and natural disaster.

Rabbi Wechsler, one of the colony's founders, complained that Bethlehem-Jehudah was "characterized by differences of opinion, quarrels and confusion, without any law or order." The causes of failure were identical with those of the other colonies: lack of farming experience and lack of trained and practical leadership.[36] When this experiment proved abortive, the AIU withdrew as an important factor in Jewish colonization in America.

Am Olam Group Settlement, Arkansas

Throughout these closing decades of the nineteenth century, there was instance after instance of other valiant but

short-lived attempts to transform into actuality the dream of
the Jew as a farmer. Sicily Island, New Odessa, and Crémieux
are only among the more notable. Because they were so transitory and because they were primarily concerned with con-
quering, literally, a new earth, only a few factual sign-posts
survive to guide researchers. The records of organizations, if
they exist; the accounts of survivors who can be traced; the
letters, if any, which passed between colonists and the outside
world; and any personal diaries—these are the chief sources of
information. But such documents do not always exist.

The difficulties of reconstructing the early colonization
efforts are illustrated by the case of the ill-fated Bethlehem-
Jehudah project. They are perhaps even better reflected in the
story of a colony in Arkansas. Here, after personal investigation, the lawyer Gabriel Davidson and his collaborator
Edward Goodwin were able to trace a handful of the colonists
and published an account based on the memories of the few
participants they discovered. As far as is known, the experience of the Arkansas colony survives only in the fragile web of
reminiscence.[37]

In the spring of 1883, a band of 150 individuals, East
European Jews and former ghetto dwellers, set out for a tract
of land near Newport on the White River in eastern Arkansas, about ninety miles northeast of Little Rock. The land had
been offered for colonization, by whom is not clear, and a
lumber company had agreed to buy staves to be cut by the
colonists. There is little else that is known about the group
except that its members were attracted by the idea of farm
life, were overwhelmed by the beauty of the virgin forest,
and wrote home to New York City of the wonders of nature
in Arkansas. A second group of thirty belonging to one of the
Am Olam societies, three families and the rest single men,
felt encouraged to follow them. They had been awaiting an
opportunity to go to the land, and thought that now they had
been given one.

Like all the previous groups, this second group were
inexperienced farmers with slender means, though abundant
enthusiasm. They did, however, include within their ranks
two men who had returned from Louisiana, Solomon Menaker and one known as Spies. Because of their background

these two were chosen to investigate the site. Unfortunately, experience does not always spell wisdom, for the tract of land they selected was near the site upon which the original 150 had settled. It was land so densely forested that not even the natives of the region had penetrated it. Worse still, it was located in a plague-infested area. Agriculture as such was obviously impossible. Menaker and Spies believed, however, that the clearing of this forest, a necessary preliminary step, could be turned to profit and could give the colonists a successful impetus, through the sale of the timber to railroad or lumber companies. "Had the colonists been more adept, they probably would have eked out a modest living."[38] But because of the inexperience of the settlers and the hard labor involved, it took two men working two weeks to cut a thousand staves. Ordinarily such work should have been accomplished in half that time by an average workman.

To add to their burden, the hot season came shortly after their arrival. Temperatures of 105–108 degrees in the shade made work quite impossible. One survivor of the Am Olam group recalls getting up to work at four in the morning, working until eleven, taking a siesta until five, and then, working again from five to nightfall, generally eight-thirty or nine o'clock.[39] The torrid weather debilitated East Europeans unused to such heat. Rainstorms broke the heat for a brief space of time, but the rain was so torrential that it proved only an additional affliction. The Mississippi overflowed and prevented the floating of logs to market, thereby cutting off a vital source of revenue. Much worse, the storms brought mosquitoes in their wake and the consequent spread of malaria and yellow fever. As there were only two log shacks in the larger settlement and only a ramshackle barn in the smaller, the women and children occupied the crude houses and the men slept out in the fields. In this way, the latter exposed themselves even more to the danger of insects, snakes, and malaria. In July 1883 when the heat was at its height, 90 percent of the colonists fell ill, and between eighteen and twenty persons died. So, the Arkansas ventures came to the same end as Sicily Island, Crémieux, and New Odessa.

Appeals to the MAAS, the patron organization of the Am Olamites, brought funds, and the survivors among the thirty who had made up the second Arkansas group were transported back to New York. The first and larger group, however, had no organization to fall back upon. If not for the MAAS, which came to their aid as generously as it had to the Am Olamites, they might have perished. By September 1883 the brief and pathetic tale had been told; the Arkansas colony was no more. Once again, the experiment had highlighted the need for informed and efficient direction if there was to be any proper development of a Jewish agricultural movement.

Cotopaxi, Colorado

Despite the record of consistent failure in the 1880s, at least half-a-dozen further attempts at colonization were made before the decade came to a close. One such venture, inaugurated under the auspices of the HEAS, was the Cotopaxi colony in Colorado. Motivated by the basic ideal of binding the immigrant to his new country and of breaking down the prejudice against Jews in agriculture, the society selected thirteen families, totaling fifty persons, and moved them on May 3, 1882, to Colorado, where they staked out claims on government land.[40] It was the intention of the HEAS to give assistance to these farmers and to help each settle on his own individual plot and to engage in individual enterprise. In its individual, rather than collective, enterprise, the Cotopaxi development differed from the communal Louisiana and New Odessa enterprises and the semi-cooperative of Crémieux. The plan anticipated a series of individual Jewish farms situated near each other in a contiguous area.

Fremont County, Colorado, on the railroad line running from Leadville to Denver, was the site selected for this group of Jewish farms. Cotopaxi, about a hundred miles southwest of Denver, was the headquarters of the rich mining district of Colorado and lay in a valley surrounded by high mountains. The Arkansas River flowed through one end of the valley and on the opposite bank were 500 acres of farming land. On this land, Julius Schwarz, a young Hungarian-born lawyer who was first clerk and then general manager of the colony and authorized agent of the HEAS, helped three farmers stake out their claims. (Schwarz was the guiding spirit of the colony. He had been entrusted with the selection of the site, the distribution of the land, and the other matters attendant upon such a new venture.)

These three claims formed the first link in the chain of Russian Jewish farms. A steep mountain range surrounded this area and beyond it lay Wet Mountain Valley, so named because of its frequent rainfall and the natural humidity of the soil. In Wet Mountain Valley, Schwarz helped six other farmers stake out their plots, and 960 more acres now came under Jewish ownership. An additional piece of land was selected as the third settlement a short distance away, and on it five more families were located. In all, the Cotopaxi colonists controlled 1,780 acres of land. By October 1882, when Schwarz wrote his report for the HEAS, nine more plots had been surveyed and staked out, which brought the total land at the disposal of the HEAS to 3,220 acres. Technically, the claims were taken out in the name of the colonists, but because the HEAS subsidized them almost entirely, the Society had power of disposal of the land.

The first colonists arrived on May 9, 1882, and to their surprise found that the land had not been as developed as they had expected. Their initial task, then, was to set up the necessary conditions of existence, homes and other facilities. They immediately began erecting log cabins. Since it was not until the latter part of May that the first settlement was accomplished, Schwarz, in view of the late start, ordered a number of acres to be cultivated in common and the crop raised to be divided according to the size of each family.

To Schwarz's great satisfaction, the crop yield was excellent. Forty acres of cabbage, potatoes, beets, berries, and turnips were grown, an auspicious start. The colonists plowed the land, built ditches, hewed rocks from the mountains, worked in mines and on the railroad. They were undeterred by distance and walked many miles to chop wood for fences. They turned to these nonagricultural labors mainly because they were a source of ready income.

The people who came to Cotopaxi were of the same character as those who had joined the other agricultural experiments: they were enthusiastic but inexperienced farmers. Socially, however, they differed from the others in that the

Coloradans had an active organized religious life, as was evidenced by their Sabbath services, Talmud Torah, and mutual relief society. In addition, they conceived their experiment in the spirit of capitalistic enterprise. Cotopaxi had no socialist program, though, as in all pioneer communities, a measure of joint activity had to be adopted.

The Cotopaxi colonists, unlike the Am Olam communards, had no intention of abandoning the Judaism which they had inherited from their ancestors in Europe. As one visitor, Morris Tuska, an observer sent out by the HEAS, wrote, the "colonists keep their religion in accordance with the ancient customs." They respected the Sabbath and holiday traditions, possessed a pentateuchal scroll donated by Rev. Dr. Herman Baar, and secured kosher meat from Denver. Others noted the extent to which the colonists troubled themselves to celebrate a ritually proper Passover.[41] Even though they were attentive to their religion, they were not inclined to separatism. On the contrary, they maintained friendly relations with their Christian neighbors.

At the end of five months, in October 1882, Schwarz, whom Tuska found to be master of the situation, reported on the experiment. There were then sixty persons at Cotopaxi and of all their efforts, said Schwarz, "I pronounce the agricultural colony in the Rocky Mountains a full and complete success." Tuska obviously agreed, for he reported to the HEAS leadership in New York that Cotopaxi, under Schwarz's tutelage, would "render evidence . . . that the Jew can make as good a farmer as any other human being."[42] Such positive estimates of an infant colony are remarkable in many ways, even after discounting the fact that they were written and/or influenced by the one person entrusted with the colony's development. It is even more remarkable, then, that barely six months later Heilprin in his *Appeal to the Jews* stated that "the Colorado colony is now breaking up."[43] What occurred between October 1882 and March 1883 can only be grasped by piecing together various items appearing in the editorial and news columns of the *Jewish Messenger* of New York and other journalistic sources.

In its issue of December 22, 1882, a news article in the *Jewish Messenger* had carried a glowing account of Cotopaxi.[44]

But in a letter the following January, Schwarz, no longer manager of the colony, took exception to the article. "The report is highly exaggerated," he complained. "The colonists have only one team together. They earn only $3–4 a day. Not all have cows, and their houses are not furnished too luxuriously. Most of them have some money."[45] He went on to suggest that they be let alone so that they could come to rely upon themselves. "Only then will this colony prove to be a monument to Jewish charity."[46]

From another source, too, came objection to the glowing account of December 22, but this time the writer, far from taking mild exception, bluntly stated that no basis at all existed for painting a picture of prosperity. A Sephardi businessman named Emanuel H. Saltiel was resident-director of Fremont County's Place Mining Company, a firm upon whose land, it later developed, some of the colonists' houses had been built. According to a letter written by Saltiel, "the farming experiment in colonies is a lamentable failure and if attempted further in the Far Western Mountain States, will cause both loss of money and great misery." He went on to say that "the potato crop, the main support [of the colony] was by the advice of Schwarz, left ungathered until severe frost had destroyed it. [The mistake] was due to the ignorance of the colonists of all practical methods for pioneering farming."

Moreover,

> the training and tastes of our Russian co-religionists are against Western farming customs, and if the experiment should ever be repeated here the only persons that will be benefited will be the clerks and managers drawing salaries. $100 given into the hands of the head of each discreet family to start business for himself will be productive of more good than thousands expended on colonization experiments . . . . We will do the best we can with those now here, but to send more would be a cruelty to a helpless people, and a total waste of money.[47]

From these two contradictory reports, Schwarz's and Saltiel's, it is hard for the impartial reader to determine whose account was the more accurate. Saltiel had appeared before the HEAS at New York to sing the praises of Wet Mountain

Valley, but it is obvious that he later became unfavorably disposed towards the farmers and their experiment, for in his own words: "when the wives of the families begged me for aid, I hired a few of [the men] to work in the mines, sorting ore. I was reluctant to hire more because some of the men had signed a paper defaming me." Possibly, as one writer has contended, Saltiel's sole interest in encouraging the Cotopaxi colony was "to boom the mining district and the town" in which he apparently had sizeable holdings. That town, curiously enough, had at one time been known as Saltiels. Certainly, it is no coincidence that Tuska spoke of Saltiel's mismanagement and accused Saltiel of having "used . . . for his own purposes" money "put in his hands" to maintain the colony. Indeed, Tuska insisted, Saltiel had "caused the colony much damage, much annoyance, and much disgrace."[48]

Saltiel, for his part, contended that Schwarz on his arrival in Colorado had been "entirely ignorant of everything pertaining to either pioneer life or methodical business"; whatever he had learned he had learned from Saltiel himself. As for Tuska, so Saltiel claimed, he had clearly "been somewhat imposed upon, otherwise a man of his standing would not have risked a heavy lawsuit for criminal libel." What had undermined the colony, Saltiel argued, was "nothing more or less than the unnecessary time consumed [by the colonists] in the preparation for every little religious feast or fast, engagement or marriage celebration." Schwarz, "by pandering to these superstitious ceremonies," had "obtained a mastery over their minds, and encouraged superstition and bigotry."[49]

Whatever the cause, the Cotopaxi colony was in trouble. In the early part of February 1883 several of the colonists had protested about conditions in the colony to Jewish citizens in Denver. The latter appointed a committee of two, the lawyer George H. Kohn and a shoestore owner, L. Witkowski, to investigate conditions. In their report they made a familiar criticism:

> As to the land, 2/5 are worthless, because the soil is rocky. With the soil definitely uncultivable the odds were too great . . . . The H.E.A.S. had promised each head of family a

house, furniture, seed and 160 acres of land. Only twelve houses were built, insufficient accommodations for seventeen families, and they were constructed at $280 when they could have been built for $100.

In further testimony to the inefficient manner in which affairs were conducted, they said, the houses had been built on land owned by Saltiel's Place Mining Company, "but no leases were ever executed by the Company to the colonists." Kohn and Witkowski were "at a loss to account for the sum of the $8,750 said to have been expended up to October 23, 1882." They were sure that "more than twice as much" had been paid than "an honest administration of the fund would warrant." The report, going on to tell of illness and lack of medical care, concluded by urging that immediate relief—clothing and food—be sent, and that as a final measure the colony be removed at once to a spot more cultivatable.[50]

The Kohn-Witkowski report, of course, evoked a response from the HEAS. The president of the HEAS, Henry S. Henry, communicated with the two members of the Denver committee and suggested that they had been exploited. As for the colonists, the HEAS notified them that if they wished to remain they would be given seeds, implements, and other necessaries. If they desired to leave, they might do so, as a number of refugees were eager to take their places. But the officers of the HEAS soon revised their estimate as to the success of the colony, for instead of others being sent to replace the discontented colonists, the entire project was quietly abandoned. By the spring of 1883, full disintegration was on, and a year after it had been inaugurated, the Cotopaxi colony wound up its existence.[51]

In determining the exact causes of failure, one factor stands out: the unwise selection of land. That Schwarz was aware of the difficulties of cultivation is quite clear, yet he pinned his hopes on the will and determination of the pioneers. To mitigate any harsh judgment of Schwarz, the time element must be considered. Once again the pressing need for a quick settlement of the people conditioned the ultimate outcome of the experiment. The lack of experience in the Western type of farming contributed to its failure. One other factor is important: the paternalism to which the colonists were encouraged to accommodate themselves.

A spirit of charity can be fatal to a colonizing enterprise. Today it is recognized that the aim in any communal or cooperative settlement should be the cultivation of a spirit of self-reliance. Indeed, certain quarters among organized American Jews even at that time endorsed this view, yet the exigencies of the moment, the crisis in Eastern Europe and the abhorrence of congestion on the East Coast, caused the harried leaders and patrons of the agricultural movement to pass over the wiser course and to take the path closest at hand.[52] All in all, the Cotopaxi colony was another monument to Jewish effort and endurance, not to Jewish agrarian or philanthropic wisdom.

Palestine, Michigan

The period of the 1880s saw two streams of emigration from Eastern Europe: one to North America; the other, much more modest in size, to Ottoman Palestine. Not all who came to America, however, were unmoved by love for or interest in the ancient biblical homeland. There were some who were at least spiritual Zionists. One miniscule group in America tried to combine its religious love for Zion with a desire to root itself in American soil. Its members aspired to create a "new Zion in free America." Appropriately, their venture was termed "Palestine." It took place in Michigan in the last decade of the nineteenth century.[53]

The actors in the drama, another unsuccessful one, were, with one exception, Russian Jews living in Bay City, Michigan. Only one of them had been in the United States more than four years, and all had engaged in peddling. In their work, they had come in contact with farmers. And because their efforts at making a living had met with scant success, they turned their minds to farming. One of them, Hyman Lewenberg, who had been in the United States for eleven years, had read of the efforts at Jewish colonization in the 1880s, and conceived the idea of establishing in Michigan a colony similar to the Colorado design, a community of

Jewish farmers. There is no evidence that the venture was to be organized along socialistic or communistic lines. The group was a homogeneous one, but individual farmers were to be settled on individual plots as in Cotopaxi. They, too, were Orthodox Jews, alike in aim, background, and, alas, inexperience.

It was while peddling that Lewenberg had met Langdon Hubbard and his son Frank, bankers and land barons who owned immense stretches of land in Huron and the adjoining counties. They agreed to sell land on easy terms if Lewenberg could get together a sufficiently large group of Jewish purchasers. In July 1891 twelve contiguous parcels of land in Huron County were sold to twelve persons.[54] One bought twenty acres, two bought forty acres each, and the rest bought sixty acres each, thus taking up an entire section of land.

The site of the Michigan venture was near the hamlet known by the picturesque name of Bad Axe. Until 1884 this district had been heavily timbered,[55] but in the fall of that year forest fires denuded the land of much of its timber. The first task was to provide some means of habitation for the colonists and to clear the ground for fall plowing in preparation for spring planting. In true pioneer spirit, the new farmers set to work with a will. They erected five or six shacks, crude one-room affairs with flimsy partitions to separate the sexes. While clearing and building, the families slept in the open. When the cold weather arrived, some of the colonists were forced to remove their families to Bay City, some 50 miles from Bad Axe, and to resume peddling for the winter. Those who remained behind, nonetheless, clung to the land and even put up more houses for the returning members in the spring.

At this point, two men entered the picture, men whose efforts on behalf of the group were truly responsible for the venture's ability to endure as long as it did. One was the Detroit clothier Martin Butzel; the other, his close friend whom he interested in the work, the Bohemian immigrant Emanuel Woodic. Butzel was a prominent merchant whose interest had been awakened by the account of the Bad Axe colonists' sufferings which a Jewish peddler had related.[56] President of the Temple Beth-El Hebrew Relief Society in Detroit and a philanthropist, he turned to Woodic for help in

Palestine Colony settlers, late 1890s: Noah and Bella Ellias. (Courtesy TB)

Palestine colony, Bad Axe, Michigan: A new Zion in America

The Ellias family home, Bad Axe, early 1900s. Previously the Palestine Colony Synagogue. (Courtesy TB)

Members of the Ellias family ready to work on their land (*above and facing*). (Courtesy TB)

Colonists in Palestine/Bad Axe: The Kahns and the Malinoffs. (Courtesy TB)

The deserted schoolhouse of the Palestine Colony, still standing 1981. (Courtesy MDS)

Emanuel Woodic, mainstay of Palestine. (Courtesy MDS)

Aaron Barony and family, North Dakota pioneers. From *An Album of the Jews in America*, by Yuri Suhl. (Courtesy YIVO)

the crisis. Woodic, known at the time as the foremost farmer of Macomb County north of Detroit, was an authority on farm problems. He responded positively to Butzel's request to investigate conditions at Palestine.

Upon his arrival at the Palestine colony in March 1892, Woodic found a population of fifty-seven: sixteen men, seven women, twenty-six boys, and eight girls. Ten shacks were occupied. Sixteen farms had been taken up, but not more than one or two acres on each farm had been cleared. As for livestock, there was a total of seven horses and two cows. Woodic returned to Detroit with a report of the colony's meager conditions. A special meeting of the Beth-El Relief Society was called by Butzel, and a supply of clothing, groceries and *matzot* for the coming Passover holiday was sent to the Palestine colonists. In addition, a fund of $1,200 was raised and given to Woodic to be spent at his discretion. On his return to Palestine after the Passover holiday, Woodic distributed livestock, implements, seed, and other necessaries to each family. Throughout the spring and summer of that year, Woodic stayed on to function as agricultural adviser, communal leader, and arbiter of the many petty disputes that arose. He kept the men constantly clearing the land and taught them the rudiments of sowing, cultivating, and harvesting. Because of the lack of housing facilities, he himself tramped to the colony four miles every day from the village of Bad Axe. He served without compensation.

While Woodic was giving of himself so unselfishly, guiding the Palestine farmers, Butzel was equally occupied in Detroit with securing financial aid for the colony. Through his efforts, Butzel called into service a much larger, international organization established almost simultaneously with the Michigan experiment—the Baron de Hirsch Fund.

The fund aimed "to extend loans to immigrants from Russia and Roumania, to actual agriculturists and settlers within the United States on real or chattel security," and also "to furnish instruction in agricultural work and in improved methods of farming."[57] The trustees regarded Butzel's request for aid as legitimate and, upon motion of the famous New York banker-philanthropist Jacob H. Schiff, granted Butzel $3,000.

In September 1892 Butzel went to the Palestine colony and personally supervised the distribution of this money.

In his report to the Baron de Hirsch Fund on the use of its appropriation, Butzel gave an account of the pioneers:

> These people, both men and women . . . through industry early and late, in all kinds of weather, seem to have accomplished all that could be expected in such a short time and have given striking proof of their sincere intention and earnestness to become farmers in fact. . . . Notwithstanding their present poverty, scanty food and poor habitation which would discourage others, these families seem willing to make sacrifices of all personal comforts and stick to farming.[58]

In further testimony to their earnestness, an exhibit of their farm products was held at Temple Beth-El in Detroit during the Sukkot holiday in the fall of 1892. It was probably the first exhibition to be held in the United States of farm products raised by Jews. As a memento, a small parcel of two potatoes was sent to each of the trustees of the Baron de Hirsch Fund.

The years 1893–94 marked the height of the agricultural activity of the colonists. In 1894, for the first time, the farmers, who had gained a few additional recruits, earned enough for their maintenance and were able to make partial payments on their annual interest. Such payments were the measure of their success. The colonists had in the meantime built a synagogue and a religious school and brought a shochet from Saginaw to see to their need for kosher meat. For a while, they even had a voluntary cantor-teacher, the Rev. Charles Goodwin, of Bay City.

In the autumn of 1895, a critical period began. It was marked by a continuing struggle to hold the lands. The colonists defaulted on their contracts with the Hubbard Company for merchandise worth over $1,300. The company pressed for a lien on the crops and movable property. Butzel came forward to plead for the colonists. "Just now when favorable indications seem to appear," were the Hubbards going to "drive them from house and home just for the reason that each one of the family heads owes less than $100 for interest past due?" He appealed for an extension: "I hope and trust that you will not only grant this request but give them aid, comfort, and advice [which] would give all parties peace of mind, [and] satisfy the teaching of the Saviour and the God of Israel alike." Initially, his pleas were ineffective, but ultimately, as a result of his protests, the company dropped its eviction suits and new contracts were drawn up. These contracts were signed with the individual purchasers, but an agreement was inserted whereby, in the event of default, the land was to be surrendered without legal process.

For a time things ran smoothly, but in 1897 the crops failed due to poor management. With ruin facing the colonists, they sent a letter to the Baron de Hirsch Fund, suggesting that the fund might buy the land outright from the Hubbard Company. The fund replied to this proposal by sending an agent to investigate. The agent was impressed by what he saw and in his report spoke of the determination of the Palestine colonists, their hardships, and the respect they had won from their neighbors.

> Some of them had to sleep on the bare ground, in weather and storm, with the animals of the field as their companions but they braved it all with the ultimate expectation of possessing what they then began to toil for. It should not be difficult to convince you how almost insurmountable were the obstacles they had to contend with and it is surprising that they did not lose heart. That they were industrious beyond measure none can gainsay as their own shoulders served as animals which they had not the means to purchase, and their Christian neighbors testify to their pluck, energy and determination.

The report notwithstanding, the trustees decided against the purchase on the grounds that "further nursing would only prolong the agony."[59] They were able, however, to modify the contracts to insure the colonists' ability to hold onto the land in the future. As a further measure of protection, quitclaim deeds were made over to Henry Rice, a trustee of the fund, conveying the purchasers' rights under their contracts. Even so, at best these measures were only palliatives. In January 1898 the Hubbard Company again notified Butzel that, because payments on the purchaser contracts had not been met and because taxes and drain assessments had piled up, eviction notices would be served. A third appeal to the fund followed, and full settlement of $825 out of the $1,552.17 debt owed the Hubbard Company was made. In January 1899 the colonists again defaulted on the principal payments due, and in the fall of that year disintegration began. In 1900, only eight families remained. These left soon afterward, and eventually all but three parcels of land reverted to the Hubbard Company. Lewenberg appealed to the Baron de Hirsch Fund for release of the quitclaim deed so that he could realize something on his land through sale. Moses Heidenrich did the same and moved to the village of Bad Axe where he remained until his death. The departure of these latter two marked the end of the Palestine venture.

The story of the venture has itself revealed the diverse causes of failure. Despite all the aid received, the odds were simply too great. Even before the colony had gotten underway, the protectionism of American economic policy plunged the country into the disastrous financial panic of 1893, spelling ruin for America's agricultural and industrial classes alike. And the Palestine colonists' inexperience as farmers contributed a sizable share to the doom of their valiant attempt. One primary cause, however, was the time period. After 1900, when the country's agricultural depression lifted somewhat and the situation of farmers began to improve, Michigan became the home of many a thriving Jewish farmer. The success of these later ventures, however, to no degree diminishes the grit and exertion of the pioneers of Huron County's Palestine Colony.[60]

Painted Woods and Iola, North Dakota

A North Dakota colony, Painted Woods—in which New Odessa's visitor, Rabbi Wechsler, took a substantial interest—was attempted near Bismarck in Burleigh County but saw a succession of natural disasters write finis to an experiment which lasted from 1882 to 1887.[61] Some of the Painted Woods colonists went further north to Ramsey County and there, near Garske, founded Iola, according to J. M. Isler "one of the

70

oldest Jewish farming settlements in the Northwest."[62] But Iola was not a colony in the sense that Palestine and Painted Woods had been. It was a neighborhood which had many Jewish farmers. In Iola, individual farmers established separate farms through individual effort, and when in distress, received generous aid from the Baron de Hirsch Fund.

Chananel, North Dakota

Not far from Iola, in Ramsey County, another North Dakota colony, Chananel, was organized around the time Painted Woods was abandoned. One Benzion Greenberg was involved in the Chananel undertaking. He was still there along with some twenty Jewish families in April 1897 when he addressed a letter to Philip Cowen, editor of the *American Hebrew*:

I came to North Dakota in the spring of 1888. When I left Michigan I had a couple hundred dollars, but the expense for myself and family from Michigan to North Dakota took all of it. When I landed at the depot at Devil's Lake [in Ramsey County] I had $2.50 left in my pocket. I took a pre-emption claim and I started farming. The first year we had a very fine crop, but a few days before harvesting a frost, and we lost all our crop. Of course we had hard times. We were assisted with provisions to live through. The next two years we lost our crop by drought, and the year '91 we had an abundant crop, the biggest that North Dakota ever had, but the winter set in so early that we could not thresh, and I lost $1,500. of grain that rotted in the shacks. A great many of our farmers lost their crops the same way, so you can see how much we had to stand. In the winter of '91 I lost six horses and four head of horned cattle, and now I have five good horses and harness, nine head of horned cattle, and all the farm implements; that is, plows, harrows, mower and rack, two self binders, a good lumber wagon, a pair of sleighs, a good frame house 18 by 24 [feet] with additional summer kitchen, a stable, and plenty of grain and all kinds of poultry, chicken, geese and turkeys, and all I owe on it is between $250 and $300. We make a fine living, and if we had taken assistance from anybody I do not believe we would have remained on the farm. But now I hope, if we get a couple of good crops, we will be well-to-do and I own 160 acres of land free from all incumbrance.

Greenberg, however, may not have remained permanently in North Dakota. Cowen observes that in later years he came to New York and interested himself there in the work of the HIAS which had been founded in 1888.[63]

No mention has been made of the colonization ventures in Utah, California, and Nevada, or of the one undertaken in 1882 by a group of philanthropic Baltimore, Maryland, Jews to establish nine families at Waterview on the Rappahannock River in Middlesex County, Virginia, or of "the forgotten colony" founded some twenty years later in Aiken County, South Carolina.[64] To cite these other instances of unsuccessful colonization is repetitious, since the motives, nature, and fate of the efforts omitted and of those described parallel each other. Yet the picture of unrelieved gloom was soon to be superseded by one of qualified success.

3 New Jersey: "Every Beginning Is Difficult"

The pattern of constant failure in colonization efforts was broken in two notable instances: the experiments at Alliance and Woodbine, both in New Jersey.[1] The names Alliance, Woodbine, Carmel, and Rosenhayn denote communities still in existence, though today they differ radically from their original conception since Jewish farming in South Jersey has become the private enterprise of individual farmers. It was in Alliance and Woodbine that Jewish farmers functioning as groups or as settlements evincing some dimension of collective enterprise attained an unprecedented measure of success.

Alliance

The name chosen for the Alliance enterprise reflected the willingness of the Alliance Israélite Universelle to support Jewish colonization efforts.[2] The colony was founded in Salem County's Pittsgrove Township by the HEAS on May 10, 1882, almost simultaneously with the launching of Cotopaxi in Colorado; it is said to have been the first Jewish colony in South Jersey to aid victims of persecution.[3] The intention in both efforts was similar: to give assistance to Jewish farmers and to enable them to engage in individual enterprise. The land for Alliance, in Salem County, thirty-five miles from Philadelphia and five miles from Vineland, was purchased by the HEAS. One hundred fifty acres were denoted common land. The remainder was divided into sixty-six fifteen-acre farms deeded to the occupant families, who were each charged $300, to be repaid in thirty-three years without interest.[4] Twenty-five families, mostly small traders and storekeepers from southern Russia, moved out to New Jersey. All their transportation expenses to Alliance were paid. In some cases, pioneers went straight from the steamer to South Jersey. Temporary shelters were erected to house them. For the first six months, the HEAS furnished all provisions and also sent an instructor to teach farming to the newcomers, who set to work immediately, clearing the land of its dense scrub oak and pine. In the first month, they had cleared one tract of thirty acres on which they planted corn. For this labor the HEAS provided a weekly wage and thus made it possible for the colonists to build up a reserve fund to meet future expenses. To supplement this income, several of the colonists also worked part-time for neighboring Christian farmers, who are said to have been impressed enough with their diligence and patience to prefer the Jewish workers over the non-Jews.

In 1883, cooperating with London's Mansion House Relief Committee, the HEAS purchased eighty additional acres of land and carved out six more farms. These farms were then distributed to the colonists in accordance with lots they had drawn the previous fall. Contracts similar to those made the previous year were drawn up with the HEAS; again, each farmer was to pay $350 for his holding within ten years. After 1884, with a grant of $10,000 by the Mansion House Fund, new contracts were drawn up whereby the farmers were to hold one-half of the farm free of charge provided the other half was paid for in equal installments over a period of thirty-five years. (In subsequent years the Baron de Hirsch Fund assumed direction of the affairs of these colonies, and new contracts were then drawn.) With the farm each family received a stove, furniture, and household goods. From time to time, the HEAS came to their aid. In the spring each family received "tools, furniture, cooking utensils, plants and farm utensils to the value of $100."[5]

Kol haskholeh koshoh ("every beginning is difficult") wrote Herman Rosenthal, one of the Am Olam founders, in

74

reviewing the experience of the Alliance settlers.[6] In order to save the expense of horses and farm tools, the colonists agreed to work four farms together, each farmer doing the work he could do best. Although the theory was reasonable enough, the practice did not work out due to the inexperience of the farmers. Each family then worked its own farm independently, planting trees, grapevines, berries, and some vegetables for its own use. During the summer and early fall of 1883, these neophyte farmers again worked for their neighbors, picking berries, digging potatoes, husking corn.

In the fall of that year, the HEAS took an unusual step. It encouraged the setting up of a factory in the community which had been intended exclusively for agricultural activity. The immediate reason was that the HEAS had to provide for the unceasing flow of immigrants which persecution was driving to these shores from Eastern Europe. Alliance seemed a good place to send them, largely, perhaps, because it was comparatively close to New York City. At first, a cigar factory was opened by a private entrepreneur on land owned by the HEAS; later, part of the building was devoted to the needlework trade to which some Jewish immigrants were well adapted. A number of the colonists found employment in these establishments during slack periods for farming. The two enterprises were shortlived, however, because of a fire which destroyed the building.

The idealism which lay behind the South Jersey ventures is worth bearing in mind. Years later Shneur (Sidney) Bailey, one of the Alliance colonists, recalled what had motivated Am Olamites like himself to settle in the South Jersey colonies. In the Ukrainian seaport of Odessa during the late spring of 1881, Bailey had been among those

> who formulated . . . the *Am Olam* idea that our brethren should go to America to become tillers of the soil and thus shake off the accusation that we [Jews] were mere petty mercenaries, living upon the toil of others. Our thought was to live in the open instead of being "shut-ins" who lived an artificial city life. We desired to be dependent for our living upon the elements of Father Sun and Mother Earth instead of depending upon the whims of others. We desired to lead a real healthy

and honorable mode of life. We were not to be, at our farm vocation, jealous and envious one of another, but to live upon our own resources with the help only of nature.

Bailey and his confrères wanted "to own a home and land as a means of earning a livelihood, and to be true citizens of [their] adopted country." Nothing seemed to them so important as the opportunity

> to live our own lives and bring up our children to be healthy, honorable and useful citizens; brought up according to our own ideas instead of being influenced by the street children or by their next door neighbors; in short, to get the blessings of a natural life from heaven and earth. For these ideals we decided to leave Russia, to become farmers in "the land of the brave and the home of the free." We came here instead of going to Palestine which was then under a Turkish [Ottoman] regime. Thus, the exodus of 1882 began rolling en masse to America, and Alliance was established in May, 1882. Though I did not come over with the first settlers, as did Israel Opachinsky and Joseph Zager, who are still in Alliance, I arrived only a few years after and missed [out on] living in barracks, sleeping on straw, digging out the stumps, laying out roads and even missed [out on] working at the cigar factory which lasted for a couple of years.[7]

The first meager fruits of the colonists' agricultural efforts were evident in the spring of 1884. Considerable replanting was necessary, both because of the inexperience of the farmers and the ineptness of the managers who had chosen neither the right types of crops nor the proper time for planting during 1882 and 1883.

Before 1885, the scene at Alliance resembled all the previous colonization experiments described: primitive facilities, optimism, frustration, confusion. In the winter of 1884–1885, some of the colonists left for Philadelphia or New York City and returned with tailoring work for their own and other Jewish families. One New York philanthropist, Leonard Lewisohn, even gave each family a sewing machine to help supplement its income. At the same time the families worked their farms. Despite these adjuncts to farming, the struggle

76

was as relentless as ever. In that winter of 1884-85, Philadelphia's Association of Jewish Immigrants, a charitable organization, came to the colony's aid, and a wealthy patron in New York gave $1,000 to reestablish the cigar factory.[8]

Signs of discontent became evident. Complaints poured into the Alliance Land Trust (ALT), which had succeeded the HEAS on the latter's dissolution in 1883. One of the colonists recorded his concern about the lack of solidarity at Alliance:

> [Its] inhabitants . . . possess many different outlooks, for in it are found Russian Jews and Polish Jews, Orthodox, Chassidim and ignorant persons, some without any belief and some who do have a belief. Each group lives unto itself. Many attempts have been made . . . to unite these groups and to set up an executive committee . . . before [which] all differences of opinion would be aired . . . [and which could] represent all the people of the colony before the leaders of the New York Committee. But even this sensible recommendation was not accepted for they could not come to an agreement and the committee was disbanded.

Early in 1885, the colonists, suffering from inexperience and a troubling paucity of supplies, described themselves as "very sadly disappointed and . . . much distressed," though as yet they were not ready to admit defeat.[9] In response, a committee made up of the ALT president and two other members was sent to investigate. The result was another direct contribution, another grant of relief. But the picture as it looked to the immigrants themselves has been preserved by the Alliance Am Olamite Bailey:

> Our wanderers, from various parts of Russia, came . . . to settle on land. Our people being Talmudists, merchants and tradesmen, knew nothing of the significance of farm life. When they came to New York and arrived at Castle Garden and talked very naively with our German-American brethren who came to meet us and help us, they (the immigrants) were warned against, and advised to give up the idea of becoming farmers, but were advised to continue at their trades or to become peddlers. . . . However, a few remained true to their [agricultural] ideals and their ambition was to be realized.[10]

Fortunately, in the spring of 1885, for the first time since the inception of their colony, the Alliance farmers began to realize a profit from their agricultural labors of the previous three years. The result was an increased enthusiasm for farming, though the farmers continued to supplement their income partly by working other farms and partly by tailoring. The nascent prosperity of 1885 blossomed the following year, with the sale of crops in the spring and summer of 1886 yielding as much as $200 to $400 for some farmers, income derived solely from agriculture. Those who had two sources of income were able to earn as much as $700.

The year 1887–88 marked the beginning of a veritable boom. Crops were plentiful and readily sold, which suggested that the agricultural experiment was successful. Newcomers from the cities and new immigrants were attracted by the achievement of the "old" settlers. "At this time," Bailey recalls,

> a group of intelligentsia came to Alliance, among whom were Messrs. Bakal, Konefsky, Peisochovitz, Spivack, Schwartz, Seldes, Gartman, Friedman, D. Steinberg and ourselves, and farming started in earnest. A team of horses were procured by Coltun and Luberoff to plow the virgin soil for the settlers. Some of the American neighbors were also hired to help break up the soil and help plant amidst the stumps. We planted all kinds of berries, grapes and fruit trees.[11]

The newcomers supported themselves as tailors during the winter and as berrypickers during the summer, but throughout the year they themselves served as a ready market for the agricultural produce. The year 1887 and the summer of 1888 marked the peak of prosperity. In July 1888 the Alliance settlers dedicated the Eben Ha-Ezer ("Rock of Salvation") Synagogue; two years later, another synagogue, Tiphereth Israel ("Splendor of Israel"), was founded. Alliance, it is clear, was not to be a New Jersey version of Oregon's New Odessa, even though its colonists included Am Olam sympathizers. In 1888, Adolphus S. Solomons, a well-known Washington, D.C., Jewish communal worker, described Alliance in the pages of the B'nai B'rith monthly *Menorah*. Alliance, he wrote, was "the first successful Jewish colony in America," and he applauded "the hard work which has made a garden out of a desert, and untold numbers of wretched human beings comparatively prosperous and happy."

The Alliance settlers, Herman Rosenthal wrote enthusiastically in 1891, could "be proud of their hard work, patience, and perseverance and of the sweet fruits of their indefatigable labor." Rosenthal hailed them as "truly pioneers contributing to the glory of all Israel." As late as March 1894, Cincinnati's *American Israelite,* basing its report on an investigation undertaken the year before by the *New York Sun,* could assure its readers that "the Hebrew colonies in New Jersey . . . are in so flourishing a condition that arrangements will at once be made for bringing over in the spring a large number of new recruits." Readers of the *Israelite,* and of the *Sun,* too, presumably, were given to believe that hard times had little or no effect upon the colonies.[12] But all this satisfaction proved premature, and after the late 1880s the fortunes of the Alliance farmers waned, resulting in a reduction in farm income and an increase in farm indebtedness.

Responsible in part for the increased debt was the colony's brief success, which had spurred the farmers to spend more for farm tools, for the improvement of the buildings, for the purchase of feed, and for other purposes. They borrowed heavily in one instance from a Salem, New Jersey, building and loan association, mortgaging their farms as security. Still, the principal source of the reduction in farm income was beyond Alliance's control; it was the general stagnation of American business and the low prices farm products fetched during the 1890s. As one historian has put it, even the "roaring '80's" had "not brought equal cheer to all," and they gave way to the "heartbreaking '90's." The panic of 1893 was what threatened to undo Alliance, along with the rest of the country:

> In February, 1893, the Philadelphia and Reading Railroad Company failed; a break in the stock market followed, and an oldfashioned panic seized the country in its grasp. A period of hitherto unparalleled speculative frenzy came thus to an end, and sober years followed in which the American people had

ample opportunity to contemplate the evils arising from their economic debauch. Prices of agricultural products continued their downward trend. Wheat touched bottom in 1894 with an average price of 49¢; corn, two years later, reached 21¢. All the other grains were likewise affected . . . it was literally cheaper to burn [the corn] than to sell it . . . and this . . . is what hundreds of despairing farmers did. [13]

Besides seeing the low prices for his produce further depressed by the rapacity of the railroads and the other intermediaries between the producer and the consumer, the farmer had to pay a high interest rate on his mortgage. Even more serious than the problem of mortgages, however, was the problem of taxes. The United States government at the turn of the century was far more protective of the interests of industrialists and big businessmen than it was of the interests of farmers. Federal revenues were raised exclusively through indirect taxes on consumer goods and commodities, which meant that an excessive share of the tax burden fell on farmers, shopkeepers, and wage earners. Henry George's observation was accurate enough: the farmer "bears more than his fair share of the burdens of society, and gets less than his fair share of its benefits." [14]

Throughout the four or five years that followed the panic of 1893, the Alliance colonists managed to hang on, although many lost their meager stock and savings and, worst of all, suffered some erosion of their spirit of perseverance. The Alliance colony also was confronted with a lack of understanding or sympathy in some quarters. Cincinnati's *American Israelite,* for example, blamed the colony's difficulties not on general economic conditions but on a presumed greediness, a shortsightedness, on the part of the colonists: "Up to two years ago," said the Cincinnati journal in June 1897, Alliance had "prospered. The colonists raised good crops of berries and fruits and received good pay for them." Some colonists, it was averred, unwisely increased the size of their farms, "and against the advice of the Alliance Land Trust, built expensive houses." The consequent second mortgages "are what are now adding to the trouble at the colony." The *Israelite* seemed unable to recognize that the problem was considerably more complex.[15]

In the winter of 1897–98, the Salem Building and Loan Association threatened to foreclose. It was then that the Baron de Hirsch Fund stepped in. After considerable negotiation, the fund arranged to buy up the mortgages of the farmers and also arranged a plan for the partial and gradual discharge of their debts. The fund's administrators sought to substitute for relief grants as much as possible sound business methods and the creation of institutions of a permanent character which would encourage the recipient of aid to become self-reliant.[16] Thus, Reis records that in 1905 the fund was encouraging the tailoring industry in Alliance.[17] A few years earlier the brothers Maurice and Joseph Fels, Philadelphia industrialists, had sought to foster the aim of self-help by establishing a large canning factory near Alliance. Before the intervention of the Fels brothers, the farmers had been dependent on commission houses in the large cities for the sale of their products. Local markets were always limited, and when the market in the cities was glutted, the farmers lost heavily. Now with the establishment of a local canning factory, farmers became independent of the commission houses for they could store their produce until they found a favorable market.

Somehow the Alliance colony managed to survive the vicissitudes of the 1890s. Speaking in an official capacity, William Stainsby, a leading authority on the South Jersey colonies, had the following to say of Alliance in 1901:

> The colony at Alliance has had a hard struggle, but has passed the experimental stage and is now fairly on the road to success. It has recently passed from the control of the Alliance Land Trust (incorporated by the Trustees of the H.E.A.S.) to the Board of Trustees of the Baron de Hirsch Fund. This, the first colony established in South Jersey, has not had the success which has crowned the colony at Woodbine, but it must be remembered that Alliance has not had hitherto, the benefit of large appropriations from the Baron de Hirsch Fund as have been given to the people of Woodbine.[18]

In 1905, an unofficial census revealed that, out of Pittsgrove

Township's total population of 2,154, some 900 persons or 165 families were Jewish.[19] Just how many of these were farmers exclusively, or how many combined farming with another industrial occupation, tailoring, for instance, is not disclosed.

Subsequently, due mainly to the efforts of the Baron de Hirsch Fund, the character of Alliance underwent a vital change. As Reis tells us, the Jews of Alliance were seldom engaged only in farming. The first limited efforts the HEAS had undertaken in 1882 to introduce an industrial dimension into Alliance were now taken up by the Baron de Hirsch Fund, and Alliance, like Cape May's Woodbine colony, became an agro-industrial community.

Still, in comparing Alliance with other ventures like New Odessa and Crémieux, it would be false to conclude that Alliance succeeded where the others failed, namely, in the establishment of a Jewish colony of farmers. But as a Jewish community in which agriculture played a vital, yet secondary part, Alliance enjoyed rather substantial success. Stainsby's praise of the Alliance farmers aptly referred to their "ready adaptability to the circumstances by which they are surrounded and to their untiring energy,"[20] as well as to the excellence of their products. Bailey offers some examples of Alliance's adaptability and energy:

It is our old maxim that not "by bread alone lives man, but on the word of God." Mr. Stavitsky brought with him a Sefer Torah, Mr. Krassenstein the Talmud, and we (my wife and I), the works of [the German poets] Schiller and Goethe. There was one public school in Union Grove and another in Willow Grove, about four or five miles apart. Our children had to walk long distances, through woods in order to reach school. Of course, they had to get up early and come home late. This was not satisfactory to our Jewish parents with whom education of children comes next in command to the "Shema!" ["Hear O Israel"—recital of Judaism's monotheistic creed]. We petitioned the Board of Education for greater school facilities, and in consequence another school was built in Alliance. In all as many as five public schools were built in our midst.[21]

The area of the settlement being rather large and the population constantly increasing, we built four synagogues.

Almost as soon as we arrived in Alliance, we inaugurated a Sabbath School where my wife read poems in Yiddish from [Morris] Rosenfeld and others, and also in German from Schiller and Goethe, and I spoke on Jewish current events and Jewish post-biblical history and on Jewish ethics generally, from the Scriptures and the Talmud. Later we had Friday night gatherings at the hall of the big synagogue where we also conducted a public library of which I was for many years librarian. We succeeded in getting Mr. [Maurice] Fels interested in our library to which he donated many valuable books. We also conducted night school for adults. Charles Spivak taught at one time, later Charles Rice and I conducted the night school for almost six years. Professor [Louis] Mounier did educational work for many years. He arranged lectures, concerts and taught music. We subscribed for Yiddish and English papers and magazines, acquired books and musical instruments.[22]

Several factors favorable to the survival of Alliance stand out. For one, the colony was near two large metropolitan centers, New York and Philadelphia, which meant access to a variety of markets and also to aid societies when the need for their services arose. In support of the "self-reliance" principle, various industrial enterprises were encouraged and established. There were times when the colonists grumbled at the meager wages paid them and at the fact that the enterprises were often enough shortlived. Still, the industrial dimension helped to tide the farmers over slack seasons, and by attracting others to the colony, expanded the local market. All these factors, singly or together, helped to carry the colony through sixteen years of struggle until the Baron de Hirsch Fund responded to the appeal for further aid. Alliance's early history, paralleling that of other ventures which failed to survive, served to emphasize that a Jewish colony founded purely on agriculture could not endure; that if colonization was to achieve any measure of success, it had to be combined with industrial or mechanical pursuits.[23] Alliance prospered sufficiently for Bailey to observe:

> Now after a lapse of fifty years from such a meager beginning, when many a rib was broken as we ran into a

stump while plowing or cultivating; after learning how to harness horses to a double plow, and to use tractors, hay-loaders, potato planters and other farm machinery, we may feel thankful and satisfied with our achievement. Our farms are all paid for; we have a good name, and credit in the bank, befitting industrious and thrifty people. We feel prosperous and can keep our heads up; we are employed steadily; we are our own bosses. We are well and fairly comfortable and happy. Even the crisis which played such havoc in the cities with our brethren who were gambling in real estate and in stocks and bonds, didn't hurt us very much. We lost neither our heads nor our homes. Indeed, we have less temptations, albeit less luxuries. We lead a natural life.[24]

Woodbine

The best example of an agro-industrial community is not Alliance but Woodbine, the Cape May County sister-colony which was begun in 1891, nine years after the founding of Alliance. At the outset, it must be stated, Woodbine, too, failed as an agricultural settlement. The aim of establishing a colony consisting exclusively of Jewish farmers soon had to be abandoned, and as Woodbine developed, the number of those engaged in agriculture continued to decline.[25] None-theless, farming played a vital, however subordinate, role in the life of Woodbine.

The history of the agricultural efforts undertaken in the 1880s was not in itself sufficient to inspire new attempts. The creation of Woodbine, the last important agricultural venture of the nineteenth century, was the result of a fresh outburst of persecution suffered by the Jews in Russia. During the years 1887–89, the German financier-philanthropist Baron Maurice de Hirsch had carried on with the czar's government negotia-tions in which he proposed to assume the cost of educating his fellow-Jews in agricultural and mechanical pursuits, provid-ing the government would repeal the harsh and discrimina-tory legislation denying Jews a position of equality in the Russian empire.[26] The negotiations had broken down when de Hirsch came to the realization that the Russian government had absolutely no desire to improve the position of the Jews,

Founders of the Alliance Colony, New Jersey. "They looked to father Sun and mother Earth." Shneur Bailey, *second row, first on left.* (Courtesy AJA, Cincinnati)

Baron Maurice de Hirsch. Agriculture held a messianic purpose. (Courtesy AJA, Cincinnati)

Hirsch L. Sabsovich, founder, champion, and mayor of Woodbine, New Jersey. (Courtesy YIVO)

Mayor and other members of the municipality, *ca.* 1905. (Courtesy YIVO)

A view of Woodbine. (Courtesy YIVO)

Woodbine: proof that the Jew "loves the beautiful, the quiet and natural life of man"

Young colonists. (Courtesy YIVO)

but rather preferred their removal from the realm. Emigration was the only solution, but de Hirsch preferred an orderly emigration with the object of "establishing Jews primarily as farmers and also as handicraftsmen in those lands where laws and religious tolerance permitted them to carry on the struggle for existence as noble and responsible subjects of a humanitarian government." For de Hirsch, too, agriculture held a messianic promise: "The poor Jew, who until now has been hated as an outcast, will win for himself peace and independence, love for the ground he tills and for freedom; and he will become a patriotic citizen of his new homeland."[27]

The actualization of this scheme led to the baron's well-known colonization ventures in Argentina and, in the United States, to the creation of the Baron de Hirsch Fund.[28] Acting on de Hirsch's suggestion, Isadore Loeb of the AIU approached a number of prominent laymen in New York City, men like Jacob H. Schiff, Meyer S. Isaacs, and Emanuel Lehman, and requested them to form a central committee to determine the disposition of the money de Hirsch would provide for the improvement of the position of persecuted Jews. The central committee held a formal meeting of organization on March 13, 1890, in New York City. Nine members were chosen to act as trustees. Later the committee adopted the name of the Baron de Hirsch Fund.

In its deed of trust, the aims of the Baron de Hirsch Fund were stated:

1) to make loans to immigrants from Russia and Rumania, to actual agriculturists, settlers within the United States, on real or chattel security.
2) to aid in the transportation of immigrants after arrival at an American port to places where they may find work and make themselves self-supporting.
3) to teach immigrants trades and to continue their support while learning such trades.
4) to furnish instruction in agricultural work and in improved methods of farming.
5) to furnish instruction in the English language and in the duties of American citizenship . . . to all in the establishment of special schools and workshops.[29]

The Baron de Hirsch Fund was not concerned exclusively with agricultural activities, nor did it aim solely to make farmers out of the Jews. Its major task was to help the immigrant adjust quickly to his new home; the fund sought to achieve its goals by whatever means seemed best. In later years when the agricultural responsibilities of the fund became pressing, it turned over all such matters to the Jewish Agricultural and Industrial Aid Society, which subsequently transformed itself into the Jewish Agricultural Society. Even before these events, however, the fund undertook the creation of Woodbine.[30]

To carry out its task of helping the harried victims of czarist bigotry, the fund appointed the Committee on Agricultural and Industrial Settlements, headed by Dr. Julius Goldman, a notable proponent of agricultural colonization. Despite the record of failure of such colonization, Goldman vigorously urged the establishment of another colony in the hope that this time the disasters of the past would be avoided. A majority of the committee, however, was not persuaded by his proposal. The majority view held that, since swift settlement of the immigrants was necessary, families should be placed in groups on small plots of ground located near a large city. The aim was to have some members of each family work the farm, while the rest secured jobs in the city or in the colony itself. In this way a steady income would be assured to tide the families over the initial period of clearing the land, plowing, planting, and sowing. The colony, wrote Rosenthal, was to "be set up, not as a charitable undertaking, but [one] founded on pure businesslike commercial principles."

From its inception, the Woodbine colony was predicated on the assumption that some form of industrial activity would be necessary to supplement farm income, though ultimately, it was hoped, all the residents of the colony would become farmers. The Committee on Agricultural and Industrial Settlements appointed a three-member subcommittee to investigate the possibilities of a South Jersey site for the projected colony. Two of the subcommittee's members, Herman Rosenthal and Paul Kaplan, were Am Olam founders. On the advice of Hirsch L. Sabsovich, an outstanding agricultural chemist,

Woodbine, part of Dennis Township in Cape May County, was the site chosen.[31]

The reasons given for this selection were that Woodbine was only fifty-six miles from Philadelphia and twenty-two miles south of Vineland, the site of another colonization scheme.[32] A large tract of land was available, or could be easily assembled. The soil, though covered with a dense growth of scrub oak and pine, had proven capable of adaptation to truck-farming and to the cultivation of fruits. Markets existed nearby in Sea Isle City (only sixteen miles away), Cape May, and Philadelphia. The West Jersey and Seashore Railroad furnished ample transportation. There were already improved farms in the neighborhood. And, lastly, the attitude of the native farmers seemed friendly toward the newcomers,[33] an important factor in the lives of persecuted Jews.

Once it had been determined that Woodbine would be the site of the venture, a corporation to manage it was created under the name of the Woodbine Land and Improvement Company. Its directors were the trustees of the Baron de Hirsch Fund, and it was capitalized at $50,000, with the fund holding all the capital stock. Goldman was elected president of the Company, and Sabsovich was named superintendent of the colony.[34] In August 1891 the Woodbine Land and Improvement Company purchased 5,300 acres of land for the sum of $37,500. Preliminary to the transfer of families, the land was surveyed and 800 centrally located acres were set aside for the town plot. The rest of the land beyond the town limits was divided into parcels of fifteen acres each. Beyond the farms there was to be pasture land. In all, the development resembled the layout of a medieval English village.

The entire venture was marked by a great effort to leave nothing to chance. The experienced New York representative, Herman Rosenthal, was assigned the task of selecting the colonists. Each family was required to invest some of its own money and to pay an additional $200, though the latter condition was not always insisted on, since it might have led to the elimination of many desirable families. A fifteen-acre plot of farm land was to be sold each farmer at a nominal sum, and in addition the purchaser could take out an option on an adjoining fifteen acres to be purchased within a reasonable span of time. The contracts made between the prospective settler and the Woodbine Land and Improvement Company called for the payment of $150 rent for the first three years and the execution of leases upon presentation at the end of that period. The colonists were to agree to pay $200 down, give a purchase mortgage for the land and house and a chattel mortgage on implements and livestock in exchange for a deed. At the end of twelve years, at an average cost of $1,100, the settlers would hold clear title to their thirty-acre farms. According to the best authority on the Baron de Hirsch Fund, the fund did not place too much stress upon the contracts, for it was never its intention to evict anyone for failure to live up to their terms,[35] a significant point in the light of developments in the year 1893.

The first arrivals, sixty heads of families, most of whom had been settled in the United States for some time, signed the contracts. As the press reports of the time make clear,

> Before the families of the settlers moved to Woodbine, the men built the houses and prepared everything for the final settlement. During this interval they lived in rude structures that afterwards became barns. A small stove, a table made of a barrel and a board, and rough bunks on the ground and in the loft were the only furniture.

The usual task of clearing the land was undertaken. For this work the Woodbine Land and Improvement Company paid them a weekly wage. They were to clear ten acres of their thirty-acre tracts, build their houses and plant four and a half acres of fruit-trees and berries. When his own plot was completed, each colonist would join the others in making a new farm. When this new farm was ready, another colonist from New York would come and occupy it. The company supplied all lumber, tools, trees and seeds beside the necessary animals. It was not an easy life, but, particularly once families were reunited, it held genuine promise.

> The diet of the men was mostly coffee and black bread. Their Russian costumes in most cases had been put aside. Some of the older men, however, clung to their astrakhan cap and the long cloak with the astrakhan trimmings. The Hebrew cast of countenance was not so marked as expected. The faces were broad and full. The hair of the young girls was cut

straight across the forehead. The children were noticeably bright and active.

According to Sabsovich, each new colonist was to begin cultivation of his tract with ten acres all ready for planting, and twenty acres wooded. The wood could be cut for fire, or sold. In 1892, a year after the project was begun, Sabsovich estimated that

> the time will now be coming when the farms will all be taken and laid out and there will be no work for which the company can offer wages to the colonists. In order to provide against this happening long before the farms begin to pay a living, any kind of industry should be encouraged.[36]

The second year, Sabsovich believed, the colonists with luck would get enough return from their vegetable patches to provide for their families, but it would be three years— 1894—before the strawberries and small fruits would begin to bear. "That year would be the test of whether the colony would pay its way or not." Woodbine meanwhile seemed to be thriving. Cincinnati's *American Israelite*, in describing the Woodbine enterprise, was more charitable or more hopeful than it would be a few years later in depicting the Alliance experience:

> According to the report for Mr. [Francis B.] Lee, the agent of the New Jersey State Board of Agriculture, the town of Woodbine, in Cape May County, under Superintendent Sabsovich of the Hirsch Fund, consists of 1,536 lots, around which are 30 acre farms and the outlying lowlands are reserved for pasturage upon the plan of medieval English communities. In a year 650 acres of farmland, 12 miles of driveway, and 170 acres of town lots have been wrested from a natural wilderness. The town houses were built by the company (composed of the Trustees of the American Hirsch Fund), cost from $850 to $1,300 each, and are models of neatness and adaptability for the colonists' needs. Active work is expected to give Woodbine 150 houses by spring. A hotel, a railway station, a synagogue, and a public school are completed, or are in course of erection. A park has been laid out with side streets and avenues lined with poplars and maples. On the farms each agriculturist has

250 fruit trees, planted in 1891, with an acre of grapes and small fruits. Early vegetables growing as readily in Cape May as in Norfolk, were also successfully raised.[37]

In an address given some months later, in August 1893, Lee described the conditions of that year.[38] Work had progressed rapidly. Six hundred and fifty acres of farmland had been cleared, and a hundred miles of farm roads had been built. Farmhouses were erected, and in his opinion, they were as well-built as town houses. They contained the latest features in scientific ventilation and plumbing. The recently established Jonasson Cloak factory was in operation and employed one hundred fifty people, and other factories for cutlery, knitting, and cigars, were soon to be built.[39] Anticipating the demands of a transient trade, a new hotel was built, and the railroad even opened a station at Woodbine to accommodate traffic. Goldman's report to the Baron de Hirsch Fund was very optimistic. The Woodbine experience would prove that mass colonization of East European Jews on agricultural land could be successful.[40]

But in the spring of the following year, 1894, all building stopped, and practically all farm work was suspended. This was the year referred to by the colonists as the "Year of the Trouble." Chiefly responsible was a failure of communication between the trustees, who were well-Americanized gentry of German Jewish background, and the colonists, who were, of course, Yiddish-speaking immigrants. The Jewish communal worker Boris Bogen, who for a while taught for the Baron de Hirsch Fund in Woodbine, has deftly summed up the characteristic attitude of Westernized Jews to the exotics from Eastern Europe: "The immigrant was a child who must be carefully kept in his place. His benefactors knew better than he what was good for him. These benefactors had made substantial business successes and, therefore, felt they were the competent guardians of the newcomers."[41] The trustees had decided to discontinue the fund's monthly aid, a course of action they justified by contending that, with the cloak factory now operating, the foundations of the colony had been secured. The farmer could find work there in his slack season; all further aid from the fund was simply unnecessary. Moreover, the capital which had been set aside for Woodbine was practically exhausted.

An anxious correspondence followed between Superintendent Sabsovich and the trustees. In a letter to Goldman, Sabsovich pointed out the unwisdom of cutting off aid to the colonists. He reminded the trustees that the Jonasson Cloak Factory had been open only since April 1892, not nearly long enough to assure the employment that the trustees assumed was available to the farmers. Only those whose children could work in the factory during the winter had acquired sufficient income; and all the farmers were burdened with great expenses like providing their families with transportation from Europe and improving their farms. They had exhausted whatever savings they may have possessed. "I strongly advocate more help for the farmers," Sabsovich asserted.

> I would suggest that we advance them $100.00 each to plow and harrow the land; for though they earned good money during the first year of Woodbine's existence, still, considering that everyone had to build a new home, and besides that, send a considerable amount of money to Russia to bring their families over, and to invest some on their farms, it is easy to realize that of their earnings they could save nothing. By helping them to improve their farms we shall the sooner free them from our wardship. After all, they are our wards.

Of the trustees, however, Goldman alone agreed with Sabsovich's suggestion.[42]

The fund's decision to discontinue its aid was the chief cause of the "Year of the Trouble." But there were other troubles plaguing Woodbine. For one, conceded by Sabsovich, too much clearing had been attempted, due as much to inexpert management as to the overenthusiasm of the farmers. As a result, few farms had been properly cleared, which limited their income-producing ability and was only further evidence of Sabsovich's contention that the farmers were not yet self-supporting. Then, in January 1893, when the leases which the original contracts called for were presented, only two of the sixty farmers signed. The fund trustees interpreted this failure to sign as evidence of willful and unwarranted spite, and they therefore instituted eviction proceedings against those who were considered the leaders of the agitation. Naturally, this course of action led to fierce controversy—what the historian Joseph Brandes has called "the Woodbine revolution"—and the fund received sharp criticism. The New York *Press*, for instance, undertook to tell the story in terms that were less than flattering to the Baron de Hirsch Fund: The colonists had

> first bought five thousand acres of the scrub oak and pine land at $6.00 an acre. It is called virgin soil. It is severely virgin. Spinster soil confirmed in old maid habits would be, perhaps, a better name for it. There is no doubt that it will make good farm land with patience, time, and scientific methods, but the battle to be waged against the stumps and the everspringing brush, is one that is taking the heart out of many a "farmer" bred to town ways, and has done much to bring about the present state of affairs.

So far as the *Press* could tell, the selection of the families who were to settle in the South Jersey wilderness was equally "ideal and chimerical." Having many children had been seen by the patrons of Woodbine as "the first requisite." The children were to be employed in the cloak factory and comparable enterprises to be set up; they were to earn needed money while the father stayed home and devoted three or four years to bringing "the wild land under subjection." The scheme thus sought to make a virtue of necessity, though it could not be "supposed that the children should support the parents while they were farm making." The would-be farmer's other resources were the seven dollars he was to be paid for each acre of the farm he cleared and whatever he could earn constructing roads in the colony. He would have a house and a cow barn, be given $40 to buy a cow, and $12.50 to buy chickens, and in addition would receive "implements, seeds, fruit trees, and plants . . . for a start."

> Sixty heads of families were chosen with care for the experiment. Most of them had settled for some time in this country. Only about fifteen were brought from the other side. They all signed contracts which would give them in fee simple, thirty acre farms in twelve years at an average cost of $1,100.

The first three years they were to pay fifty dollars rent, and execute leases upon presentation. Then they were to receive a deed upon paying $200 down, and giving a purchase mortgage for the land and house, and chattel mortgages on implements and livestock.

After the first heads of families had been selected they sent a delegation down to Woodbine to look at the site. Then the contracts were signed, and it is probable that no great stress was laid upon the contents at the time, for the simple reason that the company had no mind that the worthy beneficiary would suffer by not being able to live up to its terms. They have asked none but the agitators for the first year's rent.

The construction of housing for the settlers had been poorly planned. None had been put up until late fall and early winter, hardly the best season to begin farming in the wilderness. The consequent hardship had embittered the colonists. The New York *Press* focused in particular on two farms at the two extreme ends of the colony. The first shelter available there was "a little shanty" no bigger than "a hen's roost." The occupants of those two farms complained of having "lived in that place, sixteen in all, for five months," while their land was being cleared.

This was not a desperate matter for pioneers who, as Superintendent Sabsovich says, are glad in Dakota or Kansas to live in dugouts their first years. Yet work under these circumstances made just this significance in the case, that it gave the colonists a feeling of having put some of their lives into the soil and animating that feeling which made evictions so incomprehensibly hard for the Irish peasant, which made the interminable lease peasant of the patroons rise in this state in 1845 and set their pitchfork tines against the clauses of these manuscripts and the bayonets of the militia.

The *Press* went on to offer an account of the Woodbine difficulties and Sabsovich's admission that the inexperienced farmers had been given too many acres and too many seeds too soon. The trustees of the fund, it was implied, might have had right on their side, but would have been well advised to temper justice with mercy. "Failure will add another agony to the perplexing problems of immigration."[43]

The trustees took what seemed the only course left open to them; they appointed Colonel John B. Weber, former Immigration Commissioner of the Port of New York, to investigate. Colonel Weber interviewed fifty-five farmers and made a series of recommendations. Chief among his suggestions were that the colonists make no further extension of farm plots; that they gradually fill up the farms now vacated; that the fund develop the town of Woodbine by introducing industries; that they also introduce a non-Jewish element among the factory operators, a policy which would tend to promote the Americanization of the settlers; and, lastly, that newcomers be scattered among those having agricultural experience. "Further experience," he declared, "may develop the wisdom of another experiment of a farming colony upon lands yielding immediate returns, instead of lands requiring four or five years for clearing and putting in tillable shape."[44]

The trustees acted on Weber's recommendations and made many concessions. The Woodbine Land and Improvement Company would now furnish the farmers with work until their lands were cleared and rendered suitable for farming. Also, the terms of the leases were modified; the price of the farmhouses, land and livestock was reduced; the amounts of the installments and the interest were also reduced; and, finally, the interest payment of 1893 was postponed until October 1894. Even so, legal action was taken against a number of the Woodbine "revolutionists," those who in January 1893 had refused to cooperate with the fund trustees, and they were forced off their holdings.[45]

As for the trustees of the Baron de Hirsch Fund, profound disillusionment followed the "Year of the Trouble." For them, Woodbine had failed as an agricultural enterprise. The New York journalist-lawyer Myer S. Isaacs had already expressed his pessimism: "I do not think we should repeat the experiment of sending a certain number of families, whose capacity and history are unknown, to an uncleared tract of land and to be held responsible by them or in our own minds for their failure to become successful farmers."[46] Julius Goldman, who had pinned his hopes on having Woodbine prove a success agriculturally, was now of the opinion that agricultural settlements among Russian Jews on any extended scale were bound to fail; settlers sent to agricultural colonies in large numbers without being required to invest any means of their own would lose their self-reliance and become communal burdens.[47] Because of the discussion in the press and the dispossession of some of the settlers, Woodbine received a great deal of unfavorable publicity among East European Jewish immigrants. Sabsovich admitted that many farms were vacant because of the ouster of dissidents, and that the turn-over among the remainder was very great. Finally, as a result of the loss of interest and activity in farm work, the trustees turned toward the development of industries and toward the establishment at Woodbine in 1894 of an agricultural school named for Baron de Hirsch and intended, under Professor Sabsovich's direction, "to raise intelligent, practical farmers" in a two-year course of study.[48]

The picture of Woodbine after 1893 would change considerably. The next seven years witnessed the establishment of a number of industrial ventures.[49] The policy of the Woodbine Land and Improvement Company was to grant manufacturers subsidies of all kinds (free rent, free light, etc.) in order to encourage them to set up their factories there. The first such enterprise was a short-lived broom and basket factory. It was followed by a machine shop which later developed into the Woodbine Machine and Tool Company, one of the most successful of all Woodbine enterprises. The Jonasson Cloak Factory, initiated in April 1892, closed its doors in 1893 after the industrial depression of that year made itself felt. Other clothing factories were set up, however. In the case of one of them, Haas Brothers, the Woodbine Land and Improvement Company went so far as to give free rent for three years, as well as free light and steam for six months, and agreed to rent at nominal terms twenty farmhouses and four town houses for the use of the firm's workmen. Despite these concessions (some of the trustees felt *because* of them), Haas Brothers closed its doors in 1898. In only one instance did the Woodbine Company directly participate in the management of an industry in Woodbine, but this venture, too, lasted only five months. Before the century closed, the Universal Lock Company agreed to transfer its plant to Woodbine, the Woodbine Company in its turn undertaking to build a factory to house

Universal and to advance on mortgage 70 percent of the cost of erecting twelve new homes for their workmen. In the summer of 1897, the *American Israelite* was able to report:

> In an interview with a representative of the *New York Evening Post*, Mr. A[dolphus]. S. Solomons, agent of the Hirsch Fund, says of the Baron de Hirsch colony at Woodbine, New Jersey: "Hard times have not injured in the least the prosperity of the colony at Woodbine. There is not an idle man or woman in the settlement. There have been no reduction in wages, no strikes, no worriments of the sort that have come to the rest of the country. In the iron mills, the basket factory, and the brick-yards, the tailoring shops, and on the farms there has been no trouble such as that in the Alliance colony in Salem county, New Jersey."

Still, the *Israelite* remembered the troubles of earlier years at Woodbine:

> There are about 240 families in this colony, over 1,000 people. If Mr. Solomons is correctly reported it is an achievement to be proud of. . . . But why should so good a work be shrouded in mystery? Why do not the Hirsch Fund trustees give a public account of the discharging of their trust? They have achieved a great success and the world is anxious to know how it was done that the methods may be copied.[50]

Behind all the Woodbine ventures was the hope, even after the "Year of the Trouble," that the town population would create a market for farm products, that agriculture and industry would complement each other. This hope was, of course, far removed from the original conception of making agriculture the paramount objective, a conception which had expressed itself, for instance, in a very early decision to rent no houses in Woodbine to persons who came there merely for the sake of being employed in any industries that might be established.

As for Woodbine's Baron de Hirsch Agricultural School, though not an unequivocal success (it was plagued by curricular vacillations and student unrest), apparently it had a beneficial influence on New Jersey agriculture. Stainsby at any rate devoted much space to a description of the school and its

The main building of the school. (Courtesy AJA, Cincinnati)

Baron de Hirsch Agricultural School, Woodbine, New Jersey

Office and classroom building. (Courtesy AJA, Cincinnati)

Students spraying potatoes, 1907. (Courtesy YIVO)

Mechanics in the school shop. (Courtesy YIVO)

Students planting tomatoes, 1907. (Courtesy YIVO)

Agricultural students, 1930s. (Courtesy YIVO)

Scenes from South Jersey farming colony: Carmel, 1889. (Courtesy YIVO)

activities.[51] The school won several prizes in the Paris Exhibition of 1899, and in 1900 Governor Foster M. Voorhees of New Jersey ordered Stainsby, acting as a special agent, to give an account of it in his annual report to the state legislature. By 1912, nearly 900 students had attended the school; some 400 had completed the course of study.[52]

By the end of its first decade, Woodbine presented what Professor Samuel Joseph thought proper to call "a hopeful picture of growth." What had been at the outset "a barren wasteland with hardly a sign of habitation" presented a strikingly different appearance in 1901. Of the colony's original 5,300 acres, "1800 . . . were cleared and improved; in the town site 275 acres were cleared. Fourteen miles of street had been laid out, four miles of which had been graded and gravelled; there were twelve miles of farm roads in excellent condition. There was a population . . . of over 1400, with one hundred and sixty Jewish families and thirty-four non-Jewish families."[53] At that time, 40 percent of the population was engaged in agriculture, 60 percent in industrial pursuits.[54] Of the fifty farms (a decline from the original sixty), sixteen were already paid for in full, while the others were under leases and the farmers were rapidly clearing them. Fifty percent of all the residents owned their homes. Many public buildings had been erected; for instance, a synagogue, a Baptist church (the ground for which had been donated by the fund), a public bathhouse, and two school buildings. Industrial activities included the Woodbine Machine and Tool Company, the Universal Lock Company, a large clothing concern (Daniels and Blumenthal), two small clothing factories, and the Woodbine Brick Company. Woodbine also led in the production of fine fruits and vegetables. Speaking of the farmers of Woodbine, Stainsby said:

> The Jews who enter upon farm life are hard workers, and from earliest dawn to sundown the hours are spent in labor on the farm. They are always anxious to find the best methods to pursue in cultivation of the soil and the treatment of growing crops. In taking a tract of 15 acres of his farm, the head of the family devotes himself to that work, perhaps retaining a son to help him, the rest of the children find employment in the

factory and earn sufficient to supply the needs of the family until the farm is well-cultivated and productive.[55]

Woodbine by now possessed many of the attributes of political autonomy: an improvement association, a board of health, a volunteer fire department, a school system. Apparently it also had its share of political corruption. In March 1903 Woodbine was formally detached from Dennis Township and incorporated as an independent borough, the "First Self- Governed Jewish Community Since the Fall of Jerusalem," a New York enthusiast called it. No longer would its citizens be compelled to see their tax revenues devoted to purposes from which Woodbine derived little benefit. Woodbine would now be separated "from the hands of the surrounding politicians," would "become conscious of its civic responsibilities," and would develop "a proud citizenship scorning the corrupter." Moreover, it would no longer need to "maintain itself . . . by the philanthropy of the Baron de Hirsch Fund." Sabsovich, elected mayor in April, presided over "a Jewish administration."[56]

Writing of Woodbine a year later, in 1904, Abraham R. Levy, a rabbinical visitor from Chicago, compared the pioneer work of the South Jersey colonists to the achievement of the Pilgrim fathers.[57] Like them, the Jewish colonists had come to a new land, subdued it, and built a culture which was a blend of the old and the new. In speaking of their agricultural efforts, Rabbi Levy asserted that they were the most successful intensive farmers. Their products, particularly sweet potatoes and grapes, were famous throughout the East. The problem of keeping the children on the farms had been dealt with more successfully than in non-Jewish farming villages throughout the nation. "It is probable that fewer young men and women leave Woodbine and the other Jewish settlements than leave the average American farming villages."[58] The reason was that social institutions, schools, synagogues, social clubs, were being developed simultaneously with the economic growth. The rabbi concluded that "Woodbine proves that although the Jew is not naturally a farmer, with proper training, aid and encouragement, he can become one."[59]

As a grand experiment in agricultural colonization, Woodbine was a failure, but as an experiment in agro-industrial colonization, it must be pronounced a success. Despite the agricultural instability which dominated the closing years of the old century, as the new century began, two–fifths of the Jews in Woodbine were earning their living as successful farmers.

The largest single differentiating factor between Woodbine and the other colonization attempt was, of course, the support given by the Baron de Hirsch Fund. Woodbine was the child of the fund, the direct application of its principles. Despite the reluctance of the trustees of the fund to pour unlimited sums of money into Woodbine lest their largesse corrupt the colonists' spirit of self-reliance, they never withheld aid when it was necessary, as events even after the dismaying confrontations of 1893 bore out. The de Hirsch Fund leadership had come to understand what one student of Jewish agricultural efforts would conclude a generation later: that for Jews to succeed as farmers was primarily a matter of environment and adaptation. Jews had no instinctive aversion to farming. On the contrary, "nurture [was] more powerful than nature. Efficient training in the proper surroundings, and subsequent encouragement [were] the basic needs." Woodbine thus had the benefit of careful planning, expert direction, and large resources. Most important of all, it became evident that only as an agro-industrial community would Woodbine survive and flourish.[60]

Perhaps no one who supported these South Jersey experiments around the turn of the century ever summed up the feelings they inspired better than Bernard A. Palitz, of Philadelphia, who succeeded Sabsovich as superintendent of the Woodbine colony. In 1907 Palitz drafted an account of "The Borough of Woodbine," which concluded:

> If the South Jersey colonies have made their progress gradually and probably slower than a settlement started by a population used to the tilling of the soil and country life, they are sufficient to convince the anti-Semite that the Jewish conception of social life is not commerce, that he loves the beautiful, the quiet and natural life of man and lives it when equal

opportunities are offered to him. To the Jew who wastes away his life and the lives of his children in the filth of the tenement house, in the death-traps of the sweat shop, in the immoral and unhealthy surroundings—they cry out: come back to your natural calling, to the healthy life-prolonging occupation, to more light and purer air; harden your muscles and broaden your mind for the struggle that Israel is yet to meet before his mission is accomplished and his prophecies fulfilled.[61]

4 The American Experience

The Russian pogroms of 1881 and 1882 had taken the world of liberal opinion by surprise. And in many quarters, especially in the West, the reaction was one of shock. "One is made to blush for the name of Christian when we see it mixed up with murder, plunder and ravishment," declared the English preacher Charles Haddon Spurgeon in 1882. "Jew-baiting," asserted the *Edinburgh Review* a year later, "is an outrage on decency, a darkening of the fair face of Christendom."

One effect the Judeophobic violence had upon East European Jews was flight from the czarist empire. Organized Western Jewry in the form of agencies like the AIU went into action in Europe. In America, chiefly in New York City, the leaders of the Jewish community similarly began stirring. The immediate task was to provide for the physical needs of the newcomers, food, clothing, shelter, in the burgeoning East Coast cities to which they were attracted. The challenge of providing immediate care to the seemingly endless numbers of immigrants appeared in itself beyond bounds. But, for those of utopian bent, perhaps even more formidable was the task of diverting as many as possible of the newcomers away from urban centers and settling them in farming colonies in the New World.

Settling Jewish Colonists as Farmers: Problems

The major problem was not settling individual Jews as farmers; it was the establishment of farming colonies. Settling individual immigrants would have been a simple task in the 1880s. The few who had been farmers in the Old World would have had only to request aid enabling them to resume their previous occupation. The various philanthropic committees in charge of relief would have welcomed such requests, for in granting them, they would not only have been aiding those who sought "useful" work; they would at the same time have been helping to relieve the congestion of overcrowded cities.[1]

In the 1880s Jewish farmers in the United States, while few in number, were not unknown, e.g., Emanuel Woodic, the guiding spirit of Michigan's Palestine colony.[2] But the problem confronting the philanthropic leadership of the Jewish community was larger than that of aiding individual Jewish immigrants to get a foothold in America. Rather, it was to find some means of settling entire colonies of immigrant Jews as farmers. The immigrants were motivated by a wish to throw off the stigma of parasitism which attached to their former commercial and proto-industrial life. They were eager to eliminate the tensions created by their predominance in commercial pursuits, a predominance which both they and their philanthropic sponsors interpreted—with at least some measure of *Selbsthass* ("self-hate")—as the ultimate cause of anti-Semitism. Immigrants drawn to farming wished to integrate themselves into their new American environment by following what they considered the basic pursuit upon which all economic life depended.[3] Philanthropists responsive to a utopian goal would have to devise ways of helping these newcomers.

To establish colonies, much detailed study was necessary. But the need for hasty action by the Jews of America militated against any careful planning. Lack of time to develop a degree of expertise was among the major reasons for the failure of the colonization schemes. The organizers of the schemes allowed themselves little if any opportunity to study the prospective farmers with a view to ascertaining their experience, their abilities, even their aims. As a consequence,

109

immigrants with practically no experience as farmers, immigrants lacking an understanding of the hardships which inevitably lay ahead of them, immigrants without real financial ties to the venture, since they had little or no capital of their own to invest—these were the people who were sent out to found farming colonies.

Not only were the human materials all too often inadequate, but, in many cases, the sites of the colonies were ill-chosen. Natural disasters—floods, fire, epidemics—contributed to the collapse of colonization efforts which had been valiant in the extreme. The failure is not so hard to explain: the sponsors of the colonies were inexperienced, and just as insufficient time had been taken to study the capacities of the individuals participating in the venture of colonization, so insufficient time was devoted to a study of the sites selected with a view to ascertaining their natural properties, their adaptability to farming, their proximity to markets.[4]

If inadequate planning for agricultural colonization looms as a prime cause of failure, another major factor was reliance on the concept of colonies as an instrument for converting East European Jewish tradesmen into American Jewish farmers. A colony as a form of group life has many advantages, among them its ability to foster the economic mutuality of its members. For aliens, a colony has another special advantage: it creates an island of refuge in a sea of strangeness; it promotes a feeling of belonging among those who are sharply different from their already established neighbors. Where there is a common, pervasive ideal which a group desires to translate into a living reality, the colony is a logical organizational form. It appeared that in the case of the East European Jew, alien that he always was and pauper and idealist that he may have been and was often at least assumed to be, the colony would be the most attractive medium through which he could realize his ideal. Possibly, this second factor of "colonism" may be designated a significant organizational defect, since to be successful a colony must exhibit either unity of purpose or, at the very least, some large measure of submission to the authority of one individual.[5]

There are instances in American history of successful colonization. One of the most notable examples is that of the

Mormons, whose success appears to have resulted primarily from the complete subordination of all the members to the will of one powerful directorate or individual.[6] In none of the Jewish colonies was this subordination of will to be witnessed. New Odessa came closest to it, but even there William Frey proved to be no Brigham Young. Indeed, it would be hard to reconcile what seems to have been the characteristic individuality of the immigrant American Jew, even of utopian inclination, with the Christian selflessness, if that is the proper way to describe it, which underlay the ideological propensities of, among others, the Mormons, the Hutterites, and the Moravians.

As for unity of goal, a common ideal pervaded the Jewish colonization schemes, but it was an ideal that grew out of the common experience of persecution. The memory of that adverse experience receded, however; the hardships of farm life became daily more patent, and in consequence there was an erosion of loyalty to the great ideal of proving the Jew capable of farming, capable, that is, of pursuing a "useful" instead of a "parasitic" career. Indeed, the struggle for existence during the two decades 1880–1900 became so sharp that the problem for the Jewish immigrant, as for most Americans, became one of eking out a bare subsistence rather than the selection of "useful" as against "parasitic" forms of livelihood.[7] Failure after the grim struggle against overwhelming odds and the existence of opportunities for economic betterment in the industries of the city, both factors weakened the unity of goal so vital in a collective undertaking.[8]

Failures of Jewish Communal Farms: Causes

One reason for the failure of colonization or communitarianism is that it ran counter to the traditional spirit of American individualism. Such an assertion, however, denies the incontestable success of many of the Mormon colonies in the Far West and the impressive prosperity of such (often religiously motivated) schemes as cooperatives—the Amana enterprise in the Middle West, for example— which are not in the classical mode of American "rugged individualism." If the

Jewish colonists abandoned farming for industry, it was because opportunities existed in industry which did not exist in agriculture. The real American frontier, these colonists recognized, was now the industrialized or industrializing city. As one authority has pointed out: "The position of the Jewish farmer does not differ from that of other American farmers . . . and, not unlike their Christian neighbors, they continue in agriculture merely as long as it is profitable but exchange it for another occupation if that offers better prospects."[9] If to follow better prospects is to give evidence of individualism, then the Jew was as individualistic as his non-Jewish neighbor.

No period in American history was so ill-suited as the one, the late 1800s and early 1900s, in which Jewish immigrants sought to transform themselves into American farmer-colonists. The last two decades of the nineteenth century in the United States were marked by severe agricultural distress. (It is hardly coincidence that the United States was simultaneously undergoing a rapid expansion in industrialization and urbanization.) Indeed, Solon Buck has suggested that "agricultural unrest was not peculiar to the United States in the last quarter of the nineteenth century but existed in all the more advanced countries of the world."[10]

General financial conditions for the farmer were extremely adverse.[11] "Great Distress" characterized the 1880s, but the depression only deepened in the 1890s, reaching its climax in the panic of 1893, the worst America had ever experienced. Both industry and agriculture were affected, and even the well-favored colony of Woodbine, then in its formative period, knew intense suffering.

Ever since the Civil War, the United States had been going through a process of industrialization which brought about a resultant trend of migration from farm to city where greater opportunities existed.[12] Colonists often enough had to confront the problem of trying to keep their young people on the farm. Even in Woodbine where social institutions for the young were more developed than in other colonies, the founders enjoyed limited success. But no colony could stem the tide of history. No matter how compelling the ideal,

American Jewish youth, like the rest of American youth, would not remain on the farm while the economic and social lures of city life beckoned.

General industrialization inspired the overwhelming number of immigrants along with the great majority of Americans to by-pass agriculture for industry, where the returns appeared larger and more certain and even the work in many cases less hazardous and less exacting. A degree of agricultural industrialization was developing, too, but it automatically lessened the need for individual farm help and, in the case of the colonization of farmers, required the use of huge reserves of capital, far in excess of what the individual colonist possessed or the philanthropic societies could furnish.

Thus, agricultural colonization ran counter to the trend of late nineteenth- and early twentieth-century American life. A back-to-the-land movement undoubtedly had special significance for Jews who had been debarred from agriculture for centuries. But at the time that a number of Jewish pioneers were attempting their return to the land, the main current of American life was away-from-the-land. In 1860, less than one-fifth of the American population had been urban; forty years later, nearly a third was urban.[13] The time element, therefore, is basic to an understanding of the failure of all the Jewish agricultural colonization schemes in America.

A fundamental misconception the utopian immigrant had brought with him from Russia was the belief that he had to normalize his position by going into farming in the United States. In Russia, with her still predominantly rural economy, agriculture was indeed the only way the Jew could normalize his position. But the reverse, if anything, was true in the United States. In America, by becoming a farmer after 1880, the Jew would not be normalizing his position; on the contrary, he would be making it abnormal. In Alliance and Woodbine, the two instances in which agricultural settlement enjoyed partial success, the reason has been given: industry was combined with agriculture since the directors of the two colonies had already had sufficient experience to attempt a remedy for the prime defect of reliance on agriculture alone.

113

Jewish Agricultural Utopias: An Assessment

For all their idealism and utopian enthusiasm, the attempts at colonization of Jewish farmers in America between the years 1880 and 1900 failed. A generation later, especially from 1933 on, the American Jewish community again had to face the problem of how to provide for victims of European persecution. As far as agriculture was concerned, the well-organized Jewish Agricultural Society stood ready to lend its invaluable aid to individual farmers. The policy of the Jewish Agricultural Society was not to colonize, but to extend aid and encouragement to individual Jewish farmers.[14] During these years of the 1930s and 1940s, however, there was no need to prove the Jew capable of farming; that had already been amply demonstrated. Even in 1901 the New Jersey statistician William Stainsby had seen evidence of it:

> Yes, the Jew can be made a very successful cultivator of the soil; he bears the elements of success in his quickness to learn; his ready adaptability to the circumstances by which he is surrounded; his untiring energy and close economy. To assert the contrary is to betray the effects of prejudice and not conviction brought about by a knowledge of facts.[15]

According to figures of the Jewish Agricultural Society, the number of Jewish farmers in the United States in the 1930s and 1940s was estimated at between 80,000 and 100,000, surely a striking testimony to the adaptability of Jews to farming.[16] In addition to these American figures exists, of course, the powerful example of late Ottoman and British Mandatory Palestine which "provided conclusive proof of the qualities of the Jew as a pioneer colonist and the possibility of large scale Jewish agricultural resettlement on economically productive foundations." As early as 1921, one writer could assert: "from the reports of the Jewish agricultural colonies in the Holy Land to-day, one cannot help but conclude that [the Jew] can be a happy, progressive farmer."[17]

Colonization in Palestine/Israel and America:
A Comparison

Why did Jewish agricultural colonization in Eretz Israel (Palestine/Israel) succeed whereas in the United States it failed? Both experiences reflected utopian notions peculiar to the nineteenth century. Both reflected a desire to escape from the convulsions unleased in Eastern Europe by the decay there of feudal tradition and the often heartless transition to some form of capitalism and industrialism. Yet in America there was failure; in Eretz Israel, success.

If colonization efforts in the United States and Palestine in the same period, 1880–1900, are compared, the results show that colonization in Ottoman Palestine was as much a failure as it was in North America. But, though the agricultural colonization movements of the United States and Palestine in parallel periods suffered parallel fates, the causes for failure were not the same. Certainly industrialization as a major reason for agricultural colonization failures applied no more than minimally, if at all, in Ottoman Palestine. The years 1882–1900 were a period of "patriarchal" colonization financed, from afar, of course, by the French philanthropist Baron Edmond de Rothschild. The early Zionists who established Rishon-le-Zion, Petach-Tikvah, and other colonies in Eretz Israel proved unequal to the task they had undertaken. People of middle-class background and Occidental culture, they were innocent of agricultural knowledge and of the hazards, political and sociological as well as economic, which awaited them in the Middle East, and so, not surprisingly, they achieved little on their own. If not for the financial, administrative, and moral guidance that Baron de Rothschild was willing to offer them, their efforts would have come to nothing; soon settlers came to depend for help and direction solely upon him. They understood well enough that the primary reason for their survival was the baron's continuous fiscal and administrative support. Baron de Rothschild's spirit of charity, however, killed the idealism that had inspired the "Lovers of Zion" to go back to the ancient homeland and

115

attempt there to regenerate both themselves and the land by establishing agricultural colonies. [18]

A major obstacle to Jewish colonization in Palestine was, of course, Ottoman Turkish officialdom. [19] After 1919, however—that is, with the collapse of the Ottoman empire, the issuance of Great Britain's Balfour Declaration in support of Zionist objectives, and the granting of the League of Nations Mandate to the British who were now to help the Zionists develop a Jewish commonwealth in the country—Eretz Israel underwent an amazing transformation. [20] The salient facet of the land's development is the establishment of agricultural colonies (*kvutzot*), collectives which in the face of enormous difficulties have, unlike the American colonization attempts, more often than not survived and today continue, many of them, to operate in the form of kibbutzim.

The Palestinian colonist had greater difficulties to face in his efforts to establish a colony than did the American. Jews in Palestine before World War I had to overcome the hostility of the local Arab populace and of Turkish officials. They had to fight not only against diseases like trachoma and malaria, but also to attempt revival of a soil that had been neglected for centuries. Their capacities as farmers were as limited as those of their brethren who had migrated to America. [21] True, Palestine was less industrialized in the early twentieth century than America in the last quarter of the nineteenth century. Indeed, industrially and agriculturally, Palestine deserved to be rated among the more backward areas of the world. The Zionists not only had to revive agriculture; they had to develop an industrial foundation as well. The pioneer of Palestine who desired to rebuild the homeland through agriculture, and especially through agricultural colonies, had that real as well as apparent choice which was denied the American immigrant. In the United States, economic necessity tended to propel the Jew in an industrial direction. In undeveloped Palestine, the Jew would have the choice of devoting himself to modern agriculture or to modern industry. Both, if it can be said that they existed at all, had suffered equal neglect under the Turks and the Arabs. In physical terms, agriculture was surely the more demanding. If the *chalutz*, the Zionist pioneer, chose to found and to live in agrarian *kvutzot*, it was because he had the ideological drive, that very unity of purpose and that will to survive, needed to overcome seemingly insuperable obstacles. Arthur Ruppin, the authority on agricultural colonization in Palestine, understood well the role of ideology in the Palestinian ventures:

> The success of the Palestinian settlements is not accidental. It has its roots in specific underlying factors which distinguish Palestinian settlements from similar ventures elsewhere. For one thing, it derives its motive power from the high national ideal of the reconstruction of a Jewish homeland, which has been the source of that inspiration and enthusiasm without which the initial difficulties, hardships and disappointments of pioneering could not have been surmounted. The Jewish pioneer in Palestine knew that toil and sacrifice, not profit or comfort, would be his lot. Fired by devotion to an ideal, he was determined to stick through thick and thin to his task, even if from the purely material point of view it represented the most difficult and least profitable of the occupations he might have chosen. This devotion continues to be the prime condition for progress in the future.[22]

An American could recognize it, too. Gabriel Davidson, the managing director of the Jewish Agricultural Society, added to Ruppin's a tribute of his own:

> It is true that much money has been spent in Palestine, but there is something besides money which keeps these colonies going, and that is the innate urge of the colonies to play a part in rebuilding a National Home. The spiritual drive does not exist anywhere but in Palestine.[23]

This ideal of Zionism or Jewish nationalism was reinforced by another ideological support, that of socialism. The earlier Palestinian settlers, those who became protégés of the Rothschild administration, had not been ideologically committed to socialism, but before long from the ranks of East European Jewry came pioneers who not only desired to establish in Palestine a Jewish Commonwealth, but who, most of them at least, wanted to establish a *chevrat mofet*, a model commonwealth in which the evils of capitalistic society would never take root. In the *kvutzot*, the agricultural communal

117

settlements of the pre-Israeli decades, the ideals of Jewish national liberation and socialism found in a number of instances their finest expression. These twin ideals contributed immeasurably to the success of agricultural colonization in Palestine. [24]

One pitfall which the kibbutzim, unlike collectives in America, could avoid, probably a major factor, was the lure of the city. Turn-of-the-century America was a land of accelerating urbanization, a process generated by America's emergence as a center of industrial capitalism. Agricultural utopianism could not cope with such a pressure. By contrast, Ottoman Palestine was remote from industrialism and, hence, from any impressive measure of urbanization. The kibbutzim faced no formidable urban competition; there was no opulent urban promise to distract kibbutz members. Even during the three decades of the British Mandate, the early 1920s to the late 1940s, industrialization and urbanization, while not at all negligible, were not striking enough to be thought of as particularly distracting for kibbutzniks. Today, of course, when an independent Israeli state has achieved industrial significance, the kibbutzim must take seriously the seductions of city life. [25]

Another factor of kibbutz success was, curiously enough, the history of Jewish colonization attempts in the United States. In 1907, when the World Zionist Organization decided to foster agricultural settlements in Palestine, it was able to plan its ventures by building on the experience of previous attempts. [26]

This [American] experience . . . indicated the steps to be avoided rather than the positive measures to be taken. New methods, partly derived from the old, were developed; the result was a system based on (certain) administrative, juridical and economic principles:

1) Cooperation on the basis of mutual responsibilities.
2) A settler's wife was to receive agricultural training in order to do her share of work on equal terms with her husband.
3) Mixed farming, including the growing of corn, fodder, vegetables and orchids was to supplant the one-crop system. Moreover, semi-industrial undertakings were to be run by farms wherever feasible.

Gabriel Davidson, director of the Jewish Agricultural Society and chronicler of American Jewish agrarianism. (Courtesy AJA, Cincinnati)

4) The size and nature of the farms were to be in keeping with the working capacity of the settler and his family alone.

5) The number of families in each settlement . . . were to be not less than sixty (in exceptional cases forty) to prevent monotony from stagnating the cultural and social life of the settlers and to reduce their share in the communal budget.

6) Cooperative societies were to be formed for purchase and sale.

. . . .

8) As a rule each settler was to receive five–seven acres of irrigated land or twenty-two–thirty acres of unirrigated land . . . in most cases each settler received both.

9) From a technical-agricultural point of view, the following guiding principles in the establishment of a new settlement have been developed:

a) Town planning. A town planning expert is to prepare a layout of the settlement (roads, arrangement of living quarters and farm buildings, etc.) on the basis of a topographical map. Climatic conditions are to be taken into consideration.

b) Removal of natural obstacles. Natural obstacles likely to impede normal agricultural work excessively are to be removed. Swamps harboring malaria must be drained; scrub which prevents ploughing cleared; and stones removed.

c) Central water supply. A central water works is to be provided.

d) Suitable farming scheme. For every settlement a suitable scheme (with estimate of costs) is to be drawn up (by the Agricultural Experimental Station in Rehoboth) with the assistance of a special planning commission.

e) Settlement loan. The settlers are to receive from the Jewish Agency a promise that, as soon as its funds will allow, it will place the amounts required for the establishment of the settlement at their disposal in the form of a loan to be redeemed in forty-nine yearly installments, at an interest rate of 2 percent.

f) Selection of settlers. The choice of settlers for every new community is to be made by the Agricultural Department of the Jewish Agency in agreement with the Central Agricultural Organ of the General Federation of Jewish Labor or Mizrahi Labor Federation acting as representatives of all candidates for settlement.

g) Alternative sources of income. Opportunity must be found to help tide the settlers over their initial period on the farms. Work can sometimes be found for them outside the settlements; as a rule, however, they can be put to work erecting their own buildings and in drainage, afforestation and road building, for which they are paid. [27]

In conclusion, as Ruppin said, "it is noteworthy, that whenever these principles have not been followed either because of exceptional circumstances or undue haste the settlement has suffered." Of course, some three decades after the establishment of a sovereign Jewish state in the Land of Israel, the kibbutzim which have succeeded have done so as agro-industrial, not exclusively agricultural, enterprises. Even so, significant as the kibbutzim are in Israeli life and in the Israeli economy, no more than 3 percent of the state's entire population is made up of kibbutz members. In mid- and late twentieth-century Israel, as in late nineteenth- and early twentieth-century America, urbanization has been the norm. [28]

Clearly, the principles adopted by the World Zionist Organization, principles of which Ruppin spoke in the early 1900s, had not been followed, at any rate, not consistently or systematically, in the American Jewish colonization schemes. Yet the thought remains that the attempts at American Jewish colonization were among the factors which helped pave the way for the success of one of the most significant movements in twentieth-century Jewish life: the agricultural-industrial communes which have been so basic to the survival of the Zionist experiment and of the "Hebrew renaissance" in the Land of Israel.

On a deeper level, both experiences, that of Jewish agricultural colonists in turn-of-the-century North America and that of the *chalutzim* in Palestine during the closing decades of Ottoman rule, constitute one and the same phenomenon. Both testify to a utopian quest, a messianic urgency, which captured the imagination and guided the energies of not a few, if never anything approaching a sizable minority, of the Russian czar's Jewish subjects. An observation by the Marxist historian Isaac Deutscher on what motivated the revolutionary zeal of early converts to Soviet communism serves as a summation of Jewish agrarian utopias, too: they had all felt "the miseries of the old capitalist order to be unbearable" and had all known "experience of social injustice or degradation; a sense of insecurity bred by slumps and social crises"; and "the craving for a great ideal or purpose, or for a reliable intellectual guide through the shaky labyrinth of modern society." [29] This is the skeletal fact which stood at the base of impulses to cultivate the wilderness, whether in Oregon, in Kansas, in New Jersey, in Patagonia, or in the Valley of Jezreel.

Appendix 1: Jewish Farming Colonies in New Jersey

When the socio-economic convulsions which overtook czarist Russia during the second half of the nineteenth century sparked the pogroms of the 1880s, a mass Jewish emigration of unprecedented size got underway. Most of the immigrants would concentrate in American urban centers like New York, Boston, Philadelphia, and Chicago and would seek to adapt themselves to the rapidly unfolding urbanization and industrialization of the New World. Exceptions to the norm were those immigrants who allowed themselves utopian dreams of avoiding the city and striking roots in American soil in a more literal way, through cultivation of the soil, often enough communally or collectively. The experience of these dreamers is reflected in Herman Rosenthal's Yiddish-language journal, The Jewish Farmer, published for only one year, 1891.

Rosenthal (1843–1917), a native Kurlander, had come to the United States in 1881, and became in later years head of the Slavonic Department of the New York Public Library. The increasingly reactionary czarist policies of the 1870s and 1880s made him abandon his Russophilia and work to persuade the Franco-Jewish Alliance Israélite Universelle to assist the Am Olam colonists who were following his lead in 1880. It was with AIU funds that a tract of land was purchased for a colonizing effort in Louisiana.

Though colonizing ventures were organized in various regions of the United States, it was mainly in New Jersey that these efforts achieved a qualified measure of success. Alliance, founded in 1882, and Woodbine, established nine years later, enjoyed the greatest success of all the colonies. What enabled them to overcome the obstacles with greater effectiveness than colonies planted elsewhere in America was their willingness to combine agricultural effort with a degree of industrialism. Their leaders, colonists,

123

*and supporters, perhaps because of the colonies' proximity to Philadelphia
and New York, understood that a settlement founded purely on agriculture
was unlikely to endure in a country which was rapidly turning to industrialization. They perceived that, if colonization was to sustain itself, it had
to be combined with industrial or merchanical pursuits; it had to experiment
with agro-industrial patterns. Rosenthal's reports on the South Jersey
ventures amply testify to this understanding.*

I translated these passages from the original Yiddish periodical, Der
Yudisher Farmer: Monatliche Tsaytschrift fir Landvirtschaftliche
Kolonizatsyan, *which Rosenthal edited in 1891–92 at 205 Henry Street in
New York City. (Copies of Volume I of Rosenthal's periodical are located at
the Hebrew Union College Library, 3101 Clifton Avenue, Cincinnati, Ohio
45220, and at the YIVO Institute for Jewish Research, 1048 Fifth Avenue,
New York, New York 10028.)*

My translation was first published in Michael: On the History of
the Jews in the Diaspora, *vol. III, edited by Lloyd P. Gartner (Tel Aviv:
Diaspora Research Institute, Tel Aviv University, 1975) and appears here
with the permission of Tel Aviv University.*

Excerpts from The Jewish Farmer
The Woodbine Colony

When the great philanthropist Baron [Maurice] de Hirsch gave
ten million francs into the hands of several prominent American
Jews (Messrs. [Myer S.] Isaacs, [Jacob H.] Schiff, [Jesse] Seligman,
[Julius] Goldman, [Oscar S.] Straus, [Henry] Rice and [James H.]
Hoffman in New York and Messrs. [Mayer] Sulzberger and [Wil-
liam] Hackenburg in Philadelphia), the interest of which capital was
to be used for the training and placement of Jewish emigrants as
workers and farmers, not all the members of the committee were
agreed that farm colonies should be immediately set up. [1] This was
because they wanted the emigrants to be spread out evenly across
all of America, to procure employment for them in factories and on
farms, with the object of enabling them more quickly to become fully
productive American citizens. Those members, however, who did
indeed think at the outset that colonies could be undertaken, finally
prevailed. They convinced the committee to make an effort that a
colony be set up, not as a charitable undertaking, but founded on
pure business-like commercial principles. It was decided to take into
this endeavor also a Russian [i.e., immigrant] help committee.

It is well known to many that the activities of the colonies were called into life with the help of Messrs. Isaacs and Goldman, and thanks to the efforts of the great scholar-benefactor and most warm-hearted friend of the Jews, Michael Heilprin, who devoted the last years of his useful and work-filled life to bettering the plight of his suffering brothers. His main partner was Mr. Herman Rosenthal, who also after the death of his unforgotten friend M. Heilprin continued the colonies' activities, and thus it was proposed to him to form a help committee. Although at that time he held an important position at Edison Company [in Summit, New Jersey?], nevertheless, he left this post and gladly took upon himself the hard and thankless task of helping to lead through his beloved colony-idea. He, for his part, proposed two very worthy and experienced people in this area, Messrs. [Paul or Pavel] Kaplan and Joseph Rosenblitt [Rosenblueth?]; and these three formed the Russian Aid Committee.

The first step of this committee was to propose a plan for an industrial-agricultural colony, which was approved by the central committee. The aid committee also had the task of finding land and suitable colonists.

After long and hard inquiries the aid committee found such a piece of suitable land with the help of a knowledgeable chemical agronomist, Prof. H[irsch L.] Sabsovich, who at the bidding of the aid committee was invited to be agricultural advisor to the first colony. [2]

The purchased piece of land was 4,824 acres and lay in Cape May County, New Jersey. The climate is very healthy and invigorating, the ground is outstanding; the West Jersey Railroad cuts across the piece of land with two stations: Woodbine and Mount Pleasant. A second railroad is now being built and will also cut through the purchased land, which is very close to Ocean City, Sea-Isle City, Cape May, and other bathing places on the Atlantic Ocean. One and a half English miles from the colony runs the river Dennis Creek, where large ships are built.

Through Delaware Bay the colony is accessible by water to Philadelphia. The city is fifty-seven miles from the colony. It would be impossible to find a better piece of land for a permanent and successful industrial agriculture [colony].

It is called Industrial Agriculture Colony because the committee will build in it factories where the colonists can work when not occupied on the farms, especially in winter. They will be able, by factory work, to get through the bad times till their farms give them the chance to work only on agriculture. The latter will consist in vineyards, berries, garden produce, fruit, etc., which will have a good market in the nearby cities.

The conditions upon which the farms will be given to the colonists, the reader will find in a separate [Yiddish] translation of the contract, which was made between the colonists and the committee (printed in this same issue, below).

[Vol. I, No. 1 (Nov., 1891), p. 5]

Now we will see what has been accomplished in the colony in the short period of two months. Over 1,200 acres have been surveyed, 209 acres on thirty-eight farms have been cleared of bushes and timber; the land is ready for plowing on thirteen farms, twelve farms have already been plowed, ten acres have been harrowed for sowing, five acres are limed and sown with corn, and ten acres are ready for liming. Nearly one hundred thirty cords of wood are ready for market and fifty cords will soon be ready; besides the thirty-eight farms which are partly cleared and partly being cleared, are five farms given for clearing to an experienced man, who will with the help of seven workers, complete the job in five weeks. The remaining farms will be cleared by other contractors.

Seventy-eight Jewish and twenty-five American laborers work on the colony, a portion of whom are future colonists, and some of whom are emigrants, who could not find work in New York. The workers live in nine houses with ovens. Besides these there is a stable for three horses, and another one for four cows. Presently being built is a stable for ten horses and five houses for fifty workers. As soon as the stumppuller (a machine to grub trees) arrives, six roads will be cleared, which will connect each farm to the public road and one of the two railroad stations.

On each parcel we will plant three acres of corn, one for grass, and one for seed. Early in the year (spring) we will sow between the corn such cowpeas as will be harvested in May, and in their place will be planted Indian corn (maize) and potatoes. Through them we will receive two crops during one year; also the earth will be ready for crops which demand well-used earth.

About thirty workers attend the evening school; there would have been more students, but there is very little room right now. We have already erected fifty houses, which will have five rooms, a porch, a cellar, and for convenience, a well with a pump in the kitchen. Ten houses will be ready the first of December, another twenty, the first of January and the remaining ones on the fifteenth of January.

[Vol. I, No. 1 (Nov., 1891), p. 5]

The Contract

The form of a contract between "The Woodbine Land and Improvement Comp." on one side, and Mr. N. . . . on the other.

As the second party has agreed to become a tenant of the first party, upon the conditions enumerated below, and on the Parcel No. 0, as marked off on the plan of the company's property in Woodbine, N.J., we agree, after one has paid the other a fee of one dollar.

First: The company leases Mr. N. the Parcel No. O, as marked off on the map of the company's property, containing fifteen acres, more or less, for a period of fifteen years from the 27th of October, 1891, to the 27th of October 1906, at four percent of the agreed-upon price together with taxes and assessment. The rent for the first three years shall be . . . dollars annually.

Second: The company lends the cost of constructing roads around the aforementioned parcel, clears ten acres of it and plows five acres in the course of the first year; the sum of these loans, together with the cost of the land and improvements, shall be the price of the parcel, at . . . dollars an acre.

Third: Before or during the sealing of this contract Mr. N. shall pay to the company 200 dollars, which will be credited to him toward payment of the loan for soil, plants, seed as well as the remaining [land] when it is available for the aforesaid clearing and plowing. Mr. N. shall pay for the aforesaid land all improvements upon it, incurred in clearing, plowing, etc. in twelve equal payments, which shall begin at the start of the third year, but he has the right to pay the entire sum before it falls due.

Fourth: When Mr. N. shall pay the company, besides the aforementioned $200, the additional $200, he has the right to terminate this contract with the company and receive from the company a deed, for which Mr. N. must give the company a mortgage on the sum which he still owes.

Fifth: The company agrees to build upon the aforementioned parcel, as soon as is necessary, a house for the tenants containing not less than four rooms and a cellar, together with a stable, front-hall and well.

Sixth: Buildings, pasture, seeds, and plants, in such quantity and at such rate as the company finds practical, shall be given the tenant, and the cost, after payment of the 200 dollars, shall be secured through a mortgage and shall be paid out in three equal yearly payments, which shall begin at the end of the first year, but Mr. N. can pay back the sum before the end of three years.

Seventh: The contract shall have restrictions against disorder, sale or manufacture of alcoholic beverages, abandonment of the property. The house shall stand one hundred fifty feet from the road and the site shall be covered with grass and garden plants.

Eighth: It is agreed, that when Mr. N. shall receive the deed on the aforementioned parcel, and the same shall be fully developed, Mr. N. shall have the right to receive from the company a contract upon the adjoining fifteen acres of land, which are marked off with the number 0 on the map. This second contract has the same conditions as the first. However, Mr. N. can, before receiving the second parcel, use it as pasture free of all costs, except taxes. He can use this privilege only until the first of January, 1897, if he had not by this time received the second contract.

It is further agreed, that when Mr. N. has received the deed on the first parcel, and has not yet received the right to a contract on the second parcel, and shall at this time sell the first parcel, he shall lose all rights on the second.

[Vol. I, No. 1 (Nov., 1891), p. 5]

On the Colonies

Woodbine. As of the 20th of November [1891] we have cleared the brush on fifty-nine farms, cleared 430 acres, "cleaned it of woods," burned 300 acres, turned up 130 acres, and seeded fifty acres. "The early frosts made the soil hard to turn over, so that at this point, no more has been done." On fifteen farms, three acres apiece have been seeded with rye, and 100 bushels of lime are ready to be put on each three acres of turned-over ground.

At the colony now, over one hundred Russian Jews and fifty Americans are working. The houses are already being built and ten will be ready at the beginning of December, the remaining forty will be ready at the end of January [1892]. As the weather is presently very uncertain (today dry, tomorrow rain and then again more frost), it is very hard to set a definite time when the buildings will be ready, but we think the colonists will move in February. And the factory (40' x 60', three stories high), which is being built at the beginning of December, will already at that time (February) have its chimneys blazing, and its whistle will call together all colonists to work at the machines, which will give the colonists a chance to earn their living until they can again bring forth fruit from the earth to sustain themselves.

The chopped-up wood from the farms totals about eight hundred cord. The sum of money which it will bring, when sold, will be credited to each farmer in proportion to how many cord of wood were provided by his farm. "At the site in Woodbine, is kept a special, exact accounting of all income and expenditures."

Alliance. In order to give a tiny portion of the many helpless emigrants from Russia a chance at farming in America, the Hebrew Emigrant Aid Society leased (in the course of time it will be purchased) a piece of land near Vineland, N.J. On this land was settled, at the start of 1882, about forty families, and by the end of that year, over seventy families had settled there. Each family received fifteen acres of land, a house with a well, which cost over 125 dollars, as well as all necessities such as furniture and farming implements.

During the first few years the colonists were subsidized with small sums of money (eight dollars a month per family) and they were also given the necessities for planting fruit trees, various berries, and all kinds of seeds for gardening, and were helped in every way possible to become genuine farmers.

While the first years were the hardest ("every beginning is difficult") for the Alliance-colonists and they had to suffer because for the first three years the earth poorly rewarded the tireless novice farmers, but time and effort paid off. Through their patience and ceaseless labor they forced the earth to sustain them and finally the heroes were amply rewarded: the crude never-worked land was transformed into fragrant blooming vineyards and rich vegetable gardens, from which they have lately received the finest crop in the area, from wine to delicious potatoes.[3]

Many of the old houses have been enlarged, many entirely rebuilt, several new houses have been put up (some of stone and some of wood). In the colony there is a very fine and large public school, where about one hundred fifty children study. There are also two synagogues. They help their relatives and friends to settle in the neighborhood of Alliance, and already about three hundred Russian Jewish families are farming in the area.

Last November, Alliance sent the produce from their colony to an exhibition in New York which took place at "The Palestine Bazaar": the finest wines, preserves, sweet potatoes and other vegetables, which were praised by all the visitors, and which received the best certificates.

The men and women can be proud of their hard work, patience, and perseverance and of the sweet fruits of their indefatigable labor. They are truly pioneers contributing to the glory of all Israel.

The colonists at Alliance owe much to Mr. Isaac Eppinger, Leopold Gershel, and the Superintendent, Mr. David Sternberg, who gave many years of their time and toil to making the farmers self-sufficient. They also owe many thanks to Mr. [Henry] S. Henry, Leonard Lewisohn, M. [W.] Mendel, and the famous [British] philanthropists, Mr. Samuel Montagu, Benjamin Cohen, and Doctor [Asher] Asher.[4]

[Vol. I, No. 2 (Dec., 1891), p. 9]

Up to the publication of this issue, the work of the Woodbine colony was proceeding well. Of the fifty-six families, thirty-three now live already on their own farms, and at the beginning of March [1892] the rest of the families will be settled. The factory has been completed and the machines are being installed. We are convinced that at the end of March the factory will be in full swing. According to what we were promised at the outset, we expect to become involved in the manufacture of clothing, suspenders, and some carpenter work (turner's shop). Besides this, we are undertaking production of cigars and baskets. Many have found it possible to buy lots in Woodbine and open businesses. However, the committee is very careful not to sell many lots until the industry has been well established. At this time the farmers have already begun to plant and sow. Besides the fifty-six families [are] eight of those [people] who came six months ago as general workers, and by their great effort and ability and by their supreme behavior showed themselves able to become good farmers. These people will begin farming when their families arrive from Russia. The committee does not plan to settle more at the Woodbine colony. Now our task is to assure a decent living to those already settled. The committee can then sell parcels of ten to thirty acres at a low price to emigrants who have been in the U.S. not more than two years. And when they have paid for the land, the committee can also build houses for them with liberal repayment terms. But the rest must be accomplished by the settler himself. The committee had designated one of the houses to be equipped for a public school, and next week instruction will begin.

[Vol. I, No. 5 (March, 1892), p. 6]

The time when it was necessary to convince the Jew to take upon himself farm labor is past. We no longer need to entice or propagandize the Jew to work the land, he now runs to the land himself . . . .

If friends of colonization had spent the last two weeks at Woodbine, they would certainly have been filled with pleasure at the great progress that is being made. All sixty colonists are here, and over fifty are already living in their own houses. On every farm there is much activity, plowing and harrowing; fruit orchards are being marked off, as well as gardens for berries and vegetables. Pits are being dug for orchards, plowed, fertilized, and planted. And due to the great love that our farmers feel for agriculture, by their efforts, and on the other hand, through the generosity of the Baron de Hirsch Fund, which provided all the necessities, no one need doubt that this colony will become a model colony. The factory is all ready. The steam-powered machines are already in operation, the sewing machines have been installed, and shortly after Passover those members of the families who are not engaged in farm work will begin work in the factory. The school has opened with fifty pupils. All the Americans from the neighborhood, who often come to visit the school, are surprised by the intelligence and capability of the pupils, and the teacher, American born, is very satisfied with their progress in English. The library does not have many books at present, but members of the Baron de Hirsch Fund have promised that each one of them will contribute some of their own books soon. We take this opportunity to ask all our Russian friends in the cities who have Russian or Hebrew books that they wish to give us, to send them to Woodbine, N.J., or 205 Henry Street, N.Y.

The town of Woodbine is growing fast; in the course of this month twenty new houses will be ready for occupancy.

[Vol. I, No. 6 (April, 1892), pp. 1–2]

Russian Jews Farm in America

The colonies Alliance, Carmel, and Rosenhayn, N.J., which were founded by Russian Jewish immigrants nine years ago, are flourishing today. About six hundred families now work the land, which was a desert ten years ago, and together with their American neighbors they labor for the development of agriculture and industry in this land.[5]

[Vol. I, No. 10 (August, 1892), p. 2]

Appendix 2:
Sidney Bailey's
Memoir

Sensitivity to what he called "the expression of the soul, of spiritual life," contended the German historiographer Wilhelm von Humboldt, was a sine qua non in the reconstruction of historical events, since everything active in world history also moves within the human heart. Thus, any historical writing which failed to "recognize the uniqueness and depth, the essential nature of the individual" was defective. [1]

Simply preparing an account of the achievements and failures of the immigrant Jews who were pioneer agriculturists in late nineteenth-century America will not suffice to make their story intelligible. Equally essential is some insight into the personalities and prior experience of these pioneers.

Sidney (Shneur) Bailey was a founder of Alliance, New Jersey. His memoir was composed in the early 1940s in response to a contest sponsored by YIVO, the Yiddish Scientific Institute in New York. YIVO's leaders felt that the great mass of newcomers from Eastern Europe had not had their say in the unfolding of American Jewish history, and in 1942 YIVO announced a competition for the best autobiography on the subject: why I left Europe and what I have accomplished in America. Manuscripts submitted, it was hoped, would "be written with detail, accuracy and sincerity." Twenty-five prizes were offered, ranging from a first prize of $100 to several prizes of YIVO-published books. Whether Sidney Bailey's submission won a prize is unknown, but his memoir is not, in any case, especially important for any factual data it may preserve. Rather, it is important for its recapitulation of the mindset of the pioneers and for its projection of "the uniqueness and depth, the essential nature of the individual."

Many notable personalities in late nineteenth- and early twentieth-century East European Jewish life crossed Bailey's path. No less intriguing in his memoir is an exuberant mixture of Jewish tradition and secular

133

activity. The world Bailey knew, both in Russia and in America, was a world in transition from norms long established, but now faltering to a future whose shape was still blurred, still highly problematic. Bailey's consciousness was that of a man who lived in more than one social and temporal context: he was at once a pietist and a modernist, at once a man steeped in East European Jewish mores and a man drawn to the radical enthusiasms of a turn-of-the-century Russian intellectual. Bailey in his blend of religiosity and secularism represented something novel in the Jewish experience, though precisely what, it is improbable that he (or his comrades) could have said. The haphazard character of Bailey's account is not its least valuable feature: that haphazardness may be taken as reflective of the confusion which typified Jewish agrarian utopianism in the closing years of the nineteenth century.

I have translated the memoir from the original Yiddish typescript (YIVO Archives, Record Group No. 102: Collection of American-Jewish Autobiographies; folder No. 248) at the YIVO Institute for Jewish Research, 1048 Fifth Avenue, New York, New York 10028.

My interpolations are enclosed in brackets; Bailey's interpolations are in parentheses. Special comments by Bailey or his editor-typist are indicated by symboled footnotes.

What Am I and What Is My Life?

At the invitation of dear Dr. Max Weinreich, [2] I will set down something of my modest life, something pertinent to Jewish life in the Ukraine during the 60's, 70's, and 80's of the last century.

I was born on the 19th of Kislev, 1862, in Odessa, a firstborn son of middle-class Hassidic parents and thus held in higher esteem than all the later children. When I had just turned three, I was sent to *cheder* ["Jewish community school"] to learn Torah. At that time, there was little concern for hygiene, either in the home or the *cheder*. [The *cheder*] in particular was crowded, dirty, and full of offensive odors, [but that was] where these tiny Jews would spend [the day] from very early in the morning till nightfall, and sometimes late into the night. [Parents] would send along with the assistant a bit of food for the child and he [the assistant] would eat it up so that little would be left for the child to eat all day. The teacher used to wield the rod with a free hand.

Despite it all, somehow a child would learn something and be sent to an advanced teacher to study *Gemoreh* ["Talmud"]. I remember, as a creature seven years old, how the teacher would lead me around and have me examined on a section of *Gemoreh* and a major theme dealing with the laws of torts, or even marriage and divorce laws. I wonder, how could such a guy show off such tricks! Somewhat later Rabbi Nahum Epstein, the father of [Zalman?] and Isaac, died. [3] Later my teacher was Rabbi Abraham Moses, Dr. Nahum Slouschz's grandfather. [4] He would teach ten year old boys the [talmudic] tractates *Shabbos, Baba Basra,* and *Hulin.* My last teacher, the dearest and best, was Rabbi Moshe Leib, who would teach laboriously with not more than a few students all day and into the night, for ten rubles a month per child. In a half year, from winter to summer, he would teach a twelve-year-old pupil to know by heart one of the shorter tractates—*Rosh Hashonoh, Betzoh, Hagigoh, Sukkoh, Megilloh,* [or] *Moed Koton*—so that he would put his finger by a certain place, and ask us to recite from a folio and page number and we would do it without a mistake.

I became friendly with Yehoshua Rebbe Sirky [*sic,* Ravnitzky] in early youth. [5] Orphaned in early childhood by the death of his mother, he had no place of his own and lived with us. He was a few years my senior. He had already made the acquaintance of Moshel [Moshe Leib Lilienblum], and through him I too met Moshel. [6] A *cheder*-chum of mine, Susel Schnitkover, "the Red," saw me with Moshel and told on me at *minchoh* ["the afternoon worship service"], before the worshippers in the *bes-hamidrosh* ["synagogue"]. Do you know that Reb Shlome's son hangs around with [an unbeliever like] Moshel! A pair of hot-headed fanatics grabbed me by the collar, threw me out of the *bes-hamidrosh,* and soaked me with wash-basin water. A. Litvin (Sh. Hurvitz), [7] of blessed memory, wrote about this [incident] that here I received my first ritual purification with water.* At my bar mitzvah, when I said a *pilpul* [expounded a talmudic discourse] from *toras kohanim* [Leviticus], my father of blessed memory, gave me a set of Talmud as a gift.

My teacher advised my father to send me to a yeshiva ["rabbinical academy"], and this he did. For a full three years I had a taste of studying: "eating bread with salt and drinking water in limited measure" (Avot 6:4), "eating days" [taking meals with different families], etc.—and lying in dirt on the ground, suffering horribly [of] the third plague [lice] on Egypt in great abundance, as well as other plagues such as sores on my body. It's a miracle I'm still alive. Finally I was caught by the *mashgiach* ["supervisor"] one evening, when he visited the yeshiva and the boys before bedtime. We were

* Literally "baptism"—meaning the beginning of his deviation from the traditional path (his initiation into "free-thinking").

reading the [modernist pro-Hassidic] *Sholom al Yisroel* of Aaron Zvi Hakohen Zweifel [*sic,* Eliezer Zweifel], a teacher from the Zhitomir Rabbinical School.[8] This was a sufficiently "heretical" book for that fanatic [supervisor] to decide to call a meeting the next day after *minchoh* ["the late afternoon prayer"] concerning the boy from Odessa. I was amazed to see that there had gathered together—or rather been herded together—all the yeshiva boys "that they might see and hear and avoid doing such a foul thing" [a Hebrew clause] and they began questioning me as though I were before the Inquisition. How did I get such a book?! To make a long story short, I spat and went back home immediately to Odessa. (Too sharp a knife doesn't cut well; too strict supervision leads to no good.) And I became an infidel. To this day I am no advocate of yeshivas and haven't a good word for any of them, not even those in this country. Neither the system of education nor the way of life of the bachelor-students [at a yeshiva] is right. It is injurious and dirty everywhere. At first, when I still wore a long *kapote* ["kaftan"] and *peyes* ["traditionally lengthy side-burns"], I was stared at as though I were some strange apparition. But I began to think it was ugly, so I put on a short coat, cut my *peyes* and began to wear a regular hat. A radical reform for me at that time! I looked up Yehoshua Ravnitzky, and found him a *baal-tanach* ["biblical scholar"] who wrote Hebrew according to the style of whatever book he happened to be studying at the time. And he was also studying higher mathematics from the *Book of the Science of Geometry* by the mathematician-engineer, Chaim Zelig Slonimsky, editor of [the Hebrew periodical] *Hatzfirah.*[9] In fact, this would have ended my *cheder* and yeshiva period, in which I lived through more pain than joy from the good-for-nothing so-called teachers—with a few good exceptions, such as Rabbi Nachum Epstein, Rabbi Abraham Moshe, and the last rabbi of Odessa, Rabbi Moshe Leib. At that time, *chadorim* were forbidden in Russia, unless the rabbi passed an exam in Russian, which was at the time not usual among the Jewish communities in those places. The civil authorities would, from month to month, fall upon the yeshiva and drive the children out into the street, until they were bought off by the rabbis with a bribe ("no-bark-money").* Also the method of instruction was not according to the verse "teach a child according to his ability" (Prov. 22:6).

Of my *cheder* friends I remember only a few. There was one boy, Moshe Putran, an only son. His father had a book store, a

---

* *Lo yeheratz* money (from Exod. 11:7 ["But against any of the children of Israel] not a dog shall snarl").

genuine Jewish person. Nevertheless, his only son somehow went to a commercial school and thence to the university somewhere deep in Russia, where he converted because he fell in love with a gentile girl. Another friend was Monish Polinkovsky, Rabbi Mikhl Hirsch's son, with whom I was friendly to the end. Because of his family, he could not study in the Gymnasium [secular high school], but he knew Russian well and read the best of Russian literature. Later he married a niece who had graduated from a Gymnasium and kept a completely unkosher home, where I had my first taste of *treyfa* ["non-kosher"] food, concerning which Sholem Aleichem [10] related to me that earlier, before leaving for Odessa, he would telegraph her to prepare a borsht and pot roast for him. Ravnitzky was at one time a partner in a book business with Polinkovsky, and when the latter suddenly died, Ravnitzky immediately married his widow, with whom he left Odessa to go abroad when our intelligentsia was fleeing from the Bolsheviks. Another young *cheder*-friend was Moshe Freeman, of blessed memory, author of two books, of which one was *Fifty Years of Life in America* [sic]. [11] Of other good friends, some became *shochtim* ["ritual slaughterers"], and others businessmen.

I can add a chapter about our neighbors, Hirsch and Elka Rabinovitz. They were flour merchants with three sons and one daughter—Ephraim-Froike, Yudele, [daughter] Leike, who later administered the Pasteur Institute in Paris, [12] and Zusele, whose brilliant mind made him a banker and competitor with Wall Street magnates, who forced him to leave America. Actually, the mother was the wise one, the brilliant one, while the father was a simple man. Three children took after the exceptional mother, one after the father. I came to know the household as a boy, and would play little "baubles & beads" games with them. All the children were strong-willed. It once happened that Froike installed a pigeon coop, and one pigeon broke something in the house. When the mother came home from the store, little Leike tattled on him to her mother, who either admonished or punished him. From that time on Froike wouldn't talk to his little sister, who used to take care of him in his mother's absence. Somewhat later, Froike and I were racing each other [to see] who could read the *Megilla* ["Book of Esther"] or the *sedro* ["weekly pentateuchal portion"] more beautifully for his mother, and in the *shul* ["synagogue"]. That is how I became a *baal-koreh* ["a public reader of the weekly Torah portion"]. Froike went to study at the School of Commerce. He knew Hebrew, and together we would sing *Ha-Chemloh* ("Mercy") and other songs of Adam Ha-Cohen Lebensohn. [13] When I joined [the] "Am Olam"

137

[movement], I got him interested too. [14] He decided to give up his studies and come to America. There, being alone, he met a family he knew called Weitzman, from the Kiev "Am Olam" group, and fell in love with one of their daughters, whom he wished to marry. He asked for two hundred dollars from his father in Odessa. His father sent only half of it. Froike answered his father in Russian.*

Froike obtained a government position somewhere. The following kinds of things occurred. When my [own] daughter finished her medical studies, as did her fianc´e, who later became her husband, they lacked the money needed to establish themselves in an office in the city. They got a position for doctors in Arizona, from which [in years past] a letter would travel five days by Pony Express, and [today] three by train. My children found Froike working there as the manager. Imagine the great joy when, after three years of service, the children decided to return to civilization, he wrote me.

A few years back, while my children were visiting in Los Angeles, they found Froike a municipal employee. When Froike left for America, his sister Leike came to me and asked me to be her stand-in brother. I was preparing her for entrance into the Gymnasium. Later she went to Paris to study medicine and I went to America, where we promised each other to be reunited. But fate decided otherwise. When I first arrived, I felt very lost and soon met Mademoiselle Mashbir, a graduated *Bestuzhevka*, who ran a cooperative tailor-shop, where my friend [Moni] Bakal and others worked. [15] Her mother befriended me and advised her daughter to be more friendly to me. The first time I heard her speaking the real Berditchev Yiddish, I was amazed. And so we fell in love. Under the circumstances, I forgot my promise to Leike and married [Esther] Mashbir. I had met her brother, a functionary in Balta, in 1879. Meanwhile, Leike's parents, along with mine, arrived here. After two years of studying in Paris, Leike became homesick and arrived here, to become very disillusioned. By then I was a farmer near Vineland, not far from Philadelphia. My parents wrote me that Leike demanded that I come to Philadelphia and help her gain admission to Women's Medical College, the only school of its kind in the country. This I did. We did not see each other. She finished her studies and took a position in a New York City hospital, remained there for a short time, could not stand the way politicians ran the place, and left after making public their "noble" deeds. She left for Paris, where she became the world-famous biologist and

* Here Froike's reply in Russian is missing. What follows is not what he replied to his father, but a description of further events in America.

director of the Pasteur Institute [*sic*]. Later she married a Dr. [Walter] Kempner, had two sons, and a daughter who died young. The mother, too, died in 1935, and the sons became attorneys. When Hitler took power in Berlin, the two sons fled. At first they lived for a few years in Palestine; now they are professors here. One is at the University of Pennsylvania, and the other is also a professor of law somewhere. The older one struck up a friendship with me and called on me a number of times. Now, due to the [World War II] shortage of gasoline, etc., he writes to me from time to time. Unfortunately, the parents ended up in an old age home, forsaken and forgotten after all they gave of themselves to make their children prominent.

Somewhat later, when the idea of the Am Olam became widespread, Ephraim Feldman [16] arrived from Mohilev Podolsk; he was, by the way, a *landsman* ["a fellow townsman"] of the Rabinovitshes. I aroused his interest greatly, and he decided to come here. Feldman was exceptionally bright, a good Hebraist, a talmudic scholar, had also studied at the Gymnasium in Kishinev. I supplied him with an English Bible, because being proficient in the text of the *Tanach* ["the Hebrew Bible"], he would have little trouble learning English, with the help of this book and an English-Russian dictionary. He did not stay long in New York, and did not want to become a tailor, as did most of the immigrants. It suited [them] all to become "Columbus-tailors" with the exception of the smart Abe Cahan from Vilna and Nikolai Oleynikov from Kiev, the leader of that city's immigrant party. [17] E. Feldman, along with the Zolotarovs and others, went to Cincinnati. He came to Hebrew Union College, where he was snatched up like a "precious stone" and became a professor of several subjects. To such a *rosh yeshivoh* ["head of a rabbinical academy"] as Rabbi Carl Kaufman [*sic*, Kaufman Kohler], who ruled out circumcision (it goes without saying that he [Kohler] thought nothing of permitting leaven on Passover and other such transgressions of a trivial as well as of a more serious nature), [18] and to students like Dr. [Joseph] Krauskopf, [19] who gives a long sermon on Jesus on *Kol Nidre* [Yom Kippur, Atonement] night—it was just right for Ephraim Feldman to come out with a book in which he allows intermarriage. When Feldman heard that I, too, was already in America, was a buttonhole-maker, and intended to take up farming, he reproached me greatly. The great aristocrat and gentleman Michael Heilprin, of blessed memory, who had come here in the fifties of the last century with the Hungarian revolutionary [Louis] Kossuth, also deplored my decision. [20] Kossuth soon returned to Europe, and Heilprin remained and joined the [abolitionist] Boston party, which stood for giving full rights to the Blacks—the Negroes. Heilprin edited [in fact, he was not the editor] the weekly magazine *The Nation*, and also *Appleton's Cyclopaedia*. He knew thirty-odd languages and could speak eighteen, and he regretted terribly that my wife and I did not want to study medicine, for which only the completion of a two-year course is required with very few expenses. Another would-be dissuader was [Rabbi] Sabato Morais, who started a rabbinical school [the Jewish Theological Seminary of America] on 125th Street in New York, was looking for students, and asked me to enter his college.[21] I explained to them all that I had not come to America to be a doctor or a rabbi, but only to be a Jewish farmer [and] to find my sustenance from the soil which sustains all the living. Ephraim Feldman married and had children who became actors on the English-language stage. And he, Ephraim, died in an unusual way. On his way to deliver his defense of his thesis which could earn him the title "Doctor" [*sic*, actually to be awarded an honorary degree by the Hebrew Union College], he became nervous, took a bad fall, and died. And there is no trace of him, like all of them.

As I said before, I left yeshiva feeling insulted, but not being by nature a bad-tempered or spiteful man, I did not react like [the theologically atheistical or radical] Elisha ben Abuyah of old,[*] or like the latter-day "Other" [Lilienblum].[22] No, I got together with Ravnitzky and sharpened my mind on the mathematical problems in *Hatzfirah*, and thus was introduced to the camp of Hebrew writers—Yiddish no one even mentioned!

At that time there was no newspaper in Yiddish. Soon afterward [*sic*, actually, in 1881], EReZ [Zederbaum][23] came out with his *Folksblat* in St. Petersburg; we sometimes sent it correspondence, unsigned, holding it no great honor that two such novices were writing in Yiddish. Ravnitzky learned some Hebrew, and as was the fashion, at 18 he became a bridegroom. I planned to become a licensed teacher and prepared for the required four classes in Gymnasium; later in Nikolayev I passed the examination.

One more episode, one that would have lasting effects. There are in life small occurrences with great consequences. At the beginning of Elul [late summer] of 1879 I attended a wedding in Balta, where two of my cousins became sons-in-law of the well-known Rabbi Dovidl Balter, an author of rabbinic responsa. It was not usual for our small-town Ukrainian rabbis to write books.

---

[*] Elisha ben Abuyah is nicknamed "Aher" ("the Other") because he deviated from the tradition.

There was a cousin from Odessa there, a brother of the famous actor Moshe Funkel. Funkel was [considered] a great blemish to the family. My mother Freidl was too ashamed to show her face to her friends. His family would have nothing to do with him. [Even] in their greatest need, they refused to call on him. When Funkel had a son, no one in the family came to the *bris* ["circumcision"]. My father, may he rest in peace, Sutzki, and I were there. Freidl was so fanatical she was truly mortified that this had happened to her only sister. She had no one left in her family besides her. For a boy to go to St. Petersburg and study to become a Russian actor was such a great shame that Freidl didn't speak to her sister for the rest of her life.

Funkel's brother was touched by the modern ways; [he was] a *maskil* ["emancipated intellectual"]. He had traded in the Balkans in 1876, during the Turkish War. He dressed in modern fashion, and certainly did not observe *kashrus* ["the traditional dietary laws"] on his travels. I recall that we both left the main synagogue the same summer in which he later got married, and after the [reading of the biblical book of] Lamentations,* we met down by a soda kiosk to have a drink. I warned him that this was not a proper way for a bridegroom of Rabbi Dovidl to act, because many people came from Balta to Odessa on business. He laughed it off, but at his wedding they dressed him up in all the traditional attire: a *kitl* ["a white robe"] and a long *kaftan.* He was led through the streets to and from the synagogue with a drum. He wrote me that at Balta during the ten days of penitence [between the Jewish new year and the Atonement fast] in the main synagogue, where the rabbi usually prayed, they gave him *maftir* [let him conclude the biblical readings with the prescribed passage from the Prophet Hosea] on *Shabbos Shuvo,†* a great honor in Israel. And how amazed I was when the oldest daughter Brocho—a divorcee (the *rebitzin* ["rabbi's wife"] was already dead by then)—presented me with [a copy of] *Chatos Neurim* ("Sins of Youth") by Moshel [Lilienblum]. Sabbath morning she goes to *shul* with a thick *Korban Minchoh siddur‡* and a shawl over her eyes, and on her way back from *davenen* ["prayer"] she would pay a visit to a certain *maskil.* Here I saw her take off her head covering and sit with two long braids hanging down to her shoulders. The second son-in-law of the Balter rabbi was a spiteful one. He would send his Jewish servantgirl to market for milk, and his gentile one for wine at the Jewish tavern-keeper's. At his wedding I

* Read on the mid-summer fast of Tishah Be'Av.
† The "Sabbath of Repentance" before Yom Kippur (Atonement Day).
‡ Special all-inclusive prayer book for women, entitled *Meal Offering.*

first met my brother-in-law-to-be, Lazar Mashbir.[24] He was dressed like one of those Russian officials who steal children from rich parents and send them to a Gymnasium, thus greatly grieving the parents. Since the rabbi's daughters were intelligent, they moved in *maskil* circles. So the *maskilim* were also at the wedding, where I met many of them, but I made life-long friends only of some of them who greatly influenced my early life. Reb Mordechai Voskoboinik married a girl from the Balta region; he was learned and clever, but far too honest. He came to Odessa a bit later to take a position as bookkeeper for a wholesaler. That is what we called a businessman who bought and sold grain, groceries, etc., to the small-town businessmen and salesmen of the region. Reb Mordechai Voskoboinik understood Russian too, but could not speak it well. A bit later I taught Russian to such a group. Reb Mordechai later came here with the Brotherhood. He, his wife, and small son set up a tailor shop until they arrived in the place of their desire, the [New Jersey] colony of Carmel. There he continued tailoring until he became a grocer. He told me that as long as he was a tailor, he had a reputation as a good and honest man, but as soon as he became a grocer, his customers, who buy readily on credit but pay back with great difficulties, said he was a thief.

I also met a couple, Mr. and Mrs. Gellis, who used to visit the circle of *maskilim* on Sabbath and smoke. They also moved to Odessa, where they set up a *domashni obed* (Rus., "a restaurant where home-made dinners were served"), but later joined an acting troupe under the direction of "Shomer" [Shaikewicz] who wrote plays.[25] And last but not least, I met with my friend by destiny, my teacher Bakal—a unique specimen of a man in our time. But it would take an extra chapter to tell about the head and heart of the Brotherhood, a friend of labor, himself a worker, who became a rabbi's son-in-law and heir to all his property in the form of a dowry as well as [husband] to his beautiful daughter. Not to leave anything out, I would like to relate an episode which characterizes the generational conflict of that time. Rabbi Dovidl had a brother Avromtsi, the *shochet* of Soroki. He used to ask us, the in-laws, to sing the cantillation of the *Chumosh* [Pentateuch], and he would read according to the cantillation the text of the whole Torah; he did the reading perfectly without a mistake. But his son Shmuel was already a spiteful *maskil* and later became a market-merchant ("a stall-keeper").

Now concerning my relations for many years with Moshe Leib Lilienblum (*olov hasholom* ["may he rest in peace"]). I returned from the Balter rabbi's wedding (1879) with a new circle of worthy friends, Ukrainian *maskilim* with liberal ideas, the "nihilists" of the time. In his free time, I would meet again with Yehoshua Ravnitzky, my friend—who was like a brother. He had become a Hebrew teacher and also, more or less, a writer, a pioneer in Hebrew. Ravnitzky also seriously studied Russian and even German. Ravnitzky and I would often go to see and hear Moshel (may he rest in peace). In that troubled time it was forbidden for a large number of people to assemble in a home. We hit on the idea of meeting on Sabbath and Holy Days in the court of the big *shul*. It was in a central location at the intersection of Hebrew and Reshelia Streets. At one such meeting during [the fall] *Sukkos* ["harvest festival"] we received the sad news that Ilya Orshansky had died.[26] We quickly crowned Moshel to fill the vacant position, and thus began a new era in Moshel's activities; [now he would] occupy himself with the discriminatory laws against our brothers in Russia. As is known, Orshansky had written a few books on the discriminatory laws against Jews, as well as a book on the Jewish situation in Russia.

Here is another episode from that period. The "Saul of Tarsus," Jacob Gordin,[27] made his appearance in Odessa at that time, with the teacher Priluker as his main supporter. They had a brand-new group: "Yevreiskoye Bratstvo" ("the Jewish Brotherhood"), which rapidly gained a following among the Jewish lower classes, the downtrodden, and the socially rejected tailors and shoemakers. One Friday evening, Moshel, Ravnitzky, and I visited Gordin to talk about [his] "Bratstvo." Gordin, very rude and very egotistical, told us to leave, without letting us utter a word. Moshel too reacted to this incident in several of the articles he wrote, in Russian and in Hebrew. Moshel had learned to read and understand Russian well, though he had trouble speaking it. He never acquired the proper accent; he would speak like a Lithuanian [Jew] who says *Savuos* for *Shavuos*. Often, Moshel would read his articles to the two of us. When I became a licensed teacher, Moshel was a friend and colleague of mine. In these schools he taught religion, and I, arithmetic. We would see each other often at other times. And in the summer of 1881, when the [Am Olam] Brotherhood grew better known following the terrible Passover pogroms in South Russia and the Ukraine, I met with Moshel and spoke with him about the Brotherhood. He said to me, as if "in spite," that if he had to leave home—till the very end he spoke of "Mother Russia"—why did it have to be across the ocean, as far as to America, and not to Palestine. And thus Moshel had the honor of becoming the founder of the [proto-Zionist] "Love of Zion" [movement]. Lilienblum was then earning very little. He would get ten rubles a month for teaching and a miserable pittance for his writings—a bit more for Russian than for Hebrew articles. He lived in extreme poverty with his wife, a butcher's daughter, who would earn "water for their kasha" ["water in which to cook their groats" = very little money] by repairing torn rubber shoes, in this way helping to support quite a large family of ten people. At that time, when I would visit his house, until the end of the year 1884 Moshel still remained a heretic—he continued behaving like "Aher" [Elisha ben Abuyah], even when not intentionally, perhaps out of habit. It did not bother him that his wife went to the synagogue on the High Holy Days [in the fall—New Year and Atonement Day], and he would remain at home, reading, writing, and receiving me and others who could discuss matters of interest to him. As is known, the assimilated "Pogrebalni Obshchestvo" ["funeral society"] employed him as secretary and paid him better than "our brothers" (meaning: the religious establishments) pay their officials. And this same Moshel later became one of the regular members of the *minyan* ["worship quorum"] of the Yavneh Synagogue; and [I remember] the way Moshel later used to be called for an *aliyoh* [synagogual Torah reading], and would read a *Haftoroh* [prophetic portion] with so much feeling, although the modern Elisha ben Abuyah could not become reincarnated into a [theologically orthodox] Rabbi Akiba[28] . . . Darwin was asked, in his old age, if he still stuck to his theory of "evolution" and answered the same as Moses did when he thought about the mystery of Creation, "Show me, I beg of You, Your glory." This "secret" is not to be explained "for no man may see me and live."* Albert Einstein gave the same reply at greater length. Moshel could not change his mind; he did what he did only to please the community.

[I want to speak of] my relationship with Yehoshua Ravnitzky, "a friend like a brother to me," † who worked faithfully for seventy years in the field of our literature. Yehoshua had been orphaned by his mother at a very early age. We had met at the *bes-hamidrosh*. He was all alone, and so became a frequent and very welcome visitor at our house. He remained [virtually] a member of our household for many years, even after I left for America. He would visit my parents and comfort them. Yehoshua was a bit older than I by exactly how much I don't know. He was the more progressive of the two of us and we treated each other like close friends. He was the one who brought me closer to Moshel. We studied together in the *bes-hamidrosh* and ate dry rolls and baked potatoes. In these early times I

* Exod. 33:20.
† After Ps. 35:14.

became acquainted with Moshe Freeman, with the Zhypnik brothers, full orphans [fatherless and motherless], in whose house we had many good times, and with other fine buddies and good students. Freeman was married very young, according to custom. He married and lived through pogroms in Odessa, suffered greatly, according to the verse: "A Jew is a slave and scorned."* He joined the Brotherhood, actively participated in it, and left for America with the first party in February 1882. He came here, became a farmer for a short time, but could not put up with the hardships of changing from a yeshiva and *bes-hamidrosh* student to a farmer, an occupation unknown to his fathers and forefathers through all the years of their Exile.

We are now in the third and longest Exile of our history, begun by Constantine I [the fourth-century Roman ruler Constantine the Great, first of the Christian emperors] in the first centuries of our common era. It is a few thousand years since our Exile in Egypt. The Babylonian Exile was the shortest and easiest, from which we were saved and brought to Jerusalem by Ezra and Nehemiah, who edited the *Tanach* [Hebrew Bible] and rebuilt the *Bes-Hamikdosh* ["Jerusalem Temple"], where the Levites could sing the Psalms and the Men-of-the-Great-Assembly [precursors to Pharisaic Judaism] taught the people *Tanach:* the most rational legislation represented by the Law of Moses—the words of the Prophets burning like fire—until our downfall at the hands of those Hitlers of past ages, the Romans.

M. Freeman edited a Yiddish newspaper in Philadelphia for a short time. Later he became a well-to-do businessman. He also wrote a two-volume work about the fifty years of his life in America. He remained a stranger to me during all the years.

When I returned from the Balter rabbi's wedding I had met a circle of those so-called "evil-men," the *maskilim*. It seems to me that the Ukrainian Jews are friendlier, less egotistical, and less mercenary than the Litvaks [Lithuanian Jews]. At the time I had decided to prepare myself for the profession of teaching, yet I did not ignore my friend Yehoshua. In the free time he had from teaching Hebrew, we studied and read Russian together. Not ordinary novels, but the critics and [Nikolai Konstantinovitch] Mikhailovski—isn't this how all the *maskilim* began?—and also [Vissarion Grigorevitch] Byelinsky, [Nikolai Alexandrovitch] Dobroliubov, [Dmitri Ivanovitch] Pisarev, and even the American [John William] Draper in Russian.[29] At that time Zalman Epstein (Zeben) had come to Odessa from the Volozhin Yeshiva "full and overflowing with knowledge" to his old

* After Jeremiah 2:14.

145

teacher [?—name unclear], who had once been my Talmud teacher as well. Zeben began to study Russian from the critic Pisarev, and with his younger brother Isaac, I began to teach him Russian from the *Zecher Rav* [not clear, perhaps a teacher's manual for Russian language with Hebrew explanations]. Isaac later became the mentor of [manuscript blank here]. I was somewhat bolder than he was, so I soon took up the "theory of evolution" for which my first teacher was Dr. Aaron Porjes,[30] whom I had known in Odessa and who favored me with his epoch-making *Sefer Toras Chaim*. Yehoshua [Ravnitzky] tried writing in Hebrew, and I emulated him for a while, until my teaching and studies and other activities for the needs of our people at that time became too demanding and I had to give it up. Yehoshua, however, kept on and succeeded. He was published in the Hebrew newpapers, and in the journal *Ha-Boker Or*. Yehoshua married early. His wife bore him one child and died delivering the second. He remained a widower for most of his life. His mother-in-law and father-in-law did not want to part with the child, and so he remained quite free. He taught. He perfected himself in writing for the Hebrew and Russian press, and boarded with a lady-friend of ours, Feye Polinkovsky, granddaughter and daughter-in-law to Odessa rabbis. She had completed Gymnasium in Radomisl. Yehoshua ran a book business with her husband, our old friend Monish Polinkovsky. When Monish later died, Yehoshua married Feye. He became acquainted with [the poet Chaim Nachman] Bialik, with whom he was later a partner in the publishing firm *Sifrei Dvir*, became a friend of Ahad Ha-Am, of the Litvak Mendele, a friend of Sholem Aleichem, and he too used Yehoshua, just as had Bialik.[31] Later Yehoshua left for Palestine, published [with Bialik] the *Sefer Ha-Aggadah* and others. He finally died at a ripe old age and left an only son to take over his publishing house in Tel Aviv.

[I want to discuss] my connection with Moni Bakal. He was all "purity,"* the heart and soul of the Brotherhood. When I met him in Elul (late summer) of 1879 at a wedding, he was already suffering for an ideal. Bakal was a rare gem, whose father was mentor and educator at the home of the millionaire Toltchinsky, a sugar-magnate in Uman, Kiev province. Bakal was the son-in-law of the rabbi of Ternivke, not far from Balta, and received as a dowry rights to four positions in addition to a beauty of a woman, the rabbi's daughter. She bore him a son when he was barely eight [*sic*, eighteen]. Shortly after the wedding the rabbi issued Bakal a writ of divorcement [because he considered Bakal an unbeliever] and the

---

* Originally "tkheiles" meant the "blue thread" in the *tsitsis* (fringes) of the *talis* (prayer shawl) which makes the *talis* especially fine.

episode ended. Bakal told me that even as a boy he loved to scru-
tinize the scriptural texts. He would wonder at the words "said
Elohim." *Amar* ("said") is in the singular, while *Elohim* ("God") is a
plural noun. He would hide a volume of philosophy under his
Gemoreh and steal a peek at it. He meditated upon the maxim of the
Ethics of the Fathers: "Love work and hate the office of the Rabbi."*

I had already heard that a few [members] of the circle, including Bakal, were coming to Odessa. Later, I found Bakal an appren-
tice to a jeweler, a Mr. Cohn, the father of Mr. Lawrence, manager of
the Yiddish theatre in Brownsville.

This kind of work is called (in talmudic parlance) a "clean
trade." Another of the circle, also of refined conduct, a *maskil,*
Mordechai Voskoblinikov, had a position as bookkeeper for a
wholesaler, some sort of broker for Ukrainian businessmen in
Odessa. His low wages forced his wife to take in a few boarders.
Bakal was one of them. Another boarder was one Max Rabinovitz,
along with a brother, who later became famous here [in America] as
a champion of birth control. At Voskoblinikov's house we would
gather on Sabbaths and festivals, young men and women, to read
Russian and have discussions. I was a good deal younger than they,
but Bakal, who was a great smoker, used to stop smoking, in
deference to the ladies. Among the many visitors was also one
Shapiro, from Lithuania, who appeared to be observing his own
kind of *golus* (exile). He was a sort of a vagabond. He would read to
us from [the liberal British philosopher] John Stuart Mill in Russian,
with [Peter] Lavrov's commentary; [Shapiro was] a true *maskil,* who
many years later became known for his "Lovers of Zion" activities.[32]

In the meantime I became a licensed teacher and taught in a
school [called] Malenki Yeshibot, † where students studied without
paying. Only Moshel was paid. Through his acquaintance I became
a frequent visitor to the university, where I was a non-paying
auditor of [lectures by] Prof. Eli Metchnikov and other liberal professors.[33]

With the advent of reaction came a decree from St. Petersburg
to dismiss liberal professors, so Prof. Metchnikov was fired and
decided to go to Paris. The students gave a banquet in his honor, at
which he spoke about his ancestry; and soon revealed that his
mother was a Jewish woman.

I also became friendly with a teacher from the Trud School
("Trud" means "work" in Russian). This was a school with the

* Avot 1:10.
† "Minor Yeshivah": most likely a government-sponsored Jewish seminary
with secular subjects, set up with the assistance of the Haskalah (Enlightenment)
movement.

purpose of teaching Jewish children to be useful through labor. Although this school operated for several years, it never bore fruit, due to the discriminations against Jewish craftsmen by the Russian craft-associations. The end result was that the graduates of the school who were children from well-to-do families went abroad to study, and those from poor families were forced back into working as clerks in small stores.

This situation most likely was one of the initial incentives for the idea of farm labor-colonies initiated by the Am Olam movement.

In March, 1881, Alexander II was assassinated, and he was succeeded by his cruel son [Alexander III], who sought revenge for the ugly death of his father. Pogroms against the Jews were the most proven means of action, so horrible pogroms occurred in southern Russia during Easter week. We sensitive Jewish students were embittered. We laid aside our studies and began to think of how we could aid the community in its slavish position. Is the "Jew a slave to be scorned?"* We petitioned Petersburg for land to establish a colony in Kherson Province. This was completely refused. At that time a professor, well known in Odessa, had purportedly published a book about the joys of farming in the United States.[34] Travelling in our area at that time were agents to recruit emigrants; they gave birth to a movement to leave Step-Mother Russia and go to America, the land of democracy, to be Jewish farmers there, and perhaps even to build our own state, like the Mormans' state of "Utah." Our state would be built on humanitarian principles, such as already existed there. Bakal threw himself wholeheartedly into this movement with all he possessed. The few hundred (rubles) of his savings he put into the common fund, and for a long time he subsisted on bread and tea. One episode: It happened that Bakal's father paid a visit to Odessa to see his fine son. The father came to his lodgings and found a bunch of pranksters—his son's good friends. Bakal wore a short coat and long hair, and his friends wore their shirts over their pants, in gentile fashion. We saw in him (Bakal's father) a fine subject to ridicule. We were all embittered over *cheder* [and were] against the practices laid down in the Talmud, and we discussed Jewishness with the old man. We were aware of the fact that we were hurting the old man, very much so, with our objections to and criticisms of the Jewish code. I confess that I told him that in addition to our dissatisfaction with tradition, Talmud, *Shulchan Aruch* [a sixteenth-century rabbinic law code still considered authoritative by Orthodox Jews], customs and laws, we even had some serious disagreements

* Jeremiah 2:14.

with the *Toras Moshe* [Law of Moses: the Pentateuch]. At this the old man gave a deep sigh and said naively and painfully: It is pitiful to see how such fine noble souls are drowning. . . . It would have been more pleasant to take a slap in the face from the old man than to hear these words. I then made a vow to "be careful with my words." In the meantime the Brotherhood (Am Olam) had become widely known in the town and in the university. More students joined these folks in their time of need. At this time the word "career" was regarded with loathing by the students. Because while one was studying there could be no talk of careers. One should not even mention it and thus avoid the contempt of friends. *Frei-ibergegebene-dienst* (literally, "voluntary dedicated service") was our key-word. Some of them were: Max Rabinovitz [known as ?], Ben-Ami,[35] a descendant of *shochtim*,* Simon (his family name escapes me just now), and Konstantin Fritz. He [Fritz] later became the head doctor in a large Jewish hospital; he had received a 50,000-ruble dowry, but ended up starving in Berlin when the Bolsheviks took power in Russia. Yegor Shabshovitz, Gortenshtein, [and] Brody [were] among many others [involved in the struggle]. Also Balta with my brother-in-law Mashbir at the head, Kiev with Nikolai Oleynikov at the head, Krementchug with Chaim Spivakovsky, Poltava with Israel Isser Katsovey [Kasovich],[36]—[all] with a membership in the thousands. I also made the acquaintance of Jacob Cohen Bernstein, brother of Lev Cohen Bernstein, the famous revolutionary, who was dragged from his sick-bed and led to the gallows.[37] Jacob was an easy-going sort who had studied in Kiev University to become a mathematics teacher in a Gymnasium. He did not balk at the fact that he would have to convert. But when Lev became notorious as [a revolutionary and thus cast] a stigma on the family, Jacob was expelled from his class and forbidden to study anywhere in Russia.

The brothers B[ernstein] and a little sister Anute came from a very assimilated family. Their parents were from Vienna. The father died in Kishinev where they owned a number of houses which brought in enough income to allow them to live in Odessa and to give their children a proper education. Jacob was also a concert pianist; the mother of the household spoke only German [and] never attended a synagogue. My mother, may she rest in peace, always identified him (Jacob) as the "one who never speaks Yiddish." I also met their close friend, Professor Mikhal Philipov,[38] whom I taught Jewish subjects and who published a three-volume book: *What Is a Jew?* (in Russian: "Chto Takoi Yevrei?"). This pro-

---

* Ritual slaughterers: hence, they belonged to the lower echelon of the religious officials of the Jewish community.

fessor's father was a convert to Christianity and edited the journal *Ruskii Vestnik* ("Russian Herald"), but his mother was descended from the highest Russian nobility.

M. Bakal would address meetings and prepare texts for leaflets which we would reproduce and print in the university labs, which was a kind of state within a state, where the police had no right to enter. . . . Although no Jew should be an "accuser" against the Congregation of Israel, nevertheless I must relate several sad facts. Jewish society showed no concern about "What will the non-Jews say." Professor Philipov, who alone carried the expenses of the publication, never received a penny in return for his three volumes, *What Is a Jew?* Jacob Cohen Bernstein, after he had "sanctified the Name,"* served the Brotherhood (Am Olam) with great self-sacrifice for several years. He later became a good doctor and served in Kishinev during the years of the First World War. And when [after World War I] Kishinev became a part of Rumania—[those people] from the seed of Amalek †—Jacob Cohen Bernstein went to Eretz Yisroel [Palestine], where he received no recognition for many years, and after much hardship returned to Soviet Russia, where he died shortly thereafter. Jacob Cohen Bernstein was also the right hand of Theodor Herzl, may he rest in peace. Both had the same end. ‡

The representatives of that cirle of Brotherhood members in Nikolayev were: Paul Kaplan, who later took up studies in medicine here and became an M.D., distinguishing himself thereby. He ran the New Odessa commune in Oregon. There was also Jacob Pei-sochovitch—child and son-in-law of rich men, graduate of the "Real-Schule,"§ he and his wife Chaya were fascinated by the Brotherhood.[39] Another, Z. Rosenblith, we took great pains to protect from the police, so that no unfriendly eye should fall upon him. We disguised him in women's clothes on his leaving Russia. The emigrants were all of Jewish stock: students, who were under the surveillance of the police. There were also adventurers, fortune [hunters] and bread seekers; there were also many idealists wishing to become self-sufficient and help others to become farmers and wash away the stain of the belief that Jews could not work the land, since they had not been permitted by the Russian government to do any farming.

* This term originally implied a martyr's death. The modern usage in Yiddish implies any selfless deed for a human cause. In regard to Jacob Bernstein, the term implies also his withstanding all the enticements of conversion to Christianity.

† I.e., bitterly anti-Jewish (Deut. 25:17–19).

‡ Disillusionment (see Eccles. 2:14, 3:19).

§ Government-sponsored school offering secular subjects.

The city of Odessa was divided into small circles, each with a representative. I had the honor of being the representative for one such group. I recall one time when I was talking of the joys of farming, although the Talmud had warned us that the farmer feeds everyone else and starves himself (*der erd-arbeter shpayzt andere un hungert zelbst*). The great Margolis[40] was at the meeting, and he asked me if I had ever tried to load hay into a wagon. I, who had never in my life been on a farm—[in Russia] it is not fashionable as it is here to take a "country" vacation—could only answer: "There's nothing you can't do if you really want to do it." Where there's a will there's a way, even in so hard a task as loading hay. The leaders who were politically suspect would avoid those small group meetings. Many police, with the police colonel at their head, fell upon such a meeting in January, 1882. We were very fearful at first and felt lost, but then some of the brave ones found their tongues and said that we were discussing emigration to America. The head of the police burst into a fit of malicious laughter and wished us a smooth journey. Nevertheless they took us to the police station, where we were kept twenty-four hours. Raids began occurring in every house; they were searching for politically subversive materials. We remained under police surveillance for a whole year and would have to report each month to the police. On my visits I was witness to much cruel treatment.

The first group of Am Olam emigrants was in February, 1882, after we received information from our two delegates Ben-Ami and Simon (?), who had been sent earlier to Vienna and Paris. There they prevailed upon the Alliance Israélite Universelle to authorize Herr Carl [Charles] Netter[41] to manage the emigration at the city of Brody on the border of South Russia. Ben-Ami returned to Odessa and Simon (?) went to New York to take care of the next step of our task. He telegraphed short and sharp: "We are receiving everything we asked for." At these words many families broke up and left across the ocean with no possibility of every returning. They were ruined.

M. Bakal left with the first party of exiles, and arriving in New York, he met with the true distressing situation. The assimilated American Jews, the "allrightniks," did not empathize with the immigrants, the former heads of families who were now homeless wanderers. The by-word was "help yourself," and we were advised to forget our Am Olam ideals and take a pack of merchandise on our backs, climb the stairs, and peddle door-to-door, as had their fathers upon their arrival in America as greenhorns.[42] Many could not survive these catastrophes and went back, but Bakal withstood the disaster and did not lose his head. One must have patience. He and the whole group of student youth became shirt-makers, with the exception of two: Jacob Cohen and Nikolai Oleynikov. Levi Miller, a child of wealthy parents and a Gymnasium graduate, worked many hours all day and also found time to learn English. "As a father has mercy on his children," Bakal became a father to all the disappointed and helped everyone in many ways, even lending a hand to some good-for-nothings. He worked so that morale should be maintained and not sink lower. Bakal acquired a large circle of admirers, whom he served as a [sort of] *rebbe* [or "guru"], speaking and lecturing on Sunday evenings and not relinquishing, even for a moment, the idea of realizing the Am Olam ideal, even if only on a small scale. Several attempts were made to establish colonies in various American states. The energetic Meeker was leading some in Kansas; my brother-in-law, Mashbir, with Herman Rosenthal in Dakota.[43] Nothing remained of any of these [colonies], except for the ones in New Jersey [which] exist to this day more as stores than farms. The largest were in Alliance: Rosenhayn, Carmel, Garden Round. In Alliance there gathered Bakal, Spivakovsky, Schwartz, [George] Seldes,[44] Katsovey, Peisochovitch. I too came here in the autumn of 1885 and found Bakal living with Spivakovsky, in the same place where I boarded. As related earlier, I found in Alliance the following members of our Brotherhood [Am Olam]: Spivakovsky, Peisochovitch, Schwartz, Katsovey, Feffer, Seldes, myself, and a few more, enough for a *minyon*. It happened that Schwartz's one-year old child became sick. It was a Friday evening, and a cold rain was falling and they sent for Bakal to come immediately to look at the child. Bakal, the father of mercy, would not have stayed away even if his shoes had been torn. . . . he told me it was very risky for him to go anywhere, but he took pity on Schwartz and his family, and ignored the deadly dangers lurking in wait for him. Yes, this aggravated the illness and Bakal was sick all through the winter, and on March 7, 1886, we buried him. A couple of nights earlier he had asked me to take him outside so that he could bid farewell to the clear sky and stars. "A pitiful loss, a loss not to be replaced." And so the life of a rare and loving soul was cut off. Bakal died in his mid-twenties. The sanctimonious *chevro kadisho* ["burial society"] would not let us dig a grave in the graveyard row, and forced us [because of his radicalism] to bury him outside the fence of the cemetery as Jewish communities used to bury one who [violated Jewish law by] committing suicide.

Something worth recording from the lives of my deceased wife and from her brother. Their father was Rabbi Shlomo Mashbir. Shlomo Mashbir, by the way, was the model for the protagonist

Vecker (the "arouser") of [Sholom Jacob] Abramovitch's drama, *Die Takse* ("The Tax"). [Abramovitch's] pen name was Mendele Mocher Seforim ("Mendele the Bookseller"). Mendele was a family friend and an admirer of Rabbi Shlomo. Mashbir was a man of fine family, son of Rabbi Mordechai Mashbir, whom the city of Berditchev entrusted with the commission of bringing from Pinsk [the body of] Rabbi Levi Yitzchok, the greatest and most saintly soul after the [Hassidic founder] *Baal Shem Tov*, of blessed memory.[45] Rabbi Mordechai, the grandfather of my wife, had the honor of having his grave beside that of Rabbi Levi Yitzchok. Rabbi Shlomo Mashbir had *semikhoh* [certification] to be a rabbi, but without any claim to a [rabbinical] position, because he had no in with the tax collector, who would skin the hide of the poor.* R. Shlomo Mashbir pitied them. My future wife, Esther, was an only daughter, known in the whole city for her beauty and kindness, always modest and concerned for others. Since her childhood she had no enemy. When she was six years old, her father sent her to a modern government-supported school, where she was privileged to attend tuition-free. She was soon on the honor roll. There was a section in Berditchev known as the old city, where most of the Jewish institutions were located and where most of the orthodox and common folk lived. There were many *batei-hamidroshim* as well as the large synagogue where my cousin, Naphtali Balter, was cantor for many years. Later the famous cantor Nisan Belzer came there. Also living there was Reb Jacob Yossi Heilperin, a banker, a rich man but a devoted *hosid* ["pietist"], who prevented the liberal rabbinical school from being established in Berditchev. It was moved to Zhitomir, [a town] not far away but belonging to another province. The Mashbirs lived on the street where the *shul* was. There too lived Rabbi Yosef and other Jewish notables. In the newer part of town lived the newly rich, who had their own [more modern] choral-*shul*, with Cantor Bachman.[46] They never stopped persecuting Heilperin, and ruined him completely. They established a school for girls, run by assimilated German Jewish women. My future father-in-law, Reb Shlomo Mashbir, had two sons and only one daughter, Esther. Reb Schlomo knew that the *haskoleh*[47] ["the Haskalah, or intellectual enlightenment movement of the nineteenth century"] would reach their section of town, too, so he sent his boys to the state school and his little daughter to the "Pension," as the girls' school was called. His justification was that his children should at least be refined *goyim*

---

* Mendele's Yiddish drama, *The Tax*, is a bitter satire against the Jewish community leaders who would lay heavy taxes on kosher meat and become fat at the expense of the poor pious masses.

["gentiles"], not boors. The boys went to study at the Zhitomir Rabbinical School. Nothing came of the elder one, but the second, Lazar Mashbir, became an official and a journalist. He was also a friend of Karl Emil Franzos.[48]

When Shlomo Mashbir brought his daughter, dressed in the poor Jewish costume, to the "Pension" for the first time, she was laughed at by the spoiled children there. Esther was about six years old. She could already read the Hebrew prayerbook and knew a little *Chumosh* ["Pentateuch"], but no Russian. The teacher read [Mikhail Yurievitch] Lermontov's poem "Molitva" ("A Prayer") to the class and asked who could repeat it.[49] Nobody volunteered but they pointed at the new pupil. So the teacher called upon the new pupil and asked if possibly she could recite it. Esther got up before the class and recited the entire poem without an error. This called forth applause from everyone. From that time on she was everybody's favorite. She had a sharp intellect, good understanding, and an extraordinary memory, and so she remained on the honor roll for all five years. After her graduation, little Esther became a Russian teacher for rabbis' daughters and other young ladies. Soon after, she decided to attend the girls' Gymnasium in Zhitomir. She was strong-willed and would not give in to any obstacle. She had prepared for the fifth class, but since there were no vacancies, she enrolled in a lower one. Nothing mattered so long as she was in a Gymnasium. Here too she was greeted at first with laughter from the students, because her accent wasn't the pure Russian of the kind spoken in the Gymnasium, but here too little Esther found favor with some classmates, who corrected her pronunciation. After this, through her whole life no one could tell she was not a genuine Russian.

Several White Russians who had fled the Bolsheviks live here in Alliance. A few came from Odessa, my birthplace. One had graduated a military academy, and one was a woman who had studied at a state-school where I once taught. They all marvelled at the fact that Esther Mashbir-Bailey was still reciting Russian poetry after being here for over fifty years.

There in Zhitomir Esther once took on a job of tutoring a pupil from the first class, a dullard, to earn living expenses and pay the Gymnasium tuition. It was like chopping wood to pound some knowledge into this dullard's head. Coming out of class tired from the day's studies, she would have to begin working with this dolt, and only afterwards have time to prepare her lessons. Her parents couldn't help her. Her mother had become a money-changer, something of a job. Her father, after the ruin of the magnate Reb Jacob

Yossi Heilperin, could find nothing to do. He went to Odessa, where he barely managed to subsist by selling rags, also not much of an occupation. No matter how hard Esther's life ever became, she always found learning easy and would always distinguish herself with her skillful writing.

The principal of the Gymnasium—she had formerly been a lady's maid-in-waiting—had a daughter in Esther's class. The Gymnasium awarded a gold medal to the student who was consistently outstanding. The teacher decided that Esther must receive the medal. This upset the principal, and she fired the teacher. When the new teacher arrived, he wanted to test the class he was meeting for the first time. As little time was left for the term, he assigned a theme to be written that night and submitted the next day. The next day he collected the themes, with the names of the students on them. When he returned from grading them he called on Mademoiselle Mashbir, whose theme he had found to be the best, and he too nominated her for the gold medal.

In those years, the 70's and 80's of the last century, there were in all of Russia only two universities for women, a medical and a teacher's school. Esther decided to continue her studies, but since she could not afford medical school, she chose the teacher's school. Students were not required to attend lectures. The student would pay, get his books, and come to exams at the end of the term. None of the professors and none of the students knew one another. Esther was well suited to this method of study. She obtained a position for the whole winter in Uman, studied the lessons for the first year, and took her exams in the spring.

One of the subjects was the Old Slavonic language. The students arrived for the exam. It happened that before Esther, a great beauty had been examined. The professor was so preoccupied with this belle that he became confused and gave Esther no mark, but only said that she had gotten a three, which meant that she had failed and would have to repeat the year. But Esther felt that she had passed and that this was a mistake. She demanded to be reexamined, but this was beneath the professor's dignity, and he tried to distract her with various excuses, that he was hungry, etc. Esther replied that she would get him something to eat, and the other professors said she was in the right. The professor, after he finished his "feast," started to examine her eagerly to show how right he had been in his first evaluation. But it didn't help. She answered all the questions more than [simply] well. The other professors congratulated her with the words: "You've won." After this she studied three years, until she completed the full course. During this time she also studied to be a mid-wife. On her graduation from the university she received [the offer of] a title of nobility and also an offer to teach in the Gymnasium, but only on the condition that she would convert. She did not want to do this, and thus she "sanctified the Name of Israel."

She thought of opening a private Gymnasium. At that time the Brotherhood was organized. Her brother Lazar decided to give up all the benefits of living in Russia, and he emigrated to America with the Balta group in 1882. As hard as the life of an immigrant was here in the beginning, he never gave up, never went back. On the contrary, he, together with Herman Rosenthal, editor of a daily in Kiev, established a colony in Dakota, where much free land could be had from the state. Their colony failed and Lazar had to make a living carrying stones to a [new] college being built in a neighboring city, where he was later offered a professorship.[50] That was the custom in America! He also later persuaded Esther to leave Russia and come here, which she finally did in 1884. She brought her mother with her and soon was working at a sewing machine. She refused to go on studying; she had come here to live by working. As mentioned earlier, she started a cooperative shop with three others. In a short time Lazar called her to come to Dakota, where she became a teacher of German at the college where he taught. I was to come there later, to be a Hebrew teacher, and also a farmer, as had been my wish throughout. This was in the autumn of 1885. My friend Bakal was living in Alliance, and I came here to say goodbye to him. He said the trip [West] wasn't worth the expense and that I should use my money to buy a farm in Alliance and bring Esther here. This is what I did.

Esther came in the spring of 1886. We slowly began settling ourselves on a vacant farm, covered with brush which grew from the woods which had just been cleared away. The landlord bought the tract of land from the colony for one dollar an acre, along with the forest. He chopped down the forest [and] shipped out the wood to be made into lumber with which he built little houses for us at $150 per house; for the land he charged $15 an acre. The Alliance Israélite Universelle helped us pay, and so we began our family life.

Three daughters were born to us there, and our youngest was an only son. Now the first-born has already been a doctor for thirty years.[51] She already has a daughter who is a doctor. My second daughter became a famous teacher, married a doctor, and has three sons, two of whom will also be doctors and one a professor. All are graduates of Harvard College. One daughter of mine is in New

York, a real estate broker, and my son is a textile chemist, a very successful man.

Esther died on the 8th of the [autumnal] Hebrew month Cheshvon of 1940, after we had lived together for almost fifty-five years. Her principle in life had been that no one owed her anything, and that she must simply work for the necessities of life. At the end she asked that I arrange no ceremonies. She had lived simply and died simply. On her gravestone I aksed to have inscribed: "My saintly Esther rests here." It is already four years,* and all who knew her bless her. She was a woman of great beauty, wise, strong-willed, and honest. She served our town as secretary of the Women's Club. She was a good sister to everyone, had been a correspondent for Yiddish newspapers, and left many writings. She followed the advice of Koheles [the biblical Ecclesiastes]: "Be careful not to make books without end." † Among the colonists one who stood out was Mr. Moishe Baum [sic, Judah Moses Bayuk?[52]] from Bialystok, a very learned man. He left five books [among them] Or Toras Moshe ("The Light of the Torah of Moses"). Other fine families were the Altermans of Warsaw, the Lipmans, and the Rosases, who have a writ of family lineage that goes back to [the tenth-century Babylonian sage] Saadia Gaon. In my sixty years of life here, I can say to my credit that I remembered the maxim of our sages, "One who despises gifts shall live," ‡ and the prayer, "not to be reduced to needing gifts from others." I never willingly laid eyes on gifts, easy earnings; I gratefully accepted only what our poor South Jersey earth would provide. I cleared forty-four acres of land, developed it well, raised children [who are] not in any way inferior to any professional in the city, served our town, always stood up for them to the German Jews, occasionally got a shove from our Christian neighbors "out of eternal hate for the eternal people" (Mèsinas olom l'am Olom).

In the first years it happened that our bunch had broken up. Bakal, Schwartz, Katsovey, [and] Feffer soon died. Spivakovsky, Seldes, Peisochovitch left. And I remained here alone of the whole company. This is how Abe Cahan recommended me to Morris Winchevsky, of blessed memory.[53] I am the only one who remained faithful to the ideal of the Brotherhood (Am Olam). We used to act as correspondents for the Yiddish newspapers. I became friendly with Moishe Mintz[54] from the Biluim (a student movement for agricul-

---

* Which gives us the date of writing of this memoir—1944.
† A misquoting of Eccles. 12:12.
‡ Based on Prov. 15:27.

tural settlement in Palestine which originated after the 1881 pogroms),* editor of the *Folkszeitung*, and with Mr. Getzl Zelikovitz, editor of *Der Yiddisher Farmer*. They were writing "songs of praises" about us in all the Yiddish and Anglo-Jewish newspapers—people like Dovid Galter, Mr. Druk Zusman, and more than all of them, [my] friend A. Litvin (S. I. Hurvitz) in the *Morgen Journal* [and] in the *Yiddisher Kempfer*. Recently Daniel Charny,[55] in the *Tog*, used his column to write profound articles on this subject [of farm colonies], and Mr. L. Berman, in other newspapers, wrote on *Sixty Years of Jewish Farming*. We were also inscribed in [the Jewish National Fund's] *Pinkes Ha-Zohov* ("Golden Book") in Jerusalem. The H.I.A.S. [Hebrew Immigrant Aid Society] honored us by immortalizing us on a copper plaque in their lobby. Also the English-language press gave us much coverage, often a whole page in the *New York Herald* and the *New York Daily News*. We also had a corner in the *Congressional Record*. Recently the government wrote about me in two newspapers and published my picture as the longest and oldest in service as a crop correspondent. Elizabeth Fraser wrote such a favorable report about our farming that a farmer from Pennsylvania wanted to give us a whole farm free. I carried on correspondence with such great men of Israel as Professor [Chaim] Chernovitz, and Rabbi Levi [Louis] Feinberg of Cincinnati.[56] I also carried on a serious correspondence with great American liberals, with Elbert Hubbard, with Dr. Paul Carus of Chicago, etc.[57]

I never hid nor have been ashamed of being Jewish. In short, I do not deserve all the favors, all the acknowledgements and praises that fell to my share. [I am] a simple Jewish peasant, but one who had been privileged to be one of the fifty Am Olam partners, a pioneer among workers on the soil of [our people] Israel.

Shneur I. Bailey
Alliance, New Jersey

---

* "Bilu" is a Hebrew acronym for the scripture verse: *Bet Yaakov Lechu Venelcha* ("House of Jacob, come you, let us go." Isa. 2:5).

Notes

Introduction

1. James Darmesteter, *The Selected Essays of James Darmesteter*, trans. by H. B. Jastrow (Boston: Houghton, Mifflin, 1895), pp. 241–43.
2. Mark Wischnitzer, *To Dwell in Safety: The Story of Jewish Migration Since 1800* (Philadelphia: Jewish Publication Society, 1948), p. 62.
3. J. H. Noyes, quoted in Neil J. Smelser, *Theory of Collective Behavior* (New York: Free Press, 1962), p. 357.

Chapter 1

1. Arthur Ruppin, *Jews in the Modern World*, p. xxviii: "Our chief aim now must be normality." This idea is further expressed in his chap. X ("The Beginnings of Agriculture"). In an earlier work, *The Jews of Today*, chap. XV ("Creation of a Self-Contained Jewish Life by a Return to Agriculture"), Ruppin states his view of the need for normalizing Jewish life.
2. Samuel Joseph, *Jewish Immigration to the United States from 1881 to 1910*, p. 22. See also Bernard Pares, *A History of Russia*, pp. 264–65, 271–72.
3. Gerold T. Robinson, *Rural Russia Under the Old Regime*, p. 183. See also Lionel Kochan (ed.), *The Jews in Soviet Russia Since 1917*, pp. 1–2, 16–17; Pares, pp. 411 ff.; Jesse D. Clarkson, *A History of Russia*, pp. 330–31.
4. G. T. Robinson, p. 80; B. H. Sumner, *A Short History of Russia*, pp. 126–31.
5. Joseph, *Immigration*, p. 29.
6. G. T. Robinson, pp. 88–89.
7. *Ibid.*, pp. 59–60.
8. Joseph, *Immigration*, pp. 28, 42–45, 158. See also the study (cited by Joseph) made by I. M. Rubinow, *Economic Condition of the Jews in Russia*.
9. G. T. Robinson, p. 97.

159

10. Joseph, *Immigration*, p. 27, quoting Anatole Leroy-Beaulieu, *The Empire of the Tsars*.
11. Joseph, *Immigration*, p. 158. See also *UJE*, VIII, 346.
12. Rubinow, *Economic Conditions*.
13. Ruppin, *Jews of Today*, p. 159; Clarkson, pp. 257–58. The decree of Alexander I in 1804 regulating the position of the Jews marks the Russian government's first attempt at resettling them in agriculture. Such importance was assigned this effort that the Pale itself was, for Jewish agricultural enterprise, extended to include Astrakhan and the Caucasus (Clarkson, p. 258).
14. A comprehensive account of the Jewish farm movement in Russia is found in S. M. Dubnow, *History of the Jews in Russia and Poland*, Vol. 1, chaps. X, XII; Vol. 11, chaps. X–XXXI. See also Herman Rosenthal, "Agriculture, South Russian Colonies," *JE*, I, 252–56; Ruppin, *Jews of Today*, Chap XV; Leonard G. Robinson, "Agricultural Activities of the Jews in America," *American Jewish Yearbook, 5673*, pp. 21–115; Herman Frank, "Jewish Mass Colonization in Soviet Russia," *Reflex*, II, no. 2 (February, 1928), 54–61. See B. D. Brutzkus, *Yiddishe Landsvirtshaft in Mizrach Airopa*.
15. Frank, p. 55; Clarkson, pp. 256–58.
16. Salo W. Baron, *A Social and Religious History of the Jews*, II, 278–79.
17. *Ibid.*, II, 285–98. See also *JE*, III, 267; VII, 587; *UJE*, II, 409–10; Howard M. Sachar, *Course of Modern Jewish History*, pp. 221 ff.; Lucy S. Dawidowicz (ed.), *Golden Tradition*, pp. 46 ff. On Brafman, see Dubnow, II, 187 ff., and *EJ*, IV, 1287–88; Ismar Elbogen, *Century of Jewish Life*, p. 62. On the Kutais blood libel case, see Dubnow, II, 204. On Hippolyte Lutostanski and Alexander III, see *ibid.*, pp. 203–4, 244. Louis Greenberg, *The Jews in Russia: The Struggle for Emancipation*, I, 93–96, calls Brafman's *Kniga Kagala* ("The Book of the Kahal") "a factor contributing to anti-Jewish feeling." The Lithuanian-born Bernard Berenson, however, spoke favorably of Brafman's book as "a work . . . in Russian . . . [which] attempted to denounce [the] corruptions [of the Kahal]"; see Berenson, "Contemporary Jewish Fiction," *Andover Review*, X (1888), 600.
18. Dubnow, II, 260; Greenberg, II, 24; Philip Cowen, *Memories of an American Jew*, chap. V ("The American Hebrew and the Community"); Narcisse Leven, *Cinquante Ans d'Histoire: L'Alliance Israélite Universelle*, Vol. II, chap. XIII ("L'Émigration"); Sachar, 243 ff., 306 ff.; Zosa Szajkowski, "How the Mass Migration to America Began," *Jewish Social Studies*, IV (1942), 295 ff., and "European Attitude to East European Jewish Immigration (1881–93)," *PAJHS*, XLI (1951–52), 127 ff. Arthur Goldhaft, *The Golden Egg*, p. 23, recalls being told that in Brody, the Austrian border city, "the streets became filled with homeless refugees."
19. Cowen, pp. 94–95.
20. L. Robinson, p. 58. For the names of the founders, see Cowen, p. 96.
21. There are references to the establishment in the early nineteenth century of societies devoted to the encouragement of agriculture for Jews. As early as 1820, the "American Society for Meliorating the Condition of Jews" was established, its purpose "to repair the wrongs suffered by Jews at the hands of Christians." It was a plan for the settlement of Jewish converts. See Max J. Kohler, "An Early American Hebrew-Christian Agricultural Colony," *PAJHS*, XXII, 184 ff. In *The Asmonean*,

XII, 45–46, a letter by D. E. M. DeLara criticizing the statement "Jews as a community push exclusively the commercial interests" points to the existence of a Jewish agricultural society at that time—1855—grappling with the problem.

22. George, *Progress and Poverty*, p. 294, and *Our Land and Land Policy*, pp. 98–99; Julius Stern, "On the Establishment of a Jewish Colony in the United States," *Occident and American Jewish Advocate*, I (April, 1843), 28–32; H. L. Sabsovich, "Agricultural and Vocational Education," in R. Morris and M. Freund (editors), *Trends and Issues in Jewish Social Welfare in the United States, 1899–1952*, pp. 43–44; Philip R. Goldstein, *Social Aspects of the Jewish Colonies of South Jersey*, p. 13; Szajkowski, "The Attitude of American Jews to East European Jewish Immigration (1881–1893)," *PAJHS*, XL (1950–51), 271; *American Hebrew*, April 16, October 8, 1880; *Sholem Aleichem tsu Imigranten* (New York: Educational Alliance, 1903), p. 15 (Yiddish). The Am Olam diary is quoted in Greenberg, *The Jews in Russia*, II, 166. The novelist Mordecai Spector (1858–1925), a native of the Ukraine, advocated Zionist agricultural efforts in his *Yiddisher Muzhik* ("The Jewish Peasant") in 1884 (see *JE*, XI, 502–3; *EJ*, XV, 258). Berenson, pp. 588, 600, sees Spector as significant in "contemporary Jewish literature [which] is the expression of an effort [by Jews] to approach the modern Occident."

23. Dubnow, II, 420: "The Russian government in the 1880's merely tolerated emigration, but in the 1890's they encouraged it; viz., they permitted the establishment of the Central Committee on Emigration of Jews in 1891." Joseph, *Immigration*, p. 95, documents the tremendous influx of Jewish immigrants to the United States during the last two decades of the nineteenth century. See also Salo W. Baron, *Steeled by Adversity*, pp. 289–96.

24. See Pares, p. 59; *EJ*, II, 401 ff.; Elbogen, p. 87; Joseph, *Immigration*, p. 189; H. Sabsovich, p. 44; Marc Fried, "Deprivation and Migration," in D. P. Moynihan (ed.), *On Understanding Poverty*, pp. 112–20, 147–48.

   Manuel A. Kursheedt, secretary of New York's Russian Emigrant Relief Fund, complained to S. Hermann Goldschmidt, President of the Alliance Israélite Universelle, in 1881 that "very few [of the immigrant Jews] are farmers in the American sense. . . . Most . . . are clerks or tradesmen; they know no handicraft and wish to peddle. We are overrun with peddlars already" (*PAJHS*, XL [1950–51], 265).

25. See Hersch Liebmann, "International Migration of the Jews," in W. F. Willcox (ed.), *International Migrations*, II, 487–500; Shlomo Noble, "The Image of the American Jew in Hebrew and Yiddish Literature in America, 1870–1900," *YIVO Annual of Jewish Social Science*, IV (1954), 100. See also J. W. Jenks *et al., The Immigration Problem*, p. 91: "The Hebrew is not adapted by training or tradition to be a pioneer farmer and in general his attempts at agriculture . . . are not as satisfactory as in most colonies of other races." See also R. E. Park and H. A. Miller, *Old World Traits Transplanted*, p. 195: "The Jews tend even more than other immigrant groups to settle in cities."

   Goldhaft, *Golden Egg*, p. 32, remarks about Jewish colonizers in Kansas: ". . . what defeated those early Jewish farmers was their past. Not only their personal past, but the past of the generations that preceded them . . . city folk, students, talkers, intellectuals, and with all the willingness in the world, they couldn't make it." See Everett L. Cooley, "Clarion, Utah: Jewish Colony in 'Zion,' " *Utah Historical Quarterly*, XXXVI (1968), No. 2, 117–18, where in 1914 the leader of a Utah colonization effort tells the governor of the state that "the little work that is carried on at Clarion now is just going to be a living demonstration against the false and ironeous (*sic*) charges made against" the Jews, that they are fit only for petty trading.

26. Abraham Cahan, *The Education of Abraham Cahan*, translated by Leon Stein *et al.*, p. 186; Sumner, p. 340. Cowen, p. 99, calls the New Odessa colony "a sort of Fourierism." These older utopian traditions to which the immigrant Jewish founders of agricultural colonies gave new expression are discussed by William A. Hinds, *American Communities and Cooperative Colonies*. Jews, of course, as Hinds makes very clear, were by no means the only ones to attempt experiments in communal living. The non-Jews who thought in such terms far outnumbered them: see, for example, Ralph Albertson, *A Survey of Mutualistic Communities in America* (Iowa City, 1936); Adin Ballou, *History of the Hopedale Community* (Lowell, Mass., 1897); Thomas Brown, *An Account of the People Called Shakers* (Troy, N.Y., 1812); Katherine Burton, *Paradise Planters: The Story of Brook Farm* (London, 1939); Etienne Cabet, *History and Constitution of the Icarian Community* (Iowa City, 1917); Delburn Carpenter, *The Radical Pietists* (New York, 1975); Allan Estlake, *The Oneida Community* (London, 1900); John L. Gillin, *The Dunkers* (New York, 1906); Robert J. Hendricks, *Bethel and Aurora* (New York, 1933); Howard W. Kriebel, *The Schwenkfelders in Pennsylvania* (Lancaster, 1904); George B. Lockwood, *The New Harmony Communities* (Marion, Ind., 1902); E. O. Randall, *History of the Zoar Society* (Columbus, 1904); Jacob J. Sessler, *Communal Pietism Among Early American Moravians* (New York, 1933); and Samuel G. Zerfass, *Souvenir Book of the Ephrata Cloister* (Lititz, Pa., 1921). See also Edmund Wilson, *To the Finland Station*, pp. 98 ff.; Joel S. Geffen, "Jewish Agricultural Colonies as Reported in . . . the Russian Hebrew Press . . . ," *AJHQ*, LX (1970–71), 381.

On Charles Fourier, see Émile Poulat in *IESS*, V (1968), 548, where "a direct relationship" is seen "between Fourierism and the cooperative movement which played an important role before 1914 and of which there are . . . new developments . . . in Yugoslavia, Israel, and the countries of the Third World." See also Asa Briggs on Robert Owen in *IESS*, XI, 352, where Owen is said to have "done much to develop a constructive critique of industrialism."

Chapter 2

1. Ruppin, "Agricultural Achievements in Palestine," *Contemporary Jewish Record*, V, No. 3 (June, 1942), 275. See *EJ*, XIV, 430–32, on Ruppin.
2. Isaac Goldberg, *Major Noah*, chap. VIII ("Embarkation for Utopia"). The chief source of information about the ceremonies attending the foundation of Ararat is Lewis Allen, "Mordecai M. Noah's Ararat Project," a

paper read at the Buffalo Historical Society, March 5, 1886, and reprinted in Max J. Kohler, "Some Early American Zionist Projects," *PAJHS*, VIII, Appendix II, 97–118. It tells of the grandiloquent ceremonies that marked the opening of Ararat. Goldberg says: "[it was] a still, though not noiseless birth" (p. 203). Noah even went so far as to have a cornerstone made for the first building to be erected in the American Zion. The cornerstone tells all that is essential about the project: ". . . the Refuge for the Jews, Founded by Mordecai Manuel Noah, in the Month of Tishrei, 5568, Sept., 1825, in the 50th year of American Independence" (*PAJHS*, VIII, 105). The project was no sooner launched than it was abandoned by Noah, and nothing more came of it; see Goldberg, pp. 203–4, and Jonathan D. Sarna, "The Roots of Ararat: An Early Letter from Mordecai M. Noah to Peter B. Porter," *AJA*, XXXII (1980), 52–58. On Kirschbaum, see Bernard D. Weinryb, "Noah's Ararat Jewish State in its Historical Setting," *PAJHS*, XLIII (1953–54), 183–84. On the "Hep, hep!" riots, see Heinrich Graetz, *History of the Jews*, V, 528 ff.

3. M. U. Schappes (ed.), *A Documentary History of the Jews in the United States*, pp. 195–98, offers the text of Zeire Hazon's "Address." See also H. B. Grinstein, *The Rise of the Jewish Community of New York*, pp. 116–19. Grinstein, pp. 119–22, also speaks of the Sholem colony. See also *PAJHS*, XXIII (1915), 178–79, and XXXV (1939), 306–9; Gabriel Davidson, "The Tragedy of Sholem," *Jewish Tribune*, XXXIX, No. 24 (June 16, 1922), 1, 13; XXXIX, No. 25 (June 22, 1922), 13–14; H. David Rutman, "The Sholem Colony," *The Journal* (Ellenville, N.Y.), January 4, 1973, p. 10; January 11, 1973, p. 12; January 18, 1973, p. 10; January 25, 1973, p. 12; February 1, 1973, p. 10; and Richard Singer, "The American Jew in Agriculture," pp. 56–57.

4. "A Call To Establish a Hebrew Agricultural Society," New York, May 13, 1885 (American Jewish Historical Society, Waltham, Mass.); Grinstein, pp. 123–26.

5. See Allan Nevins and Henry S. Commager, *A Pocket History of the United States*, pp. 337 ff.; Francis G. Walett, *Economic History of the United States*, pp. 128, 135. The Jews were not the first East Europeans to attempt agricultural colonization in post-Civil War America. Polish utopians—non-Jews, including the novelist Henryk Sienkiewicz—founded a short-lived colony in Anaheim, California, during the 1870s: see Robert V. Hine, *California's Utopian Colonies* (San Marino: Huntington Library, 1953), pp. 137–40, and Leonard Leader, "Poles Apart: Southern California a Polish Commonwealth," in *Los Angeles Times*, May 4, 1980.

6. See Bernard D. Weinryb, "East European Immigration to the United States," *Jewish Quarterly Review*, XLV (1955), 512, 518.

7. For the origin of the Am Olam group, see Boris D. Bogen, *Jewish Philanthropy*, pp. 90, 130; Abraham Menes, "The Am Oylom Movement," in Joshua A. Fishman (ed.), *Studies in Modern Jewish Social History*, pp. 155 ff.; Joseph Brandes, *Immigrants to Freedom*, pp. 18–24. On the AIS, see *EJ*, II, 648–54.

Elbogen, p. 727 (note 4), makes mention of Abraham Cahan's *Bleter*: Cahan "met members of the [Am Olam] league in [Austrian] Brody and was astonished that they were not socialists." Cahan, in the

163

English version of the first two volumes of the *Bleter*, comments that, in contrast to the failure of Robert Owen's "attempt to establish a colony," the "new Jewish colonies [in America] would endure because they would be based on sound socialist ideas," but in Brody he found few Am Olamites who felt as he did: ". . . their idealism was deep and genuine, [but] they gave little thought to the doctrines of communism and socialism. They were determined only to start colonies in which life, a new kind of life for Jews, would be beautiful." Only the Odessa Am Olamites, he found, acknowledged "communist intentions." See Abraham Cahan, *The Education of Abraham Cahan*, translated by Leon Stein *et al.*, pp. 186, 204. Cahan's *Bleter* originally appeared in 1926.

8. Davidson and Goodwin, "Chalutzim in the Land of Cotton," *Jewish Tribune*, XCV, No. 13 (September 27, 1929), 2, 15; Geffen, p. 358; Zosa Szajkowski, "The Attitude of American Jews to East European Jewish Immigration (1881–1893)," *PAJHS*, XL (1950–51), 246. See also *ibid.*, p. 269. On Charles Netter, a leader of the Alliance Israélite Universelle, see *EJ*, XII, 1001–2.

9. Davidson and Goodwin, "Chalutzim," p. 2.

10. Leo Shpall, "A Jewish Agricultural Colony in Louisiana," *Louisiana Historical Quarterly*, XX (July, 1937), 821–31.

11. *Ibid.*, p. 822; *EB*, eleventh edition (1911), XVII, 61.

12. A. Stanwood Menken, *Report of the Founding of the First Russian-Jewish Colony in the United States at Catahoula Parish, Louisiana*, p. 4. On Robinson, manager of the Jewish Agricultural Society, see Brandes, p. 227. On the HEAS see *American Jewish Year Book, 5673*, pp. 58 ff.

13. Davidson and Goodwin, "Chalutzim," p. 2. See also Geffen, p. 357: B. Brodsky, one of the Sicily Island colonists, informed the editors of the Petrograd weekly *Russki Yevrei* that the original settlers numbered forty-seven men plus women and children. The colony's success, Brodsky wrote, "will depend upon whether the settlers can accustom themselves to agricultural work with which they have not had previous experience."

14. Shpall, pp. 825–31, gives the entire text of the "Constitution for the First Agricultural Colony of Russian Israelites in America." The direct quotations of the text are taken from this copy of the Constitution. Menken also appends a full copy of the Constitution.

15. See Davidson and Goodwin, "Chalutzim," which deserves to be considered the most extended analysis in this area of research. See also Menes, p. 169.

16. Davidson and Goodwin, "Unique Agricultural Colony," *Reflex*, II, No. 5 (May, 1928), 80–86; Szajkowski, "Attitude of American Jews to East European Jewish Immigration," *PAJHS*, XL, 247; Geffen, pp. 357, 359.

17. Davidson and Goodwin, "Chalutzim," p. 15.

18. Israel Kasovich, *The Days of Our Years*, pp. 175 ff.; Davidson and Goodwin, "Unique Agricultural Colony." This last is the source of much of the information on the New Odessa colony.

On the insecurity of American Jews of German background at the end of the nineteenth century, see Oscar Handlin, "American Views of the Jew at the Opening of the Twentieth Century," *PAJHS*, XL (1950), 323 ff.; Jacob Rader Marcus, "Major Trends in American Jewish Historical Research," *AJA*, XVI (1964), 9–10.

19. Gustav Pollak, *Michael Heilprin and His Sons*, chap. I ("A Brief Sketch of His Life"). See also *DAB*, VII, 502–3. On Goldman, see the Felix Warburg papers, American Jewish Archives, Cincinnati, Ohio. Brandes mentions him often.
20. Pollak, chap. XIV ("Mr. Heilprin's Work for the Russian Refugees"); Cahan, *Education*, p. 251.
21. Pollak, pp. 207–12, quotes the entire text of Heilprin's "Appeal to the Jews."
22. Cowen, p. 82.
23. *Jewish Messenger*, March 7, 1884, p. 4.
24. Davidson and Goodwin, "Unique Agricultural Colony," p. 82. "Chronicle of . . . New Odessa," in H. Rosenthal and A. Radin, eds., *Yalkut Maaravi*, I, 46 ff.
25. Cowen, p. 82.
26. This organization was a successor to the shortlived HEAS. It had been founded in New York in November, 1883, by Heilprin, Rosenthal, and Greenberg, and its object was to "select for agriculture only earnest young men and small families and to help only those able to help themselves." Thus, the MAAS was based on the idea of careful selection. See Samuel Joseph, *Baron de Hirsch Fund*, p. 9.

   "It [MAAS] left the choice of place and the internal organization of each colony to the settlers. It held no lien upon the property furnished to the colonists, relying for its reimbursement only on the honor of the colonists, if success crowned their efforts. Every settler was at liberty to leave his post without explanation or notice. New Odessa was the only colony based on Communistic principles. There was a great variety of religious views among the colonists. Mutual toleration existed everywhere, in spite of the diverse elements that made up some of the colonies. Orthodoxy prevailed at Carmel, and a glowing racial spirit animated the colony at Montefiore." See Pollak, p. 212, quoting *New York Evening Post*, October 25, 1884.
27. Pollak, pp. 207–12.
28. Davidson and Goodwin, "Unique Agricultural Colony," pp. 82–84.
29. Cahan, *Education*, pp. 246–51, 267, 341, discusses Frey and his connection with the New Odessa colony. See also Avrahm Yarmolinsky, *A Russian's American Dream*, pp. v–vii, 99–106.
30. Davidson and Goodwin, "Unique Agricultural Colony," quoted on p. 84; Singer, p. 538; Cahan, *Education*, pp. 247, 341–42. See also Geffen, pp. 374–76. On Frey, see *EJ*, II, 862; Menes, pp. 30–31. On Auguste Comte, see *EB*, eleventh edition (1911), VI, 814 ff.; Wilson, p. 103; *IESS*, III, 201–6; XI, 45–50; *ESS*, IV (1931), 151–53. On Wechsler, see *American Jewish Year Book, 5664*, p. 104, and W. Gunther Plaut, *The Jews in Minnesota*, pp. 75–78.
31. Davidson and Goodwin, "Unique Agricultural Colony," pp. 82–84; Singer, p. 537; Cahan, *Education*, pp. 341–42; Yarmolinsky, pp. v, 126, 133.
32. Yarmolinsky, pp. 105, 140.
33. *United States Statutes at Large*, XII (1862), 392. See also *DAH*, III, 41 ff. On Wise's Beersheba scheme, see *American Israelite*, June 30, 1882, reprinted along with much more Beersheba material in "A Colony in Kansas—1882," *AJA*, XVII (1965), 114–39; L. G. Feld, "New Light on the Lost

Jewish Colony of Beersheba, Kansas, 1882–1886," *AJHQ*, LX (1970–71), 159–68.

34. Davidson and Goodwin, "Epic of the Prairies," *Detroit Jewish Chronicle*, January 29, 1932.

35. Davidson and Goodwin, "Epic of the Prairies." See also Bernard Postal and Lionel Koppman, *Jewish Tourist's Guide to the U.S.*, p. 582.

36. Singer, p. 441; Menes, pp. 172–73; Geffen, p. 375; J. M. Isler, *Rueckkehr der Juden zur Landwirtschaft*, chap. VI ("Die Juden in der Landwirtschaft der Vereinigten Staaten von Amerika"). Isler emphasizes the last factor, that of natural disaster, as being chiefly responsible for the death of the experiment. On p. 100, he states: "Neben der Kolonie [Crémieux] wurde noch eine andere in demselben staate Bethlehem genannt, gegrundet diese wurde von einer Gruppe von 12 Emigranten auf Kommunistischer Basis geschaffen. Aber auch diese Kolonien erfreuten sich nicht eines langen Bestehens. Schon nach zwei Jahren wurden sie durch die klimatischen Verhältnisse (Trockenheit, Hessiche Fliege), um ihre ganze Ernte gebracht. Ein Teil der Siedler wurde entmutigt, und verliess die Kolonie; nur wenige von ihnen verblieben. Aber als im nächsten Jahre, wiederum die Ernte durch Hagel geschaedigtwurde, wanderte auch der Rest ab; die Kolonien wurden im Jahre 1885 aufgelöst."

37. Davidson and Goodwin, "An Arkansas Colonization Episode," *Jewish Tribune*, July 12, 1929. On Davidson, manager of the Jewish Agricultural Society, see *UJE*, III, 448. The colony near the White River was not the first time Arkansas had been connected with the colonization movement. In the early 1870s, one Salomon Franklin, of Pine Bluff, had offered to sponsor a settlement of East European immigrant Jews in Arkansas: see *AJA*, VIII (1956), 70–71.

38. Davidson and Goodwin, "Arkansas Colonization," p. 2.

39. *Ibid.*, quoted on p. 2; Singer, pp. 320–22.

40. Julius Schwarz, *Report . . . on Russian Refugees at Cotopaxi*. See also Dorothy Roberts, "The Jewish Colony at Cotopaxi," *Colorado Magazine*, XVIII, No. 4 (July, 1941), 124–31. Roberts offers a listing of and some data on the thirteen families (pp. 125–26). Flora J. Satt's master's thesis, "The Cotopaxi Colony" (University of Colorado, 1950), supplies additional data on the settlers (pp. 14 ff., 31 ff., 42, 44, 46, 52 ff.) and also on Saltiel (pp. 7–12, 25, 36–37, 39–40). She identifies Schwarz as a Saltiel partner (pp. 36, 63) and contends: "Too little attention has been paid to the unfortunate role [of] the [Hebrew Emigrant Aid] Society's erstwhile investigator, Julius Schwartz [*sic*], whose complicity with the motives of . . . Saltiel prevented an adequate forewarning of the problems ahead" (p. 59). Satt calls attention to the *Jewish Messenger*, July 21, 1882, for information on Schwarz, and cites the attack on Saltiel in the *Denver Republican*, February 7–13, 1883.

41. Tuska in *American Hebrew*, October 4, 1882 (quoted in Singer, p. 496); Roberts, pp. 128–29. On Baar, see *EJ*, II, 388, and *UJE*, II, 5–6.

42. Schwarz, quoted on p. 11; Tuska in *American Hebrew*, October 4, 1882 (quoted in Singer, pp. 494, 496). Saltiel claimed that Schwarz and Tuska were related: see *American Hebrew*, October 27, 1882 (quoted in Singer, p. 497).

43. Pollak, p. 210.

44. "The Russian Emigrants," *Jewish Messenger*, December 22, 1882, p. 2.

45. *Ibid.*, January 5, 1883, p. 3.
46. *Ibid.*
47. *Ibid.*, p. 2. See also Postal and Koppman, p. 72. Roberts, p. 124, identifies Saltiel as "the Portuguese-Jewish owner of a silver mine at Cotopaxi," and says it was "through [his] efforts" that the Cotopaxi colony "was brought to Colorado."
48. *Jewish Messenger*, December 22, 1882, p. 2; Roberts, pp. 124–26; *American Hebrew*, October 4, 1882 (quoted in Singer, pp. 494–95).
49. Saltiel in *American Hebrew*, October 27, 1882 (quoted in Singer, pp. 498, 504–5).
50. *Jewish Messenger*, February 23, 1883, p. 2; Roberts, pp. 129–30.
51. *Jewish Messenger*, February 23, 1883, p. 2; *American Israelite*, May 25, 1883.
52. Pollak, p. 216. Heilprin, in particular, recognized the dangers of charity, as the following passage shows: "Jewish charity has always justly been praised—perhaps slightly beyond its merits. . . . It is constantly doing a great deal of good. But it is also productive of evil consequences. It has fostered a habit of relying upon individuals and congregational institutions, and in proportion weakened the instincts of manliness, self-reliance, and honor . . . . Jewish institutions ought to be founded on the principle of aiding those who aid themselves . . . not by gifts and distributions but by affording means for enlarging the scope of honorable efforts and the field of manly energy." See also Cowen, p. 100.
53. Davidson, "The Palestine Colony in Michigan: An Adventure in Colonization," *PAJHS*, XXIX (1925), 61–74. Zionism, it is certain, was not remote from the minds of a good many who involved themselves in American Jewish agricultural colonization efforts. Herman Rosenthal, for example, wrote in 1892 of the agricultural designs being pursued at Mishmar-Hayarden and elsewhere in Ottoman Palestine: ". . . a small number of our brothers have settled in *Eretz Yisrael*. They have established colonies [to] work the land, and . . . it goes well for them . . . we hope that they will become [a] great people, and that here will be the center of the people Israel." See Rosenthal's *Yudisher Farmer*, Vol. 1, No. 6 (April, 1892), pp. 1–2 (reprinted with an English translation in Lloyd P. Gartner [ed.], *Michael*, Vol. III, pp. 71–73, 83–85).
54. Davidson, "Palestine Colony," p. 62.
55. *Ibid.*, p. 61. See also A. James Rudin, "Bad Axe, Michigan: An Experiment in Jewish Agricultural Settlement," *Michigan History* (Summer, 1972).
56. Davidson, "Palestine Colony," p. 64. On Butzel, see *EJ*, IV, 1541.
57. Joseph, *Hirsch Fund*, p. 22. On Baron de Hirsch, see *EJ*, VIII, 505–7; *American Jewish Year Book, 5686*, pp. 189 ff. See also Myer S. Isaacs, "The Baron de Hirsch Fund," *American Jews Annual* (1892–93), pp. 81 ff.
58. Davidson, "Palestine Colony," p. 67. On Schiff, see *American Jewish Year Book, 5682*, pp. 21 ff.; *EJ*, XIV, 960–62.
59. Davidson, "Palestine Colony," p. 72.
60. Singer, pp. 634–40. On the panic of 1893, see Nevins and Commager, p. 347; Morris, *EAH* (New York: Harper, 1953), p. 263. On agricultural stabilization after 1900, see *ibid.*, p. 482.
61. Milton Reizenstein, "Agricultural Colonies in the United States," *JE*, I, 259. This article records the effort, but advances no explanation for its

failure. On Painted Woods, see also Plaut, pp. 96–106, and Lois F. Schwartz, "Early Agricultural Colonies in North Dakota," *North Dakota History*, XXXII, No. 4 (October, 1965), 222–24. For Rabbi Wechsler's account of the Painted Woods effort, which he was certain would "elevate [the] manhood and womanhood" of the immigrant colonists, see *AJA*, VIII (1956), 106–9.

62. Isler, p. 102: "Ein Teil (von Burleigh County, N. Dakota) der Siedler ging weiter nach Norden, wo sie Iola-Siedlung gegruendet haben, welche heute zu den aeltesten landwirtschaftlichen Siedlungen in Nordwest gehört."

63. Quoted in Cowen, pp. 100–1. On Ben Zion Greenberg, see L. F. Schwartz, p. 225. Schwartz says that Greenberg lived his life out in Ramsey County. On the HIAS, see *American Jewish Year Book, 5675*, p. 285.

64. Cooley, "Clarion, Utah," pp. 114–31; Reizenstein, p. 259; Arnold Shankman, "Happyville, The Forgotten Colony," *AJA*, XXX (1978), 3–19. Singer discusses in considerable detail a very sizable number of these colonization attempts throughout the United States. Of particular value are the maps he provides after p. ix of his essay.

Chapter 3

1. An extensive literature exists about the South Jersey colonies. See William Stainsby, *The Jewish Colonies of South Jersey*; Boris Bogen, *Jewish Philanthropy*, chap. IX ("The Back-to-the-Soil Movement"); Jacob Lipman, "Rural Settlements in the Eastern States," in Charles Bernheimer (ed.), *The Russian Jew in the United States*, pp. 375–92; A. R. Levy, "The Jew as a Tiller of American Soil," *American Hebrew*, LXXVII (November 24, 1905), 849–64; Moses Klein, *Migdal Zophim; Yoval: A Symposium upon the First Fifty Years of the Jewish Farming Colonies of . . . New Jersey*; Joshua O. Haberman, "The Jews in New Jersey: A Historical Sketch." Brandes, *Immigrants to Freedom*, is deserving of special notice.

2. L. Robinson, p. 16. Among the accounts of the colony, a useful one was published by J. C. Reis, "History of the Alliance," *The Menorah*, XL (1906–7), 167–73. Reis resided in neighboring Norma for a number of years. His description is based on the eye-witness reports of three original settlers as well as upon his own personal observations. See also Brandes, p. 244.

3. Stainsby, p. 7.

4. *Ibid.*, p. 4. Stainsby, writing in 1901, stated the terms of the contracts as they existed after 1884. This accounts for the seeming discrepancy that the holders of the six farms (mentioned below) should have received less favorable terms than the holders of the original sixty-six.

5. Reis, p. 169; Geffen, p. 362. On Mansion House, see *JE*, VIII, 296–97.

6. See Rosenthal's short-lived monthly *Der Yudisher Farmer* (New York), I, No. 2 (December, 1891), 9. The Yiddish text, plus my translation, appears in Lloyd P. Gartner, pp. 67, 80.

7. Sidney (Shneur) Bailey, "The First Fifty Years," *Yoval*, p. 12.
8. For a description of the Association of Jewish Immigrants and its work, see Henry S. Morais, *Jews of Philadelphia*, pp. 131–35.
9. *PAJHS*, XL (1950–51), 276; Geffen, pp. 361–62.
10. Bailey, p. 9; *American Jewish Year Book, 5673*, p. 64.
11. Bailey, p. 14.
12. Goldstein, p. 15; *Yudisher Farmer*, I, No. 2 (December, 1891), p. 9, reprinted in Gartner, pp. 67, 80; *American Israelite*, March 15, 1894. Solomon's article "Alliance: The First Successful Jewish Colony in America" appeared in *The Menorah*, V (July–December, 1888), 178–87. Solomons later became director of the Baron de Hirsch Fund's American activities and also served the AIU as its treasurer for the United States: see *JE*, XI, 459.
13. Solon J. Buck, *Agrarian Crusade*, p. 104; Morris, *EAH* (1961), p. 263; *DAH*, I, 159.
14. George, *Social Problems*, p. 220.
15. Buck, *Agrarian Crusade*, p. 107; *American Israelite*, June 17, 1897.
16. Joseph, *Hirsch Fund*, pp. 15, 16.
17. Reis, p. 173.
18. Stainsby, p. 7. On Stainsby, see Brandes, p. 78.
19. Reis, p. 173. These figures were compiled by Reis in an unofficial capacity.
20. Stainsby, p. 23.
21. Bailey, p. 16.
22. *Ibid.*, p. 18. On Maurice Fels, see *American Jewish Year Book, 5673*, pp. 84–85, and *The Menorah*, March, 1900, pp. 145–48. On Mounier, see L. Mounier, *Auto-Biographical Sketch*, pp. 8–9, 14, 24, 32, 42–43, 53, 55–56; Mounier, "Retrospect," *Yoval*, pp. 28–29. Brandes mentions Mounier several times. This non-Jewish agnostic lectured at the South Jersey colonies "on all kinds of subjects, except religion," designed the synagogue in Carmel, and expressed himself as in favor of a Judaism "freed of all its cumbersome, obsolete ritualistic superstitions" (*Sketch*, pp. 8–9, 14).
23. Brandes, pp. 145 ff.
24. Bailey, p. 20. It is worth noting how even in the years after World War I there was a tendency among urban Jews to look somewhat askance at the successful South Jersey colonists. Rabbi Bernard Louis Levinthal, of Philadelphia, for example, thought it remarkable that his friend and fellow-rabbi Judah Moses Bayuk had forsaken "his ability to take his position in the world of civilization, and earthly pleasures, and [gone] to live on a farm in the wilderness of New Jersey." Another Philadelphia rabbi, Nachum Brenner, could not help "wondering why [Bayuk] a man with such profound learning . . . should have chosen to live in such [a] crude and insignificant little place like Alliance, N.J.," where he was deprived "of the advantages of mingling with his class." See the English-language *haskamot*, or endorsements, at the end of Bayuk's *Imré Torat Moshe* (New York, 1921). The same *haskamot* appear at the end of other Bayuk works, including his *Or Torat Moshe* (New York, 1921).
25. Joseph, *Hirsch Fund*, p. 89: "Clearly, the industrial progress of Wood-

bine was far outstripping the agricultural progress of the rural settlement. In this respect the ideal of the founders was not being fulfilled; for instead of a farming community with the village as an adjunct, Woodbine was developing into an industrial town with a few outlying farms." See also Bernheimer, p. 379.

26. Joseph, *Hirsch Fund*, p. 11. There are two recent biographies of Baron de Hirsch worth consulting: Kurt Grunwald, *Tuerkenhirsch: A Study of Baron Maurice de Hirsch, Entrepreneur and Philanthropist* (Jerusalem: Israel Program for Scientific Translations, 1966), and Samuel J. Lee, *Moses of the New World: The Work of Baron de Hirsch* (New York: Thomas Yoseloff, 1970).

27. Maurice de Hirsch, "Refuge for Russian Jews," *Forum*, XI (August, 1891), 627. See also Szajkowski, "European Attitude," *PAJHS*, XLI (1951), 129, 136.

28. Joseph, *Hirsch Fund*, pp. 13–15.

29. *Ibid.*, Appendix B, "Deed of Trust," pp. 279–80.

30. On the Jewish Agricultural and Industrial Aid Society, see *American Jewish Yearbook, 5663*, pp. 111 ff. On the Jewish Agricultural Society, see *American Jewish Yearbook, 5684*, pp. 270–71.

31. Stainsby's account of the founding of Woodbine differs. On p. 20 of his text, he says: "It was originally designed for a purely agricultural colony, no manufacturing being contemplated, but as the school and other farms became productive, and the farm sought to dispose of the surplus of the products above their family needs, the fact was recognized that where a battalion of producers was created, it was absolutely essential that there should also be a bridge or division of consumers. This condition of affairs was promptly seen and was immediately provided for."

Joseph, *Hirsch Fund*, asserts in his passage on "Industrial Beginnings" in Woodbine (p. 61) that "there was no clear-cut statement of aims [in establishing industry]. It was thought [in the beginning] industry might serve to divert immigrants from the cities," and therefore, the Committee on Homes, whose object was to diminish urban congestion, diverted $10,000 to the Committee on Agricultural Industrial Settlements. "Soon after the 'Trouble,' [Sabsovich] emphasized the necessity of building up industry . . . for the sake of its influence on agriculture on the ground that the town population would create a market for the farm produce and agriculture and industry would thus support each other."

On the role of Rosenthal, Kaplan, and Sabsovich, see *Yudisher Farmer*, I, No. 1 (November, 1891), p. 5, reprinted in Gartner, pp. 62, 75. Boris Bogen, *Born a Jew*, pp. 63–64, recalled Sabsovich as "a flaming spirit . . . no cloistered scientist, content among test tubes." He was "a sort of prophet" eager "to impart a portion of his spirit to the Ghetto." Bogen characterized Kaplan as "a warm-hearted, kindly fanatic who carried a dream of settling Jews upon the soil."

32. On Vineland, see *American Israelite*, May 25, 1883; Singer, pp. 297–99. Goldhaft also offers material on Vineland.

33. The friendliness of the local population may have been somewhat overstated: see Brandes, pp. 181–82.

34. On Sabsovich, see *American Jewish Yearbook, 5665*, pp. 178–79. For an interesting, if frankly biased, biography of Professor Sabsovich, see

Katherine Sabsovich, *Adventures in Idealism: A Personal Record of the Life of Professor Sabsovich*. See also Boris Bogen, *Jewish Philanthropy*, pp. 130–31.

35. Joseph, *Hirsch Fund*, p. 51.
36. *Leslie's Weekly*, April 7, 1892 (quoted in Singer, p. 303, and in Joseph, *Hirsch Fund*, pp. 50–51); M. G. Landsberg, *History of the Persecution of the Jews in Russia*, quoted on p. 7a.
37. Landsberg, pp. 6a–7a; *American Israelite*, February 2, 1893. The anti-clerical playwright Jacob Gordin reportedly thought at one point of settling with a group of his followers at Woodbine, but the existence of a synagogue there disturbed him. "His group must live separately, and . . . not one of them could attend the synagogue." Sabsovich "immediately cooled off" (see Ezekiel Lifschutz, "Jacob Gordin's Proposal to Establish an Agricultural Colony," *AJHQ*, LVI [1966–67], 161).
38. Joseph, *Hirsch Fund*, p. 51, quoting Frances B. Lee, "The Hirsch Colony at Woodbine," *American Hebrew*, August 25, 1893, pp. 530–32.
39. The Myer Jonasson Cloak Factory established in April 1892. See Goldstein, p. 21; Joseph, *Hirsch Fund*, pp. 51–52, 62–63.
40. Joseph, *Hirsch Fund*, p. 52.
41. Bogen, *Born a Jew*, p. 70.
42. *Ibid.*, pp. 52–53. See Brandes, pp. 117–21.
43. Brandes, p. 117; Joseph, *Hirsch Fund*, pp. 53–54, quoting New York *Press*, April 2, 1893.
44. Joseph, *Hirsch Fund*, pp. 55–56.
45. *Ibid.*, p. 55.
46. *Ibid.*, quoted on p. 56. On Isaacs, see *American Jewish Yearbook, 5667*, pp. 19 ff.
47. Joseph, *Hirsch Fund*, quoted on p. 56. This opinion is similar to the one held by Heilprin.
48. Goldstein, pp. 22–23.
49. Joseph, *Hirsch Fund*, pp. 61–66.
50. *American Israelite*, July 8, 1897 (quoted in Singer, pp. 309–10).
51. Stainsby, pp. 11–19.
52. Joseph, *Hirsch Fund*, pp. 66–76; Bogen, *Jewish Philanthropy*, pp. 133–34.
53. Joseph, *Hirsch Fund*, p. 66.
54. Stainsby, p. 20.
55. *Ibid.*, p. 23.
56. Brandes, pp. 235, 256–58; Bogen, *Born a Jew*, pp. 66–68.
57. Levy, p. 856.
58. *Ibid.*, p. 856. Even so, Goldstein, pp. 60, 69, had to concede in 1921 that "younger Jews . . . because they see the apparent drudgery of farm life and no very bright prospects, have little if any inclination to remain on the farms"; there were "fundamental defects," a want of community spirit and civic pride, inadequate educational and social facilities, inefficient and unscientific agricultural methods, etc., which impelled "particularly the younger element of the settlements [to] leave the farm and go to the city." Goldstein recognized, to be sure, that "the problem of the Jewish farmer [was] but a part of the larger problem embracing farming in general throughout the country" (p. 59).

See also Louis J. Swichkow, "The Jewish Agricultural Colony of Arpin, Wisconsin," *AJHQ*, LIV (1964–65), 91: "For the boy and girl reaching manhood and womanhood, [farming] meant no pursuing of

the arts, no chance to meet a mate, no future! So the children left for the cities—and the parents followed, one by one."
59. Levy, p. 860.
60. Goldstein, p. 69.
61. Bernard A. Palitz, "The Borough of Woodbine," *ca.* 1907 (Typescript, American Jewish Archives, Box 2112). See also Bogen, *Born a Jew,* p. 66, where Palitz is characterized as "a man oppressed by the world-wide tragedy of his people and looking for light in the darkness." See also Brandes, p. 44.

Chapter 4

1. The passages quoted from Spurgeon and the *Edinburgh Review* are found in Montagu F. Modder, *The Jew in the Literature of England,* pp. 252–53. Fear of overcrowding the cities was made evident by the leaders of the Jewish community when first confronted with the problem of mass migration to the United States. See Cowen, chap. V ("The American Hebrew and the Jewish Community"); also Szajkowski, "The Attitude of American Jews to East European Jewish Immigration (1881–1893)," *PAJHS,* XL (1950–51), 235–41. See also Joseph, *Hirsch Fund,* pp. 184–210, for a detailed description of the work of the Industrial Removal Office of the Jewish Agricultural Society and the work of the leaders of the "Galveston Movement." On the "Galveston Plan," see *EJ,* VII, 294–95.

2. Letter from Gabriel Davidson, Managing Director, Jewish Agricultural Society, May 10, 1943: "No census [of Jewish farmers] was ever taken, and therefore the figures are simply estimates. There are no figures until 1900, but a record made at about that time of the Jewish farms in Connecticut and New Jersey disclosed 216 families, probably somewhat over 1000 souls. There is no knowledge of how many Jewish farmers there were in other parts of the country at that time."

3. That a certain measure of *Selbsthass* was evident among both immigrant Jews and already well established American (or, for that matter, West European) Jews is incontestable. The Yiddish dramatist Jacob Gordin, for instance, in the early 1880s—he had not yet quit Russia for the United States—argued: "It is our love for money, our arrogance, our usury, innkeeping and the middleman occupations and all the other dishonest deeds that enrage the Russian population against us [Jews]" (Lifschutz, p. 154). In fact, however, the "ultimate cause" of anti-Semitism was not the Jew or anything he did or left undone; it was the changing socio-economic structure of the larger non-Jewish society, primarily, in the period with which we are dealing here, the change from agrarianism to industrialism and the fears of those whose domination of the old agrarian society was now facing a serious challenge. See Ellis Rivkin, "A Decisive Pattern in American Jewish History," *Essays in American Jewish History,* pp. 38–39; Oscar Handlin, "American Views of

the Jew at the Opening of the Twentieth Century," *PAJHS*, XL (1950–51), 340 ff.; S. F. Chyet, "Ludwig Lewisohn: The Years of Becoming," *AJA*, XI (1959), 135–36; Barbara M. Solomon, *Ancestors and Immigrants: A Changing New England Tradition*, p. 39; Modder, pp. 254 ff., 302 ff.

4. Interesting data about an abortive Jewish colony in Western Kansas, Beersheba, are available: see "A Colony in Kansas—1882," *AJA*, XVII (1965), 114 ff.

5. Julius Goldman, *Report on Colonization of Russian Refugees in the West*, p. 23.

6. How this concentration of power was made possible is shown by a brief description of the organization of the Mormon Church. The church was based upon the Old Testament idea of priesthood, the priest serving as God's lieutenant on earth and hence endowed with complete authority. Actually there were two sets of priests. The Aaronic priesthood dealt mainly with temporal affairs such as the collection of tithes, general care of properties, and distribution of charities. The second set of priests, superior to the first, was the Melchizedek order, made up of three high priests, one of whom was the bishop, the other two counsellors. Together, the three made up the general presidency which regulated spiritual affairs and supervised temporal affairs. This controlling body was also self-perpetuating. To this higher hierarchy belonged Brigham Young.

Another factor in the success of Mormon colonization was Young's skillful planning and meticulous attention to detail, as shown in the following passages from an "Epistle of the 12 to the [Mormon] Church of Jesus Christ of Latter Day Saints in England, Scotland, Ireland, Wales, and the Isle of Man," quoted in Daniel P. Kidder, *Mormonism and the Mormons*, p. 200:

> It will be necessary in the first place for men of capital to go on first and make large purchases of land, and erect mills, machinery, manufactories, etc., so that the poor who go from this country may find employment. Therefore, it is not for the poor to flock to that place extensively, until the necessary preparations are made. Neither is it wisdom for those who feel a spirit of benevolence to expend all their means in helping others to emigrate and thus arrive in a new country empty handed. In all settlements there must be capital and labour united in order to flourish. The brethren will recollect that they are not going to build cities and inhabit them. Building cities cannot be done without means and labour. . . . Sovereigns are more profitable than silver or any other money, in emigrating to America; and the brethren are also cautioned against the American money when they arrive in that country. Let them not venture to take paper money of that country until they become well informed in regard to the different banks.
>
> It is much cheaper going to New-Orleans than by New York. But it will never do for emigrants to go by New-Orleans in the summer, on account of the heat and sickness of the climate. It is therefore advisable for the saints to emigrate in autumn, winter or spring.

See also Morris Robert Werner, *Brigham Young*. Young's penchant for detailed planning is reminiscent of Theodor Herzl's Zionist advocacy in his *Judenstaat* (1896).

7. Ernest Ludlow Bogart, *Economic History of the American People*, Part III ("Industrialization, 1860–1914"). On Amish, see *DAH*, I, 68. On Hutterites, *DAH*, I, 440–41, and J. W. Smith and A. L. Jamison, editors, *The Shaping of American Religion*, I, 192, 209. On Moravians, see *DAH*, IV, 22, and J. W. Smith and A. L. Jamison, pp. 25, 53, 192, 454. On the socio-economic struggle of changing from a primarily agrarian to a primarily industrial society in America, see Morris, *EAH*, pp. 257, 262 ff.; John Higham, "Anti-Semitism in the Gilded Age," *Mississippi Valley Historical Review*, XLIII (1957), 562, 572; Davis Rich Dewey, *Financial History of the United States*; John R. Commons *et al.*, *History of Labour in the United States*; A. H. Sanford, *The Story of Agriculture in the United States*; Nathan Fine, *Labor and Farmer Parties in the United States 1828–1928*.

8. Best typified by the experiences, respectively, in the Louisiana and Arkansas colonization attempts. On Amana, see *DAH*, I, 53–54; J. W. Smith and A. L. Jamison, I, 192, 209.

9. Arthur Ruppin, *Jews in the Modern World*, p. 172. See also J. R. Marcus, *Studies in American Jewish History*, pp. 10–11.

10. Buck, *Agrarian Crusade*, p. 99.

11. *Ibid.* See also Buck, *The Granger Movement*; John D. Hicks, *The Populist Revolt*; Sanford, *Agriculture*; Fine, *Labor*; Frederick L. Paxson, *History of the American Frontier*; B. H. Hibbard, *A History of the Public Land Policies*.

12. Bogart, *Economic History*; Victor S. Clark, *History of Manufactures in the United States*, II; Burton Hendrick, *The Age of Big Business*; National Industrial Conference Board, *A Graphic History and Analysis of the Census of Manufacturing, 1849–1919*; Walett, p. 145; Morris, *EAH* (1953), p. 442. In 1790, there were ten times more farmers than city dwellers; in 1890, three times as many city dwellers as farmers: see Buck, *Agrarian Crusade*, p. 99.

13. Morris, *EAH* (1953), p. 442.

14. Letter from Davidson: Since 1933 "we have helped 423 refugee families directly and probably another hundred families have established themselves through contacts made with refugees who had been settled through our direct instrumentality."

15. Stainsby, p. 23. As late as the mid-1930s, farming, at least on a part-time basis, in a sort of latter-day shtetl in America still had its appeal: see Edwin Rosskam, *Roosevelt, New Jersey*.

16. Letter from Davidson: "Our estimates now are between 80,000 and 100,000 individuals engaged in whole, or in part, in farming."

17. Ruppin, "Agricultural Achievements in Palestine," *Contemporary Jewish Record*, V, no. 3 (June, 1942), 280; Goldstein, p. 69.

18. Ruppin, "Agricultural Achievements," pp. 269–71; Dan Giladi, "The Agronomic Development of the Old Colonies in Palestine (1882–1914)," in Moshe Maoz, ed., *Studies on Palestine During the Ottoman Period*, pp. 176–79. On Edmond de Rothschild, see *EJ*, XIV, 342–46. On the Lovers of Zion (Hibbat Zion) movement, see *EJ*, VIII, 463. On the development of Rothschild's colonies in Palestine, see Walter Laqueur, *A History of Zionism*. On the cruelties involved in the development of capitalism and industrialism in Eastern Europe, no one has painted a more vivid picture than the novelist Israel Joshua Singer in his *Brothers Ashkenazi*.

19. David Farhi, "Documents on the Attitude of the Ottoman Government towards the Jewish Settlement in Palestine . . . ," in Maoz, pp. 191, 196, 204 ff.; Ben Halpern, *The Idea of the Jewish State*, pp. 121 ff.
20. Ruppin, *Jews in the Modern World*, pp. 374–77: "Achievements in Palestinian Industry and Agriculture." On Arthur Balfour and the Balfour Declaration, see *EJ*, IV, 130–35. On the British Mandate, see *EJ*, XI, 861–63. On Jewish agricultural enterprise in Palestine, see Amos Elon, *The Israelis: Founders and Sons*, pp. 92–95, 111–12; Laqueur, p. 75 ff.; Ludwig Lewisohn, *Israel*, pp. 157 ff.
21. Ruppin, *Jews in the Modern World*, p. 368. See also Giladi, "Agronomic Development," in Maoz, pp. 175 ff.
22. Ruppin, "Agricultural Achievements," p. 280.
23. Letter from Davidson.
24. Giladi, "Agronomic Development," in Maoz, p. 176; Frank E. Manuel, *Realities of American-Palestine Relations*, pp. 265–66, is critical of American Zionists on this score: "Only the old Zionist experts such as Ruppin knew in detail the real problems of land settlement in Palestine." The people who looked to Louis Brandeis for leadership "would neglect the *Kibutz* (*sic*), that unique form of cooperative labor on the land, and concentrate almost completely on settlers with individual means. They had no feeling for the idealism of the pioneers."
25. Gloria Deutsch observes: "Critics of the movement . . . can be heard to sneer that today kibbutzniks are just like anyone else, out to make money, competitive, concerned only for themselves." See 'The Kibbutz—A Tarnished Dream," in *Jewish Chronicle* (London), May 19, 1978, p. 21.
26. Ruppin, "Agricultural Achievements," p. 271. On the World Zionist Organization, see *EJ*, XVI, 1096 ff.
27. Ruppin, "Agricultural Achievements," pp. 271–72. On the Agricultural Experiment Station, see *UJE*, I, 120–21. On the Jewish Agency, see *EJ*, X, 26–35. On the General Federation of Jewish Labor, the Histadrut, see *EJ*, VIII, 534–41. On the Mizrachi (Religious) labor movement, see *EJ*, VII, 1320–23.
28. Ruppin, "Agricultural Achievements," p. 272; Allon Gal, *Socialist-Zionism*, pp. 167, 216; *EJ*, X, 965, 967. Even among Israelis whose training is exclusively industrial and technological, the cooperative spirit appears not to be moribund. As recently as the spring of 1976, a group of Israelis employed in the country's defense industries was heard to declare its intention of organizing in the Galilee, i.e., in territory which was included in Israel before June, 1967, a community (*kehillah*) devoted to intensive social concern and principles of mutual aid (*Ha-Aretz*, April 26, 1976, p. 20).
29. Isaac Deutscher, *Heretics and Renegades and Other Essays* (Indianapolis: Bobbs-Merrill Co., 1969), pp. 10–11.

Appendix 1

1. On Isaacs (1841–1904), see *UJE*, V, 594. On Schiff (1847–1920), see *EJ*, XIV, 960–62. On Goldman, see Jacob H. Schiff and Felix Warburg

papers, American Jewish Archives, Cincinnati; Wiernik, pp. 289, 412. On Straus (1850–1926), see *EJ*, XV, 432–33. On Seligman (1827–1894), see *Who Was Who in America: Historical Volume*, p. 474. On Rice (1835–1914), see *American Jewish Year Book, 5666*, p. 96; *Who Was Who in America*, I, 1026. On Hoffman, see Joseph, *Hirsch Fund*, pp. 14–15. On Sulzberger (1843–1923), see *American Jewish Year Book, 5677*, pp. 68–75. On Hackenburg (1837–1918), see *American Jewish Year Book, 5666*, pp. 65–66; *EJ*, VII 1037–38. On Baron de Hirsch (1831–1896), see Grunwald, *Tuerkenhirsch*; Lee, *Moses of the New World*; *EJ*, VIII, 505–7; and Avni, *Argentina*, pp. 19–34.

2. On Heilprin (1823–1888), see Pollak, *Heilprin and Sons; DAB*, VII, 502–3. On Rosenthal (1843–1917), see *JE*, X, 478–79; Eisenstein, *Otsar Zichronotai*, Part I, p. 280; and *EJ*, XIV, 293. On Kaplan, see Cahan, *Education*, pp. 425 *et passim; EJ*, II, 862. On Sabsovich (1861–1915), see *American Jewish Year Book, 5665*, pp. 178–79; Katherine Sabsovich, *Adventures in Idealism*.

3. See Eisenstein, pp. 273–74.

4. On Eppinger, Gershel, Sternberg, Mendel, and Henry, see Brandes, *Immigrants to Freedom*, pp. 56, 82, 84, 212, 302. On Sternberg, see also Eisenstein, p. 274. On Lewisohn (1847–1902), see *EJ*, XI, 177. On Montagu (1832–1911), see *EJ*, XII, 264. On Cohen, see *EJ*, X, 44. On Asher (1837–1889), see *JE*, II, 180–81.

5. Eisenstein, p. 279, designates Woodbine as "more important and of greater value than all the colonies founded by Russian émigrés in America." Eisenstein, writing in 1929, goes on to say (p. 284): "Of the first colonies founded after the pogroms of 1881, none lasted but Alliance, Rosenhayn, and Carmel, and they are only colonies of workers employed in the garment industry, except for the Alliance colony, which is to some degree an agricultural colony." Of the colonies founded under auspices such as those of the Baron de Hirsch Fund, Woodbine alone remained, but "has yet to achieve the distinction [of becoming] a colony of genuine farmers."

Appendix 2

1. See Von Humboldt's essay "On the Historian's Task" (1826), in G. G. Iggers and K. von Moltke, eds., *The Theory and Practice of History: Leopold von Ranke* (Indianapolis: Bobbs-Merrill Co., 1973), pp. 5 ff.

2. On Weinreich (1894–1969), see *EJ*, XVI, 404–5.

3. Bailey is referring here to Zalman Epstein (1860–1936), a notable Hebrew essayist, critic, and Hibbat Zion leader, and his brother Isaac Epstein (1862–1943), also notable as a Hebrew writer, linguist, and educator. On the Epstein brothers, see *EJ*, VI, 826–27, 836–37.

4. Nahum Slouschz (1871–1966) was a Lithuanian-born scholar and Zionist leader. In 1909, Henrietta Szold published an English translation of his *Renascence of Hebrew Literature* (1902). See *EJ*, XIV, 1677–78.

5. On Ravnitzky (1859–1944), see *EJ*, XIII, 1588–89.
6. On Lilienblum (1843–1910), see *EJ*, XI, 240–42; "Rebel and Penitent: Moses Leib Lilienblum," in Lucy S. Dawidowicz, *Golden Tradition*, pp. 119–32. His acronym was variously "Moshel" and "Malal" in Bailey's memoir, though the translator, hoping to avoid confusion, has preferred "Moshel."
7. Shmuel Hurwitz (1862–1943), the Yiddish journalist and folklorist, used the nom de plume "A. Litvin." See *EJ*, XI, 405.
8. Bailey means Eliezer Zweifel (1815–1888), who wrote sympathetically of Hassidism. His multi-volume *Shalom al Yisrael* appeared 1868–73. See *EJ*, XVI, 1245–46.
9. On Slonimsky (1810–1904), see *EJ*, XIV, 1674–75. *Ha-Zefirah* ("The Dawn"), the Hebrew weekly he founded at Warsaw in 1862, was initially less a newspaper than a scientific-technological journal, though later Slonimsky published articles on literature and politics as well as reports from abroad. On *Ha-Zefirah*, see *EJ*, VII, 1529–30; also Sanford Ragins, "The Image of America in Two East European Hebrew Periodicals [*Ha-Zefirah* and *Ha-Melitz*]," *AJA*, XVII (1965), 143 ff. Slonimsky's grandson Henry Slonimsky (1884–1970) was a notable American philosopher and academician.
10. On Sholem Aleichem (*né* Sholem Rabinowitz, 1859–1916), see *EJ*, XIV, 1272–86.
11. Freeman, born in 1859, published in 1929 and 1934 his two-volume *Fuftzig Yor Geshichte fun Idishen Leben in Philadelphia*, a fifty-year history of Jewish life in Philadelphia.
12. Lydia Rabinovitz-Kempner (1871–1935), born in Kovno, Lithuania, had no connection with the Pasteur Institute in Paris, but worked with the celebrated Robert Koch (1843–1910) at his Institute for Infectious Diseases in Berlin, married Koch's assistant Dr. Walter Kempner, and in 1920 became director of the bacteriological laboratory at the Berlin-Moabit City Hospital. See Wininger, *Grosse Juedische National-Biographie*, V, 120; VII, 387.
13. On Abraham Dov (known as Adam Ha-Cohen) Lebensohn (1794–1878), see *EJ*, X, 1548–49.
14. Throughout Bailey's memoir, the Am Olam group is often referred to as "The Brotherhood." On the Am Olam, see A. Menes in J. A. Fishman, *Studies in Modern Jewish Social History*.
15. By "Bestuzhevka," Bailey means a disciple of Konstantin Nikolaevitch Bestuzhev-Riumin (1829–1897), a liberal historian at the University of St. Petersburg and the founder of "free courses" for girls in St. Petersburg, where Jews were permitted as denizens. From 1878–81, he was director of the Higher School for Women. On Bestuzhev-Riumin's work, see *EB*, XXIII, 919. Moni Bakal (Bakl, Bokal)—Cahan, *Education*, calls him Michael—was deemed by Cahan "one of the most important and . . . most interesting personalities of our [Am Olam] . . . group. . . . [We] all respected him because Bokal [was] free of egotism, honest, peaceful" (*Education*, pp. 245–46, 416).
16. On Feldman (1860–1910), see Abraham Cronbach, "Autobiography," *AJA*, XI (1959), 21–25, 38–39. See also Feldman's essay "Intermarriage Historically Considered," *CCAR-YB*, XIX (1909), 271–307.

17. On Cahan (1860–1951), see *EJ*, V, 14–15; *American Jewish Year Book*, LIII (1952), 527–29. Cahan, *Education*, mentions Oleynikov (Aleinikoff) a number of times. Cahan's editor, Leon Stein, identifies Oleynikov as the "first Russian-Jewish lawyer in New York's Jewish quarter" (*Education*, p. 415). According to Wiernik, p. 287, Oleynikov, Paul Kaplan, and Spivakovsky participated in the ill-fated Jewish Alliance of America at Philadelphia in 1891.

18. On Kohler (1843–1926), who in 1903 became president of the Hebrew Union College, see *EJ*, X, 1142–43. Actually, Kohler opposed circumcision only in the case of proselytes: see *CCAR-YB*, II (1891–92), 115–17; III (1892–93), 15–16; Kohler, *Jewish Theology*, p. 449.

19. On Krauskopf (1858–1923), see *CCAR—YB*, XXXIII (1923), 155–56; *American Jewish Year Book, 5685*, pp. 420–47; *EJ*, X, 1246–47.

20. On Heilprin (1823–1888), see the biography by Pollak; *DAB*, VIII, 502–3; Morais, *Jews of Philadelphia*, pp. 322–24; Morais, *Eminent Israelites*, p. 130. Heilprin was an unofficial co-editor of and contributor to *Appleton's Cyclopaedia*, Appleton's *New American Cyclopaedia*, and the *Nation*. On Kossuth (1802–1894), the Hungarian patriot and revolutionary leader, see *EB*, XV, 916–18.

21. On Morais (1823–1897), see *EJ*, XII, 294–95.

22. On Elisha ben Abuyah (early 2nd century C.E.), see *EJ*, VI, 668–70, and Avot 4:20.

23. On Alexander Zederbaum (1816–1893), the pioneer of Jewish journalism in the Russian empire, see *EJ*, XVI, 964–65. Zederbaum ("EReZ"—"cedar"—he was called) became founder-editor of *Yiddishes Folksblat* in 1881.

24. According to *EJ*, XIV, 1124, during the pogroms of 1881–82, at Balta in the Ukraine, "the teacher Eliezer Mashbir organized a self-defense unit largely made up of porters, coachmen, and apprentices, and even set up a form of . . . signaling with blasts of the *shofar* ["ram's horn"]." See also Cahan, *Education*, pp. 204, 362; Davidson, *Our Jewish Farmers*, p. 220. A translation in typescript of Mashbir's article "From Brody to New York," published originally in a Russian periodical, is to be found under "Maschbir, Elieser" in the Biographies file, American Jewish Archives, Cincinnati.

25. "Shomer" was the nom de plume of Nahum Meier Shaikewicz (1849–1906), the Yiddish novelist and playwright. See *EJ*, XIV, 1454.

26. On Ilya Grigoryevitch Orshansky (1846–1875), a notable journalist, jurist, and historian, see *EJ*, XII, 1480–81.

27. On Gordin (1853–1909), see *EJ*, VII, 787–89. Jacob Priluker, a teacher at a government-sponsored Jewish school in Odessa, sought to reconcile Judaism and Christianity through a new religious group to be known as "New Israel." Gordin and Priluker are discussed in Dubnow, II, 334–35.

28. On Akiba (*ca.* 50–*ca.* 132), see *JE*, I, 304–8.

29. On Byelinsky (1811–1848), see *EB*, XXIII, 918; *WBD*, p. 128. On the sociologist and populist leader Mikhailovski (1842–1904), see *EB* (Chicago, 1973), XV, 436. On Dobroliubov (1836–1861), see *WBD*, p. 425. On Pisarev (1840–1868), the critic and nihilist, see *EB* (1973), XVII, 1109. On Draper (1811–1882), see *DAB*, V, 438–41, and *WBD*, pp. 438–39. Draper's *History of the Intellectual Development of Europe* (1863) was translated into many languages.

30. Aaron Porjes, born in 1848, published his *Torat Ha-chaim* at Vienna in 1879.
31. On Bialik (1873–1934), see *EJ*, IV, 795–803. On Ahad Ha-Am (*né* Asher Hirsch Ginsberg, 1856–1927), see *EJ*, II, 440–48. On Mendele Mokher Seforim (*né* Sholom Jacob Abramowitsch, 1835–1917), see *EJ*, XI, 1317–23.
32. By "Shapiro," Bailey must mean Hermann (Zvi Hirsh) Schapira (1840–1898), a well-known rabbi, journalist, mathematician, and academician: see *EJ*, XIV, 941–43. On Mill (1806–1873), see *DNB*, XIII, 390–99. Lavrov (1823–1900) was a leading Russian Populist philosopher: see *WBD*, p. 868.
33. By "Lev Metchnikov," Bailey must mean Ilya Ilich Metchnikoff (1845–1916), professor of zoology and anatomy at Odessa from 1870 to 1882, when he left Russia for Paris. He worked with Pasteur from 1888 on, became director of the Pasteur Institute in 1895, and was a Nobel Prize laureate in 1908: see *WBD*, p. 1013; Greenberg, I, 25 (n. 18).
34. Is Bailey alluding here to the work of Nikolai Ignatievitch Bakst (1843–1904), the celebrated Russian Jewish physiologist who was an ardent champion of Jewish emancipation in Russia and an advocate of ORT, founded in 1880 for the purpose, among others, of "help[ing] the Jewish agricultural colonies, model farms, and agricultural schools" in the Russian empire? On Bakst, see *UJE*, II, 40; *EJ*, IV, 118–19; Greenberg, I, 177; on ORT, see *EJ*, XII, 1481–82. Bakst worked closely with Samuel Salomonovitch Poliakoff (1837–1888), the Russian Jewish industrialist who was a founder of the Jewish Agricultural Fund, the basis for ORT. On Poliakoff, see *UJE*, VIII, 580. Another luminary Bailey may have had in mind when he wrote his memoir some four decades later is Jean de Bloch (*né* Ivan Stanislavovitch Bloch, or Blioch, 1836–1901): see *UJE*, II, 399–400. Bloch, a Polish-born financier, was a Protestant convert and a pacifist; he retained a love of his Jewish ancestry and in 1901 published a voluminous work on the plight of Russian Jewry. See also Ragins, pp. 150–52.
35. Mordecai Ben-Ami (1854–1932) was born Rabinowicz (identical with the Max Rabinovitz of Bailey's text?). He was a writer, journalist, organizer of Jewish self-defense, and Zionist leader: see *EJ*, IV, 461–62.
36. Israel Isser Katsovey (or Kasovich) (1859–1934) in later years became co-editor of the American Yiddish monthly *Yiddisher Farmer*; in 1924, he published his memoirs in a Yiddish volume whose foreword was written by the famed Yiddish playwright and novelist David Pinski (1872–1959). Kasovich's memoir appeared in 1929 in an English translation, *The Days of Our Years*. See *UJE*, VI, 340. On Pinski, see *EJ*, XIII, 549–51. Chaim Spivakovsky (1861–1927), on settling in the United States, would become the notable physician Charles David Spivak: see *UJE*, X, 15; Marjorie Hornbein, "Dr. Charles Spivak of Denver: Physician, Social Worker, Yiddish Author," *Western States Jewish Historical Quarterly*, XI (1979), 195–211; also n. 17, *supra*.
37. Jacob Cohen Bernstein (1859–1929), Kishinev-born, was perhaps better known as Jacob Bernstein-Kogan. He was a Zionist leader and a physician: see *EJ*, IV, 691. He discusses his brother Lev—Lyuba, he calls him—in *Sefer Bernstein-Kohen*, pp. 79 ff., 92 ff. Lev was executed in 1889.
38. By "Professor Mikhal Philipov," Bailey means either Mikhail Avraamo-

vitch Filippov (1828–1886) or Mikhail Mikhailovitch Filippov (1858–1903); the latter wrote on Jews in 1882.

39. On Paul (Pavel) Kaplan, see *EJ*, II, 862; he is mentioned several times in Cahan, *Education*; see also n. 17, *supra*. Jacob Paisochovitz (Peisachovich) is described by Cahan as having "more than all others . . . exemplified in our [Am Olam] crowd the new awareness of Jewishness aroused by the Russian pogroms" (*Education*, pp. 266–67).

40. "The Great Margolis" is most probably Haim Margolis-Kalvariski (1868–1947), the distinguished Hibbat Zion leader and agriculturist: see *EJ*, XI, 968. On the Hibbat Zion ("Lovers of Zion") movement, see Dawidowicz, pp. 52–53. See also the summary by Eli Shaltiel, "Zionism—Thought and Deed," in *Ha-Aretz*, May 7, 1976, pp. 18–19, especially p. 19, where in reviewing David Vital's *The Origins of Zionism* (1975) Shaltiel represents the "Lovers of Zion" as a movement of Jewish revolutionaries whose hopes for Jewish emancipation in Eastern Europe had been bitterly disappointed; the preparatory work accomplished by the "Lovers of Zion" was indispensable to the emergence of Herzlian political Zionism.

41. On the Franco-Jewish philanthropist and agriculturist Netter (1828–1882), see *JE*, IX, 233–34.

42. On the reception Am Olamites received in New York, see Kasovich, *Days of Our Years*, pp. 173–79.

43. Meeker is probably Ohio-born Ezra Meeker (1830–1928), who pioneered in the Pacific Northwest (*DAB*, XII, 495–96); Nathan Cook Meeker (1817–1879), the agricultural editor of Horace Greeley's New York *Tribune* and the founder of a colony in northeastern Colorado, died before the Am Olamites arrived from Europe (*DAB*, XII, 497–98; *EB*, XII, 533). On Rosenthal (1843–1917), see Gartner, pp. 59–61.

44. George Seldes was the father of Alliance-born Gilbert Seldes (1893–?), a well-known journalist and writer.

45. On the emergence of Hassidism and the bitter rivalry between the Hassidim and their opponents, the so-called *Mitnagdim*, see *EJ*, VII, 1390 ff.; Dawidowicz, pp. 14 ff. Israel ben Eliezer (the "Baal Shem Tov," or Master of the Good Name), credited with the founding of the Hassidic movement, is presumed to have lived from about 1700 to 1760. Levi Yitzchok of Berditchev (1740–1809) was among the most notable Hassidic leaders.

46. On Belzer (*né* Spivak), cantor in Belz, Bessarabia (Moldavia), and subsequently in Kishinev and Berditchev, see Wininger, V, 600. On Jakob Bachmann (1846–1905), the famous Kishinev-born cantor who sang in Odessa, Rostov, Berditchev, and Lwów, see Wininger, I, 214–15.

47. On the Haskalah, see *EJ*, VII, 1434 ff., 1445–52; Dawidowicz, pp. 14 ff.; Greenberg, I, 22 ff., 52–53, 172, 188.

48. On the Austrian writer Franzos (1848–1904), see *JE*, V, 498–99; *UJE*, IV, 419.

49. On Lermontov (1814–1841), see *EB*, XVI, 484.

50. Bailey may be referring here to Fargo College, founded in 1887 at Fargo, North Dakota. See *EB*, XIX, 783.

51. On Bailey's eldest, Margaret Bailey Herman, see Brandes, p. 234.

52. On Bayuk, who served as a judge in Alliance, see Eisenstadt, *Sefer Dorot Ha-Achronim*, Book 2. Brandes mentions him a number of times.

53. On the poet Winchevsky (*né* Lippe Benzion Novchovitch, *alias* Leopold Benedict, 1856–1932), see *DAB*, XX, 379–80.
54. On Mintz (1859–1930), see Wiernik, p. 396.
55. On the Yiddish poet and journalist Daniel Charney (1888–1959), see *EJ*, V, 361.
56. On the renowned Talmudist and Hebraist Chernovitz (Tchernovitz, 1871–1949), see *EJ*, XV, 883–84. On Feinberg (1887–1949), see *EJ*, V, 563; *American Israelite* (Cincinnati), February 24, 1949.
57. On the journalist, novelist, and publisher Hubbard (1856–1915), see *DAB*, IX, 323–24. On the philosopher Carus (1852–1919), see *DAB*, III, 548–49.

Selected Bibliography

Avni, Haim. *Argentina, Ha-aretz Ha-y'udah, Mifal Ha-hityashvut Shel Ha-Baron de Hirsch b'Argentina*. Jerusalem: Magnes Press, 1973.

Bailey, Shneur (Sidney). "Mo Oni u-Ma Hayoy." New Jersey, *ca.* 1944. [Original ms., YIVO, New York City.]

———. "The First Fifty Years." In *Yoval* (Philadelphia: Westbrook Pub. Co., 1932).

Baron, Salo Wittmayer. *A Social and Religious History of the Jews*. 3 vols. New York: Columbia University Press, 1937.

———. *Steeled by Adversity: Essays and Addresses on American Jewish Life*. Philadelphia: Jewish Publication Society of America, 1971.

Berenson, Bernard. "Contemporary Jewish Fiction." *Andover Review*, X (1888), 587–602.

Bernheimer, Charles (ed.). *The Russian Jew in the United States*. Philadelphia: J.C. Winston Co., 1905.

Bogart, Ernest Ludlow. *Economic History of the American People*. New York: Longmans, Green and Co., 1941.

Bogen, Boris D. *Jewish Philanthropy*. New York: Macmillan Co., 1917.

———. *Born a Jew*. New York: Macmillan Co., 1930.

Brandes, Joseph. *Immigrants to Freedom*. Philadelphia: University of Pennsylvania Press, 1971.

Brutzkus, Baer Davidovitch. *Die Yiddishe Landsvirtshaft in Mizrach Airopa*. Berlin: "Ort," 1926.

Buck, Solon J. *The Agrarian Crusade*. New Haven: Yale University Press, 1921.

———. *The Granger Movement*. Cambridge: Harvard University Press, 1913.

Cahan, Abraham. *The Education of Abraham Cahan*. Translated by Leon Stein *et al*. Philadelphia: Jewish Publication Society of America, 1969. [The original Yiddish appeared in 1926.]

Clark, Victor S., *History of Manufactures in the United States*. Vol. II. Washington: Carnegie Institution, 1916.

Clarkson, Jesse D. *A History of Russia*. New York: Random House, 1962.

"Colony in Kansas—1882, A." *American Jewish Archives*, XVII (1965), 114–39.

Commons, John R., *et al*. *History of Labour in the United States*. 2 vols. New York: Macmillan Co., 1918.

Cooley, Everett L. "Clarion, Utah: Jewish Colony in 'Zion.' " *Utah Historical Quarterly*, XXXVI (1968), No. 2, 113–31.

Cowen, Philip. *Memories of an American Jew*. New York: International Press, 1932.

Davidson, Gabriel. "The Jew in Agriculture in the United States." In *American Jewish Year Book: 5696* (Philadelphia: Jewish Publication Society of America, 1935), XXXVII, 99–134.

———. *Our Jewish Farmers and The Story of the Jewish Agricultural Society*. New York: L. B. Fischer, 1943.

———. "The Palestine Colony in Michigan: An Adventure in Colonization." *Publications of the American Jewish Historical Society*, XXIX (1925), 61–74.

———. "The Tragedy of Sholem." *Jewish Tribune*, No. 24 (June 16, 1922); No. 25 (June 22, 1922).

Davidson, Gabriel, and Edward A. Goodwin. "A Unique Agricultural Colony." *Reflex*, II, No. 5 (May, 1928), 80–86.

———. "An Arkansas Colonization Episode." *Jewish Tribune*, No. 2 (July 12, 1929), pp. 2, 9.

———. "Chalutzim in the Land of Cotton." *Jewish Tribune*, No. 13 (September 27, 1929), pp. 2, 15.

———. "An Epic of the Prairies: Hitherto Unrecorded History of a Pioneer Jewish Colony." *Detroit Jewish Chronicle*, January 29, 1932, pp. 1, 6–7.

Dawidowicz, Lucy S. (ed.). *The Golden Tradition*. New York: Holt, Rinehart and Winston, 1967.

Dewey, Davis Rich. *Financial History of the United States*. New York: Longmans, Green and Co., 1939.

Dictionary of American Biography. New York: C. Scribner's and Sons, 1946.

Dictionary of American History. New York: C. Scribner's and Sons, 1946.

Dictionary of National Biography. London: Smith, Elder and Company, 1908–1909.

Dubnow, S. M. *History of the Jews in Russia and Poland*. Translated by Israel Friedlander. Vols. I, II. Philadelphia: Jewish Publication Society of America, 1916–1920.

Eisenstadt, Benzion. *Sefer Dorot Ha-Achronim*. Book 2. Brooklyn, N.Y.: Moinester Publishing Co., 1936 (1937?).

Eisenstein, Judah David. *Otsar Zichronotai*. Part I. New York: Privately published, 1929.

Elbogen, Ismar. *A Century of Jewish Life*. Philadelphia: Jewish Publication Society of America, 1953.

Elon, Amos. *The Israelis: Founders and Sons*. New York: Holt, Rinehart and Winston, 1971.

Encyclopaedia Britannica. Eleventh edition (1911).

Encyclopaedia Judaica. Jerusalem: Keter, 1971.

Encyclopedia of Social Sciences. 15 vols. New York: MacMillan Co., 1930–1935.

Feld, Lipman Goldman. "New Light on the Lost Jewish Colony of Beersheba, Kansas, 1882–1886." *American Jewish Historical Quarterly*, LX (1970–71), 159–68.

Fine, Nathan. *Labor and Farmer Parties in the United States, 1826–1928.* New York: Rand School of Social Sciences, 1928.

Fishman, Joshua A. (ed.). *Studies in Modern Jewish Social History.* New York: Ktav, 1972.

Frank, Herman. "Jewish Mass Colonization in Soviet Russia." *Reflex,* II, No. 2 (February, 1928), 54–61.

Freeman, Moshe. *Funftsich Yor Geshichte fun Idishn Lebn in Philadelphia.* 2 vols. Philadelphia: Mid-City Press, 1929–34.

Fried, Marc. "Deprivation and Migration: Dilemmas of Causal Interpretation." In *On Understanding Poverty,* edited by Daniel P. Moynihan, pp. 111–59. New York: Basic Books, 1969.

Gal, Allon. *Socialist-Zionism: Theory and Issues in Contemporary Jewish Nationalism.* Cambridge, Mass.: Schenkman Publishing Co., 1973.

Gartner, Lloyd P. (ed.). *Michael: On the History of the Jews in the Diaspora.* Vol. III. Tel Aviv: Diaspora Research Institute-Tel Aviv University, 1975.

Geffen, Joel S. "Jewish Agricultural Colonies as Reported in the Pages of the Russian Hebrew Press, *Ha-Melitz* and *Ha-Yom:* Annotated Documentary." *American Jewish Historical Quarterly,* LX (1970–71), 355–82.

George, Henry. *Progress and Poverty: An Inquiry into the Cause of Industrial Depressions and of Increase of Want with Increase of Wealth.* New York: Henry George and Co., 1880.

―――. *Our Land and Land Policy.* New York: Doubleday and McClure Co., 1901. [Originally published 1871.]

―――. *Social Problems.* New York: Doubleday and McClure Co., 1889. [Originally published 1883.]

Giladi, Dan. "The Agronomic Development of the Old Colonies in Palestine (1882–1914)." In *Studies on Palestine During the Ottoman Period,* edited by Moshe Ma'oz, pp. 175–89. Jerusalem: Magnes Press, 1975.

Goldberg, Isaac. *Major Noah.* New York: Alfred A. Knopf, 1935.

Goldhaft, Arthur D. *The Golden Egg.* Edited with an introduction by Meyer Levin. New York: Horizon Press, 1957.

Goldman, Julius. *Report of the Colonization of Russian Refugees in the West.* New York, 1882.

Goldstein, Philip R. *Social Aspects of the Jewish Colonies of South Jersey.* New York: League Printing Co., 1921. [A Ph.D dissertation for the University of Pennsylvania.]

Goren, Arthur A. *New York Jews and the Quest for Community.* New York: Columbia University Press, 1970.

Graetz, Heinrich. *History of the Jews.* Translated by Henrietta Szold *et al.* 6 vols. Philadelphia: Jewish Publication Society of America, 1949. [The original edition appeared in 1895.]

Greenberg, Louis. *The Jews in Russia: The Struggle for Emancipation.* Two volumes in one. New York: Schocken Books, 1976. [Originally published in 1944 and 1951.]

Grinstein, Hyman B. *The Rise of the Jewish Community of New York, 1654–1860.* Philadelphia: Jewish Publication Society of America, 1947.

Grunwald, Kurt. *Tuerkenhirsch: A Study of Baron de Hirsch, Entrepreneur and Philanthropist.* Jerusalem: Israel Program for Scientific Translations, 1966.

Haberman, Joshua O. "The Jews in New Jersey: A Historical Sketch."

Unpublished manuscript, New Jersey Collection. New Brunswick: Rutgers University, 1953.

Halpern, Ben. *The Idea of the Jewish State.* Cambridge: Harvard University Press, 1961.

Handlin, Oscar. "American Views of the Jew at the Opening of the Twentieth Century." *Publications of the American Jewish Historical Society,* XL (1950), 323–44.

Hendrick, Burton. *The Age of Big Business.* New Haven: Yale University Press, 1917.

Herscher, Uri D. "Herman Rosenthal—The Jewish Farmer." In *Michael: On The History of the Jews in the Diaspora,* edited by Lloyd P. Gartner, vol. III, pp. 60–87. Tel Aviv: Diaspora Research Institute–Tel Aviv University, 1975.

Hibbard, B. H. *A History of the Public Land Policies.* New York: P. Smith Co., 1924.

Hicks, John D. *The Populist Revolt.* Minneapolis: The University of Minnesota Press, 1931.

Higham, John. "Anti-Semitism in the Gilded Age." *Mississippi Valley Historical Review,* XLIII (1957), 559–78.

Hinds, William A. *American Communities and Cooperative Colonies.* Chicago: C. H. Kerr and Company, 1908.

Hirsch, Maurice de. "Refuge for Russian Jews." *Forum,* XI (August, 1891), 627–33.

Idisheh Farms in Amerika. New York: Educational Alliance, 1906.

International Encyclopedia of Social Sciences. New York: Macmillan Co., 1968.

Isler, J. M. *Rueckkehr der Juden zur Landwirtschaft.* Frankfurt am Main: J. Kauffmann, 1929.

Jenks, Jeremiah W.; W. Jett Lauck; and Rufus D. Smith. *The Immigration Problem: A Study of American Immigration Conditions and Needs.* Fifth edition, revised and enlarged. New York: Funk & Wagnalls Co., 1922.

Jewish Encyclopedia. New York: Funk & Wagnalls Co., 1905.

Joseph, Samuel. *History of the Baron De Hirsch Fund.* Philadelphia: Jewish Publication Society, 1935.

———. *Jewish Immigration to the United States from 1881 to 1910.* New York: Columbia University, 1914.

Kasovich, Israel. *The Days of Our Years: Personal and General Reminiscence (1859–1929).* Translated [from Yiddish] by Maximilian Hurwitz. New York: Jordan Publishing Co., 1929.

Kidder, Daniel P. *Mormonism and the Mormon: A Historical View of the Rise and Progress of the Sect Self-Styled Latter Day Saints.* New York: G. Lane and C. B. Tippett, 1842.

Klein, Moses. *Migdal Zophim.* Philadelphia: Jewish Publication Society, 1932.

Kochan, Lionel (ed.). *The Jews in Soviet Russia Since 1917.* London: Oxford University Press, 1970.

Kohler, Kaufmann. *Jewish Theology.* New York: Macmillan Company, 1918.

Kohler, Max J. "An Early American Hebrew-Christian Agricultural Colony." *Publications of the American Jewish Historical Society,* XXII (1914), 184–86.

Landsberg, Moses G. *History of the Persecution of the Jews in Russia.* Boston, 1892.

Laqueur, Walter. *A History of Zionism*. New York: Holt, Rinehart, and Winston, 1972.

Lee, Samuel J. *Moses of the New World: The Work of Baron de Hirsch*. New York: Thomas Yoseloff, 1970.

Leroy-Beaulieu, Henri Jean Baptiste Anatole. *The Empire of the Tsars and the Russians*. New York: G. P. Putnam's Sons, 1896.

Leven, Maurice. *Les Origines et le Programme de l'Alliance Israélite*. Paris: Rousseau et Cie., 1923.

Leven, Narcisse. *Cinquante Ans d'Histoire; L'Alliance Israélite Universelle*. Vol. II. Paris, 1920.

Levy, A. R. "The Jew as a Tiller of American Soil." *American Hebrew*, LXXVII (November 24, 1905), 849–64.

Lewisohn, Ludwig. *Israel*. London: Ernest Benn, 1926.

Liebmann, Hersch. "International Migration of the Jews." In *International Migrations*, edited by Walter F. Willcox, Vol. II, pp. 471–520. New York: National Bureau of Economic Research, 1931.

Lifschutz, Ezekiel. "Jacob Gordin's Proposal to Establish an Agricultural Colony." *American Jewish Historical Quarterly*, LVI (1966–1967), 151–62.

Manuel, Frank E. *The Realities of American-Palestine Relations*. Washington, D.C.: Public Affairs Press, 1949.

Maoz, Moshe (ed.). *Studies on Palestine During the Ottoman Period*. Jerusalem: Magnes Press, 1975.

Marcus, Jacob Rader. "Major Trends in American Jewish Historical Research." *American Jewish Archives*, XVI (1964), 9–21.

———. *Studies in American Jewish History*. Cincinnati: Hebrew Union College Press, 1969.

Menes, Abraham. "The Am Oylom Movement." In *Studies in Modern Jewish Social History*, edited by Joshua A. Fishman, pp. 155–79. New York: Ktav, 1972.

Menken, A. Stanwood. *Report of the Founding of the First Russian-Jewish Colony in the United States at Catahoula Parish, Louisiana*. New York: M. Thalmessinger, 1882.

Modder, Montagu F. *The Jew in the Literature of England*. New York: Meridian Books, 1960.

Morais, Henry S. *The Jews of Philadelphia*. Philadelphia: The Levytype Co., 1894.

———. *Eminent Israelites of the Nineteenth Century*. Philadelphia: Edward Stern, 1880.

Morris, Richard B. (ed.). *Encyclopedia of American History*. New York: Harper & Bros., 1953.

———. *Encyclopedia of American History*. Revised and enlarged. New York: Harper & Bros., 1961.

Mounier, Louis. *Auto-Biographical Sketch*. Vineland, N.J.: Privately published, 1936.

National Industrial Conference Board. *A Graphic History and Analysis of the Census of Manufacturing, 1849–1919*. New York, 1923.

Noble, Shlomo. "The Image of the American Jew in Hebrew and Yiddish Literature in America, 1870–1900." *YIVO Annual of Jewish Social Science*, IX (1954), 83–108.

Palitz, Bernard A. "The Borough of Woodbine." Typescript, Box 2112. Cincinnati: American Jewish Archives, *ca.* 1907.

187

Pares, Bernard. *A History of Russia*. New York: Alfred A. Knopf, 1937.

Park, Robert E., and Herbert A. Miller. *Old World Traits Transplanted*. New York: Harper J. Brothers, 1921.

Paxson, Frederick L. *History of the American Frontier*. New York: Houghton Mifflin Co., 1924.

Plaut, W. Gunther. *The Jews in Minnesota: The First Seventy-Five Years*. New York: American Jewish Historical Society, 1959.

Pollak, Gustav. *Michael Heilprin and His Sons*. New York: Dodd, Mead and Company, 1912.

Postal, Bernard, and Lionel Koppman. *A Jewish Tourist's Guide to the U.S.* Philadelphia: Jewish Publication Society of America, 1954.

Powderly, Terence Vincent. *The Paths I Trod*. New York: Columbia University Press, 1940.

Ragins, Sanford. "The Image of America in Two East European Hebrew Periodicals." *American Jewish Archives*, XVII (1965), 143–61.

Reis, J. C. "History of the Alliance Colony." *The Menorah*, XLII (1906–7), 167–73.

Reizenstein, Milton. "Agricultural Colonies in the United States." *Jewish Encyclopedia*, Vol. I (1901), 256–62.

Rivkin, Ellis. "A Decisive Pattern in American Jewish History." *Essays in American Jewish History*. Cincinnati: American Jewish Archives, 1958, 23–61.

Roberts, Dorothy. "The Jewish Colony of Cotopaxi." *Colorado Magazine*, XVIII, No. 4 (July, 1941), 124–31.

Robinson, Gerold Tanquary. *Rural Russia Under the Old Regime*. New York: Longmans, Green and Company, 1932.

Robinson, Leonard G. "Agricultural Activities of the Jews in America." In *American Jewish Yearbook, 5673* (Philadelphia: Jewish Publication Society of America, 1912–13), XIV, 21–115.

Rosenthal, Herman. "Agricultural Colonies in South Russia." *Jewish Encyclopedia*, Vol. I (1901), 252–56.

———— (ed.). *Der Yudisher Farmer: Monatliche Tsaytshrift fir Landvirtshaftliche Kolonizatsyan*. [Periodical.] New York, 1891–92.

Rosenthal, Herman, and Adolf M. Radin, eds. "Chronicle of the Communist Colony Known as New Odessa" (Hebrew). In *Yalkut Maaravi: Maasaf Shnati*, Vol. I (1904/1905), 46–54.

Rosskam, Edwin. *Roosevelt, New Jersey: Big Dreams in a Small Town and What Time Did to Them*. New York: Grossman Publishers, 1972.

Rubinow, Isaac M. *Economic Condition of the Jews in Russia*. Washington, D.C.: Bureau of Labor, Department of Commerce and Labor, 1907.

Rudin, A. James. "Bad Axe, Michigan: An Experiment in Jewish Agricultural Settlement." *Michigan History* (Summer, 1972), 119–30.

Ruppin, Arthur. "Agricultural Achievements in Palestine." *Contemporary Jewish Record*, V, No. 3 (June, 1942), 269–81.

————. *The Jews in the Modern World*. London: Macmillan and Co., 1934.

————. *The Jews of Today*. New York: G. Bell and Sons, Ltd., 1913.

Rutman, H. David. "The Sholem Colony." *The Journal* (Ellenville, New York). Jan. 4, 11, 18, 25; February 1, 1973.

Sabsovich, Hirsch L. "Agricultural and Vocational Education." In *Trends and Issues in Jewish Social Welfare in the United States, 1899–1958*, edited by

Robert Morris and Michael Freund, pp. 43–47. Philadelphia: Jewish Publication Society of America, 1966.

Sabsovich, Katherine. *Adventures in Idealism: A Personal Record of the Life of Professor [Hirsch Lieb] Sabsovich*. New York: Stratford Press Inc., 1922.

Sachar, Howard M. *The Course of Modern Jewish History*. Cleveland: World Publishing Co., 1958.

Sanford, A. H. *The Story of Agriculture in the United States*. Boston: D. C. Heath & Co., 1916.

Satt, Flora J. "The Cotopaxi Colony." Unpublished M.A. thesis, University of Colorado, 1950.

Schappes, Morris U. (ed.). *A Documentary History of the Jews in the United States, 1654–1875*. Third edition. New York: Schocken Books, 1971.

Schwartz, Lois F. "Early Jewish Agricultural Colonies in North Dakota." *North Dakota History*, XXXII, No. 4 (October, 1965), 217–32.

Schwarz, Julius. *Report of Mr. Julius Schwarz on the Colony of Russian Refugees at Cotopaxi, Colorado, Established by the Hebrew Emigrant Aid Society of the United States*. New York: Hebrew Emigrant Aid Society, 1882.

Shankman, Arnold. "Happyville, The Forgotten Colony." *American Jewish Archives*, XXX (1978), 3–19.

Sholem Aleichem tsu Imigranten: A Kurtseh Erklerung vegn dem Leben in Amerika, Aroysgegeben far dem Nutsen fun di Nayeh Eingevanderteh Iden. New York: Educational Alliance, 1903.

Shpall, Leo. "A Jewish Agricultural Colony in Louisiana." *Louisiana Historical Quarterly*, XX (July, 1937), 3–13.

Singer, Richard E. "The American Jew in Agriculture, Past History and Present Condition." Unpublished Prize Essay, Hebrew Union College Library. Cincinnati: Hebrew Union College, 1941.

Smith, J. W., and A. L. Jamison (editors). *The Shaping of American Religion*. Princeton: Princeton University Press, 1961.

Solomons, Adolphus S. "Alliance: The First Successful Jewish Colony in America." *The Menorah*, V (1888), 179–87.

Stainsby, William. *The Jewish Colonies of South Jersey*. Camden, N.J.: Bureau of Statistics, 1901.

Statistical Review of Immigration, 1820–1910. Washington: Government Printing Office, 1910.

Stern, Julius. "On the Establishment of a Jewish Colony in the United States." *Occident and American Jewish Advocate*, I, No. 1 (April, 1843), 28–32.

Sumner, B. H. *A Short History of Russia*. Rev. ed. New York: Harvest/ Harcourt, Brace & World, 1949.

Swichkow, Louis J. "The Jewish Agricultural Colony of Arpin, Wisconsin." *American Jewish Historical Quarterly*, LIV (1964–65), 82–91.

Szajkowski, Zosa. "The Attitude of American Jews to East European Jewish Immigration (1881–1893)." *Publications of the American Jewish Historical Society*, XL (1950–51), 221–80.

———. "The European Attitude to East European Jewish Immigration (1881–1893)." *Publications of the American Jewish Historical Society*, XLI (1951–52), 127–62.

———. "How the Mass Migration to America Began." *Jewish Social Studies*, IV (1942), 291–310.

Universal Jewish Encyclopedia. New York: Universal Jewish Encyclopedia, Inc., 1939–1943.

U.S. Congress, House. Executive Document No. 73. *Report on the Lands of the Arid Regions of the United States.* 45th Cong., 2nd Sess. Washington: Government Printing Office, 1879.

Vizetelly, Frank H. "Herman Rosenthal." *Jewish Encyclopedia,* X (1916), 478–79.

Walett, Francis G. *Economic History of the United States.* New York: Barnes & Noble, 1955.

Warburg, Felix, Papers. American Jewish Archives, Cincinnati, Ohio.

Webster's Biographical Dictionary. First edition. Springfield, Mass.: G. & C. Merriam Co., 1964.

Weinryb, Bernard D. "Noah's Ararat Jewish State in Its Historical Setting." *Publications of the American Jewish Historical Society,* XLIII (1953–1954), 170–91.

————. "East European Immigration to the United States." *Jewish Quarterly Review,* XLV (1955), 497–528.

Werner, Morris Robert. *Brigham Young.* New York: Harcourt, Brace and Company, 1924.

Who Was Who in America. Five volumes. Chicago: A. N. Marquis Co., 1960–73.

Who Was Who in America: Historical Volume, 1607–1896. Chicago: A. N. Marquis Co., 1963.

Wiernik, Peter. *History of the Jews in America.* Second edition. New York: Jewish History Publishing Co., 1931.

Wilson, Edmund. *To the Finland Station.* Garden City, N.Y.: Doubleday and Co., 1953.

Wininger, S. *Grosse Juedische National-Biographie.* Chernovitz: "Arta," 1925–31.

Wischnitzer, Mark. *To Dwell in Safety: The Story of Jewish Migration Since 1800.* Philadelphia: Jewish Publication Society of America, 1948.

Yarmolinsky, Avraham. *A Russian's American Dream: A Memoir on William Frey.* Lawrence, Kansas: University of Kansas Press, 1965.

Yoval: A Symposium upon the First Fifty Years of the Jewish Farming Colonies of Alliance, Norma and Brotmanville, New Jersey. Philadelphia: Westbrook Publishing Co., 1932.

Index

Abramowitsch, Sholom, 146, 153
Agricultural utopianism. *See* Ideology
Agriculture (Jewish), 10–11, 15–20, 23–26, 29–40, 51, 54, 61, 67–68, 70–72, 75, 77–84, 88–99, 104–6, 109, 112–21, 124, 131, 133, 157–58, 160, n. 13. *See also* Farm colonies; Farming
Agro-industrialism in colonies, 82–84, 89, 92, 99, 104, 106, 113, 118, 120–21, 123–32
Ahad Ha-Am. *See* Ginsberg, Asher
Aiken County, S.C., 72
Alexander I, 19
Alexander II, 16, 20, 148
Alexander III, 20–21, 148
Alliance, N.J., 73–84, 99, 113, 123, 129–30, 132–33, 152, 154, 156
Alliance Israélite Universelle, 21, 24–25, 32, 35, 37, 49, 52, 73, 88, 108, 123, 151, 156
Alliance Land Trust, 77, 80–81
Alterman family, 157
Amana enterprise, 111
American Hebrew, 23, 71
American Hebrew Agricultural and Horticultural Association, 31
American Israelite, 49, 79–80, 92, 99
Americanization of immigrants, 88–89, 97, 109, 124
Am Olam, 24, 32, 34, 37–39, 45, 49, 53–55, 57, 74–77, 89, 123, 137–39, 142–43, 145–46, 148–52, 156–58
Anshe Chesed Congregation, New York City, 30

Anti-Semitism, 10, 19–25, 29, 31–32, 37, 49, 52, 73, 84, 89, 106, 108–9, 114, 123, 143, 145, 148, 155, 157–58, 172, n. 3
Apostasy, 137, 149–50, 156
Ararat, N.Y., 29–30
Argentina, 88, 121
Aristocracy, 16, 18, 25, 45–47, 84, 88, 115, 139, 150, 156
Arizona, 138
Arkansas, 37, 53–55
Arkansas River, 55
Asher, Asher, 130
Asmonean, 31
Association of Jewish Immigrants, 77
Atheism, 46, 48, 51
Austria, 15, 21, 37. *See also* Galicia; Vienna

Baar, Herman, 57
Bachman, Jakob, 153
Bad Axe, Mich., 62, 67, 70
Bailey, Esther Mashbir, 82–83, 138, 140, 152–57
Bailey, Sidney, 11, 75–78, 82–84, 133–58
Bailey family, 134–35, 138, 141, 144, 149, 156–57
Bakal, Moni, 78, 138, 142, 146–52, 156–57, 177, n. 15
Balfour Declaration, 116
Balta, 138, 140–42, 146, 149, 156
Balter, Avromsti, 142
Balter, Dovidl, 140–42, 145
Balter, Naphtali, 153
Balter, Shmuel, 142

191

Baltimore, Md., 72
Baptist church, Woodbine, N.J., 104
Baron de Hirsch Agricultural School, 98–99, 104
Baron de Hirsch Fund, 24–25, 67–71, 81–84, 88–99, 104–6, 124, 131
Baton Rouge, La., 33
Baum, Moishe. *See* Bayuk, Judah Moses
Bay City, Mich., 61–62, 68
Bayuk, Judah Moses, 157, 169, n. 24
Beersheba, Kans., 49
Belzer, Nisan, 153
Ben-Ami, Mordecai, 149, 151
Berlin, Germany, 37, 139, 149
Berman, L., 158
Bernstein, Anute, 149
Bernstein, Jacob Cohen, 149–50
Bernstein, Lev Cohen, 149
Beth-El. *See* Temple Beth El, Detroit
Bethlehem-Jehudah, S.D., 52–53
Bialik, Chaim Nachman, 146
Bible, 82–83, 135–37, 139, 141–45, 147, 149–50, 154, 157–58
Bien, Julius, 39
Bismarck, N.D., 70
Blacks, 36, 140
B'nai B'rith, 22, 30, 78
Bogen, Boris, 93
Borowick (Sicily Island colonist), 35
Boston, Mass., 123, 140
Bourgeoisie, 18, 23, 25, 37, 115
Brafman, Jacob, 21, 160
Brandes, Joseph, 95
Brody, 21, 32, 37, 151
Brody (Am Olamite), 149
Brownsville, N.Y., 147
Buck, Solon, 112
Buffalo, N.Y., 29
Burleigh County, N.D., 70
Butzel, Martin, 62, 67–69
Byelinsky, Vissarion Grigorevitch, 145

Cahan, Abraham, 38, 45–47, 139, 157, 163–64, n. 7
California, 48, 72
Cape May, N.J., 82, 84, 90, 93, 125
Cape May County, N.J., 90, 92, 125
Capitalism, 10, 17, 57, 67, 84, 112–13, 115, 117–21, 137, 153
Carmel, N.J., 73, 132, 142, 152
Carus, Paul, 158
Castle Garden, N.Y., 22, 77
Catahoula Parish, La., 33
Chananel, N.D., 71
Charny, Daniel, 158
Chernovitz, Chaim, 158
Chicago, Ill., 105, 123, 158

Church. *See* Religion in colonies
Cincinnati, Ohio, 49, 79–80, 92, 124, 139, 158
Circumcision, 139, 141
Cities. *See* Urbanization
Clarion, Utah, 162, n. 25
Clergy, 16, 57, 68, 108, 111, 153. *See also* Rabbis, role in colony establishment
Cohen, Benjamin, 130
Cohen, Jacob, 152
Colonization. *See* Farm colonies
Colorado, 55–61, 73
Coltun (Alliance colonist), 78
Commerce, 18, 30, 32–34, 52, 59, 62, 77, 79, 89, 106, 109–10, 141–42, 151, 161, n. 21
Committee on Agriculture and Industrial Settlements, 89
Communes, 38, 45, 48, 111, 150
Communism, 45, 47, 52, 121, 137, 149–50, 154
Community (Jewish), 28, 39, 45, 48, 51, 61, 62, 67, 73, 78, 82, 108–11, 114, 118–20, 123, 144, 148, 161, n. 21
Comte, Auguste, 45–46
Congressional Record, 158
Connecticut, 38
Constitutions of colonies, 34, 164, n. 14
Contracts for colony establishment, 69, 74, 90–91, 94–97, 126–28, 168, n. 4
Cotopaxi, Colo., 55–62, 73
Cowen, Philip, 71–72
Crémieux, Adolphe, 49
Crémieux, S.D., 49–55, 82, 166, n. 36
Crops, 36, 39, 50–51, 56, 58, 68, 71–72, 74–78, 80, 90, 92, 104–5, 118, 125–26, 128–31
Cultural life in colonies, 35, 46, 48, 51, 82–83, 115, 119, 139, 145, 147. *See also* Education in colonies; Literature in colonies; Music in colonies; Social clubs

Dakota Territory, 37, 49, 96, 152, 156. *See also* North Dakota; South Dakota
Daniels and Blumenthal (Woodbine firm), 104
Darmesteter, James, 9
Darwin, Charles, 144
Davidson, Gabriel, 53, 117
Davison County, S.D., 49, 52
Delaware Bay, 125
Dennis Creek, N.J., 125
Dennis Township, N.J., 90, 105
Denver, Colo., 55, 57, 59–60
Detroit, Mich., 62, 67
Deutscher, Isaac, 121

Devil's Lake, N.D., 71
Disease in colonies, 35–37, 49, 54, 60, 110, 116, 135
Distilling, 34, 128
Dobroliubov, Nikolai Alexandrovitch, 145
Douglas County, Ore., 39
Draper, John W., 145

Eastern Europe, 11, 28, 33, 49, 53–54, 61, 75, 93, 98, 108, 110, 115, 117, 133, 136, 138–40, 142–43, 145–56. *See also* Lithuania; Poland; Russia; Ukraine
Eben Ha-Ezer Synagogue, Alliance, N.J., 78
Education in colonies, 31–35, 38, 67, 74, 82–84, 88, 92, 98, 104–5, 124, 126, 129, 131, 134–40, 143, 145–57
Eichoff, Lydia, 45
Einstein, Albert, 144
Elisha ben Abuyah, 140, 144
Ellenville, N.Y., 30
Emigration. *See* Immigration
English language, 35, 39, 83, 88, 131, 139–40, 152, 158
Eppinger, Isaac, 130
Epstein, Isaac, 135, 146
Epstein, Nahum, 135–36
Epstein, Zalman. *See* Zeben

Factories. *See* Manufacturing
Farm colonies, 10–11, 19, 22, 28–40, 45–55, 68, 70–84, 88–99, 108–11, 115–21, 123–34, 148, 152, 156, 158. *See also* Farming (non-collective)
Farming (non-collective), 55, 62, 71, 73–74, 90–92, 99, 114, 139–40, 145, 151
Farm prices, 51, 78–83
Farm products exhibits, 68, 130
Feffer (Alliance colonist), 152, 157
Feinberg, Louis, 158
Feldman, Ephraim, 139–40
Fels, Joseph, 81
Fels, Maurice, 81, 83
Feudalism, 16–18, 25, 115
Filippov, Mikhail Mikhailovitch, 149–50
Financial panics, 70, 79–80, 84, 112
Fires, 48, 50, 62, 75, 110
First Agricultural Colony of Russian Israelites, 34
Floods, 36–37, 54, 110
Fourier, Charles, 26
France, 17, 104, 115. *See also* Alliance Israélite Universelle
Franzos, Karl Emil, 154
Fraser, Elizabeth, 158
Freeman, Moshe, 137, 145

Fremont County, Colo., 55, 58
Frey, Maria Slavinskaya, 45–47
Frey, William, 45–47, 111
Friedman (Alliance colonist), 78
Fritz, Konstantin, 149
Funkel, Moshe, 141

Galicia, Poland, 15, 21, 29
Galter, Dovid, 158
Garden Round, N.J., 152
Garske, N.D., 70
Gartman (Alliance colonist), 78
Gellis family, 142
George, Henry, 23, 26, 80
German language, 83, 143, 149, 156
Germany, 20, 25, 37, 84, 133
Gershel, Leopold, 130
Ginsberg, Asher, 146
Gobineau, Arthur de, 20
Goethe, Johann Wolfgang von, 82–83
Goldman, Julius B., 37, 89–90, 93–94, 97, 124–25
Goodwin, Charles, 68
Goodwin, Edward, 53
Gordin, Jacob, 143, 172–73, n. 3
Gortenshtein (Am Olamite), 149
Government, municipal, 105, 138
Grand Island, N.Y., 29
Great Britain, 116, 130. *See also* London
Greenberg, Benoir, 49–50
Greenberg, Benzion, 71–72

Haas Brothers (Woodbine firm), 98
Hackenburg, William, 124
Harvard College, 156
Haskalah, 141–43, 145, 147, 153
Hassidism, 77, 134, 136, 153
Hebrew Emigrant Aid Society, 22–25, 33, 37–39, 50, 55–60, 73–77, 81–82, 129
Hebrew Immigrant Aid Society, 72, 158
Hebrew language, 131, 136–38, 139–40, 143–47, 154, 156–57; press, 146
Hebrew Union College, 139–40
Heidenrich, Moses, 70
Heilperin, Jacob Yossi, 153, 154–55
Heilprin, Michael, 37–38, 40, 49–50, 57, 125, 139–40
Henry, Henry S., 60, 130
Herman, Margaret Bailey, 138, 156
Herzl, Theodor, 150
Hirsch, Maurice de, 84, 88, 124. *See also* Baron de Hirsch Agricultural School; Baron de Hirsch Fund
Hirsch, Mikhl, 137
Histadrut. *See* Labor
History (Jewish), 9, 15, 23, 25, 36, 83, 95, 112, 118, 121, 133
Hoffman, James H., 124

Holidays, 143–44, 147. *See also* Passover; Rosh Hashanah; Sukkot; Yom Kippur
Homestead Act, 48–49
Housing in colonies, 35, 39, 54, 56, 60, 62, 68, 71, 76, 80, 91–94, 97–99, 104, 119–20, 126–29, 131, 156
Hubbard, Elbert, 158
Hubbard, Frank, 62
Hubbard, Langdon, 62
Hubbard Company, 68–70
Humboldt, Wilhelm von, 133
Hungary, 38, 139
Huron County, Mich., 62, 70
Hurvitz, Shmuel, 135, 158

Ideology of agricultural utopianism, 26, 34, 45–48, 52, 75–78, 106–7, 117, 121, 150. *See also* Communism; Religion in colonies; Socialism, influence on colonies
Immigrant Aid Society, New Orleans, 34
Immigration, 10–11, 15, 17, 21–26, 28–40, 45, 49, 53, 55, 61–62, 67, 74–78, 88–89, 95–98, 108–11, 113, 123–34, 139, 143–45, 148, 150–52, 154, 156–57
Indiana, 38
Industrialism, 10–11, 16–18, 26, 70, 80–83, 89, 92, 97–99, 104, 111, 115–20, 123–25, 129–32. *See also* Manufacturing
Industrial revolution, 10, 26
Iola, N.D., 70–71
Isaacs, Meyer S., 88, 97, 124–25
Isler, J. M., 70, 166
Isolation, 33, 39, 48
Israel. *See* Kibbutzim; Palestine (Ottoman Empire)

Jerusalem, 105, 145, 158
Jewish Agency, 120
Jewish Agricultural and Industrial Aid Society, 89
Jewish Agricultural Society, 89, 114, 117
Jewish-Christian relations, 33, 35, 45–47, 51, 62, 68–70, 74, 90, 97, 104, 126, 131–32, 158. *See also* Anti-Semitism
Jewish Farmer, 11, 32, 123
Jewish Messenger, 39, 57
Jewish National Fund, 158
Jewish Theological Seminary of America, 140
Jonasson Cloak Factory, 93–95, 98
Joseph, Samuel, 104

Kansas, 37, 45, 49, 96, 121, 152, 161
Kaplan, Paul, 47, 89, 125, 150, 170, n. 31
Kasovich, Israel Isser, 149, 152, 157
Katsovey. *See* Kasovich, Israel Isser

Kempner, Walter, 139
Kibbutzim, 116, 118
Kiev, Russia, 32, 138–39, 149, 156; University, 149
Kirschbaum, Eliezer, 29, 31
Kishinev, 139, 149–50
"Know-Nothings," 30
Kohler, Kaufman, 139
Kohn, George H., 59–60
Konefsky (Alliance colonist), 78
Kossuth, Louis, 38, 139
Krassenstein (Alliance colonist), 82
Krauskopf, Joseph, 139

Labor, 11, 17, 24, 30, 33, 38, 45–46, 54, 69, 74–76, 78, 88, 93, 99, 104, 120, 126, 130–31, 142, 148, 156; federations, 120
Lavrov, Peter, 147
League of Nations, 116
Lebensohn, Adam Ha-Cohen, 137
Lee, Francis B., 92–93
Lehman, Emanuel, 88
Leib, Moshe, 135–36
Lermontov, Mikhail Yurievitch, 154
Leroy-Beaulieu, Henri, 17
Levi Yitzchok of Berditchev, 153
Levy, Abraham R., 105
Lewenberg, Hyman, 61–62, 70
Lewisohn, Leonard, 76, 130
Libraries in colonies, 34, 46, 48, 83, 123–24, 131
Lilienblum, Moshe Leib, 135, 140–44, 147
Lipman family, 157
Literature in colonies, 29, 32, 35, 82–83, 137, 142, 144–46, 153–54
Lithuania, 143, 145–47
Litigation, 59, 68–70, 94–95, 97
Little Rock, Ark., 53
Litvin, A. *See* Hurvitz, Shmuel
Livestock, 50, 71, 75, 78, 84, 91, 95–97, 126
Loans to colonists, 32, 39, 52, 62, 67–71, 74, 79–80, 91, 94, 96–97, 99, 120, 127, 131
Loeb, Isadore, 88
London, England, 22, 47, 74
Long Island, N.Y., 38
Los Angeles, Ca., 138
Lousiana, 33–38, 45, 48–50, 52–53, 55, 123
Luberoff (Alliance colonist), 78
Lumber. *See* Timber, as source of colony income
Lutostanski, Hippolyte, 20

Macomb County, Mich., 67

Mandelkorn, Israel, 48
Mansion House Relief Committee, 22, 74
Manufacturing, 18, 75–77, 81, 93–99, 104–5, 124, 129–31
Margolis-Kalvariski, Haim, 151
Marxism, 45, 121. *See also* Socialism, influence on colonies
Maryland, 72
Mashbir, Lazar (Eliezer), 142, 149, 152, 154, 156, 178, n. 24
Mashbir, Mordechai, 153
Mashbir, Shlomo, 152–55
May Laws, 19
McEnery, Samuel D., 33
Medicine. *See* Professionals, influence on colonies
Meeker, Ezra, 152
Menaker, Solomon, 53–54
Mendel, M. W., 130
Mendele. *See* Abramowitsch, Sholom
Menorah (B'nai B'rith monthly), 78
Metchnikov, Ilya Ilich, 147
Michigan, 61–62, 67–71, 109
Middlesex County, Va., 72
Mikhailovski, Nikolai Konstantinovich, 145
Mikveh Israel School, 32
Mill, John Stuart, 147
Miller, Levi, 152
Mining, 55–56, 58–60
Mintz, Moishe, 157
Mississippi River, 33, 54
Missouri, 45
Mitchell, S.D., 49–50
Mizrahi. *See* Labor
Montagu, Samuel, 130
Montefiore Agricultural Aid Society, 24, 40, 50, 54–55, 165, n. 26
Morais, Sabato, 140
Mormonism, 111, 148, 173, n. 6
Moses, Abraham, 135–36
Mounier, Louis, 24, 83, 169, n. 22
Mount Pleasant, N.J., 125
Music in colonies, 35, 46, 51, 83, 137, 142, 149, 153

Nation, The, 140
Netter, Charles, 21, 32, 151
Nevada, 72
New Jersey, 24, 73–84, 89–99, 104–6, 121, 123–33, 138, 142, 152, 157; State Board of Agriculture, 92; state legislature, 104
New Odessa, Ore., 37, 39–40, 45–48, 51, 53–55, 70, 78, 82, 111, 150
New Orleans, La., 33–36
Newport, Ark., 53

New York City, 22, 26, 29–32, 36–39, 48–50, 53, 55, 57–59, 67, 72, 75–77, 83, 88, 90, 105, 108, 123–24, 131, 133–34, 138–39, 151, 156–57
New York Evening Post, 99
New York State, 29–30, 38, 96
New York Sun, 79
Nicholas I, 16, 19
Noah, Mordecai M., 29, 31, 162–63, n. 2
North Dakota, 70–72

Ocean City, N.J., 125
Odessa, Russia, 20, 37, 75, 134, 136–38, 141–43, 145–49, 151, 154–55
Oleynikov, Nikolai, 139, 149, 152
Opachinsky, Israel, 76
Oregon, 37–40, 45–48, 50, 78, 121, 150
Orshansky, Ilya, 143
Orthodox Judaism, 37, 57, 59, 62, 68, 77, 135, 140–42, 148–49, 152–54, 157. *See also* Hassidism
Owens, Robert, 26

Painted Woods, N.D., 70–71
Pale of Settlement, 15, 18, 53, 160, n. 13
Palestine (British Mandate), 114–21, 139, 150
Palestine (Ottoman Empire), 28, 32, 61, 76, 114–21, 143, 146, 158, 167, n. 53
Palestine, Mich., 61–62, 67–71, 109
Palitz, Bernard A., 106–7
Paris, France, 104, 138, 147, 151
Passover, 57, 67, 131, 139, 143
Paternalism, 61, 93–94
Paul I, 19
Peasants, 16–18, 21, 25, 96, 158
Peisochovitch, Chaya, 150
Peisochovitz (Paisochovitz), Jacob, 78, 150, 152, 157
Pennsylvania, 139, 158. *See also* Philadelphia, Pa.
Petach-Tikvah, 115
Philadelphia, Pa., 73, 76–77, 81, 83, 90, 106, 123–24, 138, 145
Philanthropy, 22–26, 31–32, 34, 36–40, 54–62, 67–70, 74–77, 81, 83–84, 88–99, 104–6, 108–11, 113, 115, 124–31, 151, 156, 167, n. 52
Pisarev, Dmitri Ivanovitch, 145–46
Pittsgrove Township, N.J., 73, 81–82
Place Mining Co., Colo., 58, 60
Pobyedonestsev, Constantin, 20
Poland, 15, 25, 77, 157, 163, n. 5. *See also* Galicia, Poland
Polinkovsky, Monish, 137, 146
Politics, influence on colony establishment, 30, 33, 105, 138, 140, 151

Porjes, Aaron, 146
Portland, Ore., 39–40
Press (New York), 95–96
Priluker, Jacob, 143
Professionals, influence on colonies, 37, 48, 53, 55, 59, 78, 93, 97, 130, 138–40, 149–50. *See also* Scientists, role in colonies
Protectionism, U.S., influence on colonies, 70, 80
Prussia, 15
Putran, Moshe, 136–37

Rabbis, role in colony establishment, 46, 49, 52, 70, 105, 135–37, 139–42, 146–48, 152–54, 158
Rabinovitz, Elka, 137
Rabinovitz, Ephraim-Froike, 137–38
Rabinovitz, Max, 147, 149
Rabinovitz family, 137, 139
Rabinovitz-Kempner, Leike (Lydia), 137–39
Rabinowitz, Sholem, 137, 146
Racialism, philosophy of, 20
Railroads, influence on colonies, 39–40, 56, 79–80, 90, 93, 125–26, 138
Ramsey County, N.D., 70–71
Rappahannock River, 72
Ravnitzky, Feye Polinkovsky, 146
Ravnitzky, Yehoshua, 135–37, 140, 143–44, 146
Reis, J. C., 81–82
Religion in colonies, 16, 37, 46, 51, 57, 59, 61, 67–69, 77, 82, 104, 107–8, 111, 134–37, 139, 144–45, 148, 152. *See also* Orthodox Judaism; Synagogues, role in colonies
Rice, Charles, 83
Rice, Henry, 69, 124
Rishon-le-Zion, 115
Robinson, Leonard, 33, 36
Rosas family, 157
Rosenblith, Z., 150
Rosenblitt (Rosenblueth?), Joseph, 125
Rosenfeld, Morris, 83
Rosenhayn, N.J., 73, 132, 152
Rosenthal, Herman, 11, 32, 35–36, 49–50, 74, 79, 89–90, 123–32, 152, 156
Rosh Hashanah, celebration of, 141
Rothschild, Edmond de, 115, 117
Roumania, 67, 88, 150
Ruppin, Arthur, 28, 117, 120–21, 159, 175
Russia, 10–11, 15–23, 26, 32, 37, 45, 49, 67, 74, 76–77, 84, 88, 91, 94, 108, 113, 121, 123, 128–31, 134, 137, 142–43, 148–56

Russian Emigrant Relief Fund Committee, 22
Russian language, 35, 131, 136–39, 142–47, 149, 154
Russo-Jewish Committee, 22
Russophilia, 32, 123, 143

Sabbath, celebration of, 57, 143, 147
Sabsovich, Hirsch L., 24–25, 89–90, 92, 94, 96, 98, 105–6, 125
St. Petersburg, Russia, 35, 45, 140–41, 147–48
Salem, N.J., 79
Salem Building and Loan Association, 79, 81
Salem County, N.J., 73, 99
Saltiel, Emanuel H., 58–60, 166
San Francisco, Ca., 48
San Francisco Overland Monthly, 47
Schiff, Jacob H., 67, 88, 124
Schiller, J. C. F. von, 82–83
Schnitkover, Susel, 135
Schwartz (Alliance colonist), 78, 152, 157
Schwarz, Julius, 55–60
Scientists, role in colonies, 89, 125, 136–38, 144, 157
Sea Isle City, N.J., 90, 125
Seldes, George, 78, 152, 157
Self-hate, 109, 172, n. 3
Seligman, Jesse, 124
Sephardic Jews, 58, 157
Shabshovitz, Yegor, 149
Shaikewicz, Nahum Meier, 142
Shapiro (Lithuanian intellectual), 147
Sholem, N.Y., 30
Sholem Aleichem. *See* Rabinowitz, Sholem
Sicily Island, La., 33–37, 45, 48–49, 52–54, 164, n. 13
Simon (Am Olamite), 149, 151
Slonimsky, Chaim Zelig, 136
Slouschz, Nahum, 135
Social clubs, 105
Socialism, influence on colonies, 32, 34, 117–21
Solomons, Adolphus S., 78–79, 99
South Carolina, 72
South Dakota, 49–52
Spies (Am Olam colonist), 53–54
Spivack (Spivak), Charles D., 78, 83, 152, 157
Spivakovsky, Chaim. *See* Spivack (Spivak), Charles D.
Spurgeon, Charles H., 108
Stainsby, William, 81–82, 99, 104, 114
Stavitsky (Alliance colonist), 82
Steinberg, D. (Alliance colonist), 78

Sternberg, David, 130
Stoecker, Adolf, 20
Straus, Oscar S., 124
Sukkot, 68, 143
Sulzberger, Mayer, 124
Synagogues, role in colonies, 30, 62, 68, 78, 82–83, 92, 104, 129, 135, 137, 141, 143–44, 153

Tailoring, as colony industry, 75–76, 81–82, 99, 138–39, 142–43
Talmud, 77, 82–83, 134–35, 139–40, 144, 146–48, 151
Taxes, U.S., influence on colony finances, 80, 105, 128
Tel Aviv, Palestine, 124, 146
Temple Beth-El, Detroit, 68
Temple Beth-El Hebrew Relief Society, Detroit, 62, 67
Texas, 38
Timber, as source of colony income, 35, 39–40, 53–54, 56, 62, 90–92, 126, 129, 156
Tiphereth Israel Synagogue, Alliance, N.J., 78
Toltchinsky (Ukrainian millionaire), 146
Treitschke, Heinrich von, 20
Tuska, Morris, 57

Ukraine, 19–20, 32, 37, 74–75, 134, 140, 143, 145–46. See also Kiev, Russia; Odessa, Russia
Ulster County, N.Y., 30
Union Grove, N.J., 82
United States government, 48, 55, 80, 158. See also Homestead Act
Universal Lock Company, 98–99, 104
University of Pennsylvania, 139
Urbanization, 18, 24, 26, 38, 83, 112–13, 118, 120, 123
Utah, 72, 148, 162, n. 25
Utopianism. See Ideology of Agricultural Utopianism

Vienna, Austria, 149, 151
Vincennes, Ind., 38
Vineland, N.J., 24, 73, 90, 129, 138
Virginia, 72
Voorhees, Foster M., 104
Voskoblinikov, Mordechai, 147
Voskoboinik, Mordechai, 142

Washington, D.C., 78

Washington (state), 38
Waterview, Va., 72
Wawarsing, N.Y., 30
Weber, John B., 97
Wechsler, Judah, 46, 48, 52, 70
Weil (South Dakota businessman), 50
Weinreich, Max, 134
Weitzman family, 138
Wet Mountain Valley, Colo., 56, 58
Willow Grove, N.J., 82
Winchevsky, Morris, 157
Wines, 129–30
Wischnitzer, Mark, 11
Wise, Isaac M., 49
Witkowski, L. (Denver merchant), 59–60
Women's Club, 157
Women's Medical College, 138
Women's rights, colony attitude toward, 52, 118
Woodbine, N.J., 73, 81–82, 84, 89–99, 104–7, 112–13, 123–31, 170, n. 31, 176, n. 5
Woodbine Brick Company, 104
Woodbine Land and Improvement Company, 90–91, 97–98, 127
Woodbine Machine and Tool Company, 98, 104
Woodic, Emanuel, 62, 67, 109
World Zionist Organization, 118, 121

Yiddisher Farmer, 158
Yiddish language, 32, 83, 93, 123–24, 126, 134, 138, 140, 145, 149–50, 157–58; press, 11, 32, 123, 140, 145, 157–58
Yiddish Scientific Institute (YIVO), 133–34
Yom Kippur, 50, 139, 141
Young Men's Hebrew Association, 22
Youth, role in colonies, 105, 113, 152, 171, n. 58

Zager, Joseph, 76
Zeben, 135, 145–46
Zederbaum, Alexander, 140
Zeire Hazon Association, 29–30
Zelikovitz, Getzl, 158
Zhypnik family, 145
Zionism, 28, 61, 115–21, 143, 147, 167, n. 53
Zolotarov family, 139
Zunser, Eliakum, 26
Zusman, Druk, 158
Zweifel, Eliezer, 136

Uri D. Herscher is associate professor of American Jewish history and executive vice-president of Hebrew Union College–Jewish Institute of Religion. He holds degrees from the University of California at Berkeley (B.A., 1964) and Hebrew Union College (M.A.H.L., 1970; D.H.L., 1973). Rabbi Herscher is the author of a book and numerous articles on Jewish history.

The manuscript was edited by Jean Spang. The book was designed by Don Ross. Typeface for the text is Palatino, designed by Hermann Zapf for Linotype about 1950. The display type is Windsor, designed by Stephenson Blake about 1905.

The text is printed on International Paper Company's Bookmark paper and the book is bound in Holliston Mills' Kingston Natural Finish cloth over binder's boards. Manufactured in the United States of America.